"LIEUTENANT, YOUR CAP'S ON BACKWARD!"

A Warm Story of the Cold War

John J. Thomason

ISBN: 1-4033-7357-4 (e-book)
ISBN: 1-4033-7358-2 (Paperback)
ISBN: 1-4033-7359-0 (Dust Jacket)

Library of Congress Control Number: 2002094392

This book is printed on acid free paper.

Printed in the United States of America
Bloomington, IN

1stBooks – rev. 03/21/03

Dedication:

To my grandchildren, Alyson, Hans and Sarah, and to the soldiers and civilians, men and women of many nationalities, who fought for liberty and won the cold war so that my grandchildren and children all over the world can be free.

Thanks:

To my wife for her generous and enthusiastic help in editing this manuscript and to my friends, Jürgen Sabarz, of Duisburg, Germany, and Michael D. Terry, of Memphis, Tennessee, whose valuable editing and suggestions have significantly improved the text, and for their much appreciated enthusiasm and encouragement.

TABLE OF CONTENTS

A NOTABLE NEW YEAR'S EVE
December 31, 1954

"After what happened last week," I said, "I don't think I want to go skiing."

George protested. "That was just a fluke." That's not likely to happen again. Besides, you can't spend your last New Year's Eve in Germany playing liar's dice at the officer's club!"

George Gallup, nephew of the famous founder of the Gallup Public Opinion Poll, was fresh from the States. He was the new public information officer for the Army VIIth Corps. Now a second lieutenant in the Army, a few months previously George had been in the advertising business in New York City. He was in charge of our corps newspaper, *The Jayhawk*.

I was an Army lawyer with almost two years service in Germany, soon to be heading home. After thirty months in the Judge Advocate General's Corps, I would shortly begin my career as a civilian attorney in Memphis, Tennessee.

George wanted us to spend our New Year's holiday skiing in Garmisch where there was an American Army recreational center at which a friend of his was stationed.

"What happened last week," was that while skiing with my friend, Jerry Hall, a civilian court reporter from Boston, Jerry fell and fractured his left leg in two places. We had been on the Nebelhorn, near Orberstdorf. Having been snow bound in a mountaintop hotel for three days and then having to get painfully injured Jerry off the

1

mountain, into a hospital, and from the hospital back to Kelley Barracks had been a difficult and irksome experience.

"Anyway, I've been to Garmisch," I said.

George persevered. "You haven't been skiing there. That's where they held the 1936 Winter Olympic games," he reminded me. "It's probably the best ski resort in Europe. You can't go back to the States without having skied Garmisch, especially since we're so close!" Then he played a trump. "Anyway, you've got a car, and I haven't had time to get one. If you won't go, I won't be able to go, either."

We went.

Soaring, high alpine mountains surround the picturesque towns of Garmisch and neighboring Partenkirchen. The highest mountain in Germany, the Zugspitze, is nearby and the more accessible Kreuzeck is even closer. We skied the latter and stopped for lunch at the Höllentalklamm Hütte, a cheery hiking hut, ski lodge and restaurant on the summit, listening to the sparkling music of a zither, when in walked two very attractive young ladies in ski togs. The restaurant was crowded but a table became available across the room. We paused and watched as the athletic, enthusiastic newcomers, chatting and laughing, made their way to the empty chairs. From the moment of their entrance, the two good-looking female skiers were the topic of our discussion.

"Those girls are Americans," said George. "We ought to go over to their table and introduce ourselves."

"No, George," I corrected. "They are clearly German."

"How can you tell that?"

"It's an acquired talent." I explained.

2

Enlarging upon the point, I opined, "After you've been over here for a while you'll learn to notice certain significant characteristics."

"Like what?" asked George.

I assumed a knowledgeable attitude. "Like their shoes, their hair styles, the cut of their clothes, the way the move their hands when they talk, their posture. You can tell a lot about what language they speak by just watching them, even if you're too far away to hear. See how rosy their cheeks are?" I queried. "You see that a lot in German girls."

"I think their cheeks are rosy because they've been out in the snow," said George.

I ignored his unenlightened comment.

"Notice how animated they are when they talk," I observed. "That's also typically German, although, conceivably, it might be French, or even Italian."

"I still think they're Americans." George remained firm, yet curious, willing to listen.

"When you've been here as long as I have, George, you'll be able to make a determination of female nationality and ancestry with more accuracy," I rejoined, reasonably reminding him of my senior status in this particular area of expertise.

"I think they're speaking English," George rejoined.

This dialogue went on for some time until, abruptly, the subjects of our scrutiny, apparently having finished their lunch, paid their check, gathered their belongings and left the dinning room.

I moved quickly.

"Pay the check, George. I'll pay you back later. While you're doing that I'll intercept them outside before they can put on their skis."

Outdoors, at the ski rack, I approached the young ladies. Affecting an attitude of amiability, I said, "Guten Tag. Wie geht's Ihnen?"

They looked at me curiously. Then, one of the young ladies replied, but not in German.

"Sprechen Sie Deutsch?" I asked uncertainly.

Again, there was a reply, but I did not recognize the language.

"Sprechen Sie English?" I persisted. "Verstehen Sie die Frage nicht?"

Then George appeared. "Have you figured it out?" he asked. "Are they Germans?"

"I don't know," I replied. "They are speaking some language I have never heard before."

Next I tried my college French, with the same unsuccessful result.

"I speak Spanish," said George. "Maybe they're from Spain."

"I don't think so. But give it a try."

From the young ladies we heard more of the same mysterious speech.

We didn't realize it, but the young ladies could understand everything we said. We incorrectly assumed that English was foreign to them. Then, suddenly, to my surprise, one of them said, in unmistakable American English, "We're speaking Swedish. We go to school in Sweden."

"Really? Is that so?" Was all I could say.

She continued. "But we didn't come down here to meet Americans. We're in Europe to meet Europeans. So, why don't you two guys buzz off?"

George moved in from the flank. "No offense," he said. "We noticed you in the restaurant and were debating your nationality. My friend here thought you were Germans, but I said you were Americans, so, I win the bet."

"What bet?" asked one of the Swedish students.

Thinking quickly, George lied, "A beer, we bet a beer."

In a flash the game plan became apparent to me. "That's right," I said. "We have to buy you a beer!"

I could tell they didn't believe us, but they were softening.

They exchanged a sort of "What the hell" look, and one said, "Well, maybe, but not now. We want to ski."

"Sure, so do we." We responded obligingly and seized the initiative. "But we can't renege on the bet. We'll meet you back here at four and buy you both a beer."

They communicated by a glance, in some mysterious code that, I have observed, is understood by women of all nationalities.

"O. K., make it four-thirty and we'll meet you; but, for just *one* beer."

We accepted, suspecting the final qualification would not likely be binding.

*   *   *

Fashionably a few minutes late, they appeared as promised a little after four-thirty and, as we had expected, did not enforce the one beer restriction. The conversation was easy in the warm afterglow of a strenuous, but fun, day of skiing. We all had a great time. Without formality, we paired off, but I seemed drawn to George's "date," Sally Palmer from Bakersfield, California, more than to my own.

After a couple of hours, several good German beers and very pleasant conversation, the girls said that they had to get back to their ski lodge, a mile or so along the trail. George had agreed to meet his friend in Garmisch for supper, which required him to catch the next cable car down from the mountaintop to the valley. Apparently, I was the only one without plans for the evening.

Sally rescued me. "Why don't you have supper with our group at the Stulben Hütte?" She suggested. "It's another ski lodge below the cable car station. We're with a bunch of mostly Dutch students. They'll be having a New Year's Eve party and you can join us. It's all very informal. We're sleeping in two big rooms -- boys on one side, girls on the other. You don't have to go back down to Garmisch; you can stay right here on top of the mountain."

Her invitation sounded pretty good. Although I had accommodations in a military hotel in Garmisch, I quickly decided to stay on the Kreuzeck.

Supper was served in a rather primitive restaurant next to the ski lodge. I ate alone because Sally was with the other students. I was beginning to think I had made a mistake, but there was nothing I could do about it. The cable car terminal was half a mile away and the last car of the day had descended. It would soon be dark. There was no way I could walk down.

The situation improved after supper. Although I'd thought I was Sally's date and was disappointed when we did not sup together, she had intended that I would simply join the group. That became

6

obvious when she, accompanied by several of her Dutch friends, appeared at my table inviting me to join the New Year's Eve party at the ski lodge.

The festivities were in a large room, warmed by a tile pottery oven such as I had seen as a child in my illustrated *Grimm's Fairy Tales*. There was recorded music, mostly American, and room enough to dance. Around the dancing area people sat at tables and drank beer, tea, coffee and glühwein, warmed Claret, sweetened and spiced.

I sat next to Sally. I considered myself a pretty good dancer. Because I had an older sister who liked to practice dancing with me, I knew most of the popular American steps and, after coming to Europe had learned some others, including the Viennese Waltz. I was especially proud of my ability to dance the "Memphis Shuffle," a regional variation of the "jitterbug," which I tested that night.

Sally was terrific. She could dance to anything and followed with just the right amount of opposing hand pressure so that leading her was easy. I later learned that she had three brothers, perhaps explaining her facility on the dance floor.

Sally was from Bakersfield, California. Regularly a student at Occidental College in Pasadena, she had been selected for an exchange scholarship and was studying Political Science for a year at an English speaking university in Stockholm, Sweden.

Coincidentally, I had visited Sally's hometown. Five years before I had worked in Santa Ana and spent a weekend with Sue Howell, in Bakersfield. Sue had been selected "Maid of Cotton" in a competition in Memphis. I had met her during the Memphis Cotton Carnival. She had invited me to visit her in Bakersfield at the conclusion of her world tour during which she promoted women's cotton fashions.

Sue's parents and Sally's were neighbors. Sally knew Sue and Sue's younger brother.

We laughed and speculated that when I was visiting Sue, Sally was probably riding her tricycle on the sidewalk in front of the Howell's house. That humorous speculation was not actually accurate, since there was only five years difference in our ages.

As the evening progressed, others noticed Sally's dancing expertise. As a result, she was seldom seated. During one of her forays onto the dance floor with a different partner, I became aware of being encircled by four or five of the male Dutch students in her group, one of whom asked me to accompany them outside. In America, that sort of invitation usually meant trouble. I didn't know what to expect. With serious misgivings I went outside.

"Are you aware that Sally is dancing with a German?" one asked.

Bewildered by the question and not comprehending its significance, I explained myself.

"Well, I don't know her dancing partner, or his nationality, but he asked her to dance and she accepted. She can dance with whomever she wants."

"You are her escort," they persisted, "and you are an American Army officer. You should be responsible for her and make sure she doesn't dance with Germans."

I was becoming a bit exasperated. "Look," I said, "the war is over. Anyway, she's not answerable to me. If you don't want her to dance with Germans, take it up with her." .

We went back inside and the Dutch students huddled for a while but didn't do anything more about Sally's "fraternizing with the enemy." After all, *we were* in Germany. Later, I learned that this was the first time, since World War II, that students from this particular part of Holland had visited Germany. Feelings were still hostile.

At the stroke of midnight, everyone wished everyone else a happy 1955 and then, to my surprise and disappointment, the party broke up. The skiers headed for bed, saying they wanted to be fresh in the morning, ready for an invigorating day on the slopes.

Turning to Sally, I optimistically exhorted, "Look, it's too early to go to bed. It's New Years Eve. There's an American officer's club up by the cable car station at the Kreutzeck Hütte. I saw a notice on the kiosk; they're having a party tonight. They have an American dance band and everything. Let's go up there and dance some more. We don't want to go to bed *now!*" If Sally vacillated, it was not apparent.

"Let's go," she replied enthusiastically.

We walked on a packed snow trail to the top of the mountain. Sally wore saddle oxford low cut shoes. I had on army boots, having danced in my socks. When we got to the top of the mountain, the party was in full swing. Until 4:00 a.m. we had a blast, dancing to almost every number.

When the band stopped and began packing their instruments, we headed back down to the ski lodge; but my, oh my, how things had changed!

While we danced it had snowed. Fourteen inches of new snow covered everything, including the trail. We couldn't be sure which way to go and Sally wasn't dressed for glacial hiking. However, the moon was full and its gentle radiance reflecting off the new snow enabled us to see pretty well. We made it back to the Stulben Hütte, pausing from time to time to admire the mountains, the moonlight, and each other.

Next day, Sally was up and gone skiing by the time I roused myself. Without notable Incident, I made my way back down the mountain to Garmisch, to my unused hotel room and found George. He was on his way to a ski jumping competition that afternoon at the site of the Olympic games. It sounded interesting, so I went along.

Surprisingly, at the ski jump I ran into Sally. We talked a while and she suggested I come back up the mountain that evening for supper. I wasn't too interested. George and I had made other plans for the evening. Furthermore, I didn't see much point in becoming more captivated by this young lady; I was headed back to Memphis in a month or so and she was returning to Sweden. I'd probably never see her again or have any kind of relationship with her. Anyhow, there were plenty of attractive single girls in Tennessee. Pursuing Sally was a dead end street. We talked for awhile and then, without exchanging addresses, we said good-bye.

Back in Stuttgart, at Kelley Barracks, George repeatedly took me to task for not following up with Sally and especially for not getting her Swedish address. Whenever we met he brought up the subject, criticizing my judgment and persistently urging me to write her a letter. After about two weeks of his constant nagging, somewhat against my better judgment, I complied with his suggestion.

*　　　*　　　*

Dear Sally, 　　　　　　　　　　　*13 January 1955*
　　The reason I am writing you is because George Gallup was in my room tonight and we were talking about you. Earlier we had been playing liar' s dice with some other guys.

That is a game which provides the winner with free beer. Since I am a better liar at liar's dice than the other liars around here, I was the recipient of several free beers.

Please forgive me for typing this letter rather than writing in long hand. I want to be sure you will be able to read it – if you ever receive it.

The fact of the matter is, I have serious doubts that this epistle will ever reach you. Since I don't have your address, I must rely on the industry and imagination of the postal authorities to find you. I find it peculiar to be writing a letter without knowing whether the addressee will receive it. Be that as it may be, I'll give it a try.

George and I were reminiscing about a wonderful last New Years Eve afternoon about two weeks ago on top of the Kreuzeck, and since you were also present, it is understandable that your name was mentioned. The previous sentence is really an understatement. We talked mostly about Sally.

I am, presently listening to some New Orleans jazz records which will be packed for shipment on Tuesday, after which time for several weeks I shall be without recorded music. Listening to these records reminds me of some really terrific dancing with you on the evening – and morning – in question. (I must change the record).

I have been thinking since I left you in Garmisch that I acted rather badly when I saw you on New Years Day at the ski jump meet. I recall that as we talked you indicated that I would be welcome back up on the mountain that night for supper and perhaps more dancing and I, not so gracefully, declined. I remember also that as I stood talking with you I was avoiding eye contact, which is really not the way I usually behave. I think the reason I wouldn't look you in the eye is because, as you know, I shall soon depart for the States, and you are in Sweden and I thought that it would be better for the two of us to just call it quits at that time rather than get involved in something which, between you and me, I could very easily get involved in. (Pardon the long sentence and the ending preposition).

Well, since then I have more than once thought that I would have been a lot smarter if I had gone back up on the mountain so that I could have had a date with you and enjoyed myself in a manner similar to the night before. Such fun as we had is not often afforded an occupation troop such as myself. So, it may be said, and I will not contradict, that I goofed.

It all boils down to the fact that I think Sally is a very wonderful person and I am sorry that I did not bend every effort to see as much of her as I could, when I could. And, this thought occurs to me: unless going by way of China, when Sally journeys home to California from Europe she must of necessity pass somewhere in the vicinity of Memphis. Such being the case, I hope with all the hope powers available to me that she will select a route near Memphis and inform me of it so that I may meet her along the way and see her once again.

Also included in my hopes is that somehow she will receive this letter, so that as she passes Memphis on her way to California, she will think of and want to be with me – rather than proceeding on her way, unaware of my affection.

I wonder. Did you have as much fun as I did?

    Love,

      Bud

New address:

    Mr. John J. Thomason, Attorney at Law

    1894 Central Ave.

    Memphis, Tennessee

       *   *   *

I left my room and proceeded back to the officer's club bar. George was having a cup of coffee.

"Well, I've done it, George," I said. "I've written her."

"How did you address the envelope?" he inquired.

I showed him:

"Miss Sally Palmer, An American Graduate Student studying at a University which teaches Political Science in English, and which, I believe, is located in Stockholm, Sweden."

George was doubtful. "I don't think that's good enough," he observed.

"I don't either," I agreed, "But, I don't know what else to say."

Without much optimism, I walked to the mailbox and dropped in the letter.

THE COLD WAR

This is a warm story about the Cold War; more particularly about that period of the Cold War from 1953 to 1955, as seen through the eyes of an American Army first lieutenant stationed at that time in what was feared might be the flash point of World War III, Germany. It is a *warm* story because most of it is taken from letters written by that soldier to his parents back home in Tennessee and from his personal recollections. Interspersed throughout the text and designated as "THE TIMES" are descriptions of important events that were then taking place, mostly in Europe.

This is a true story. These events really happened. The names are real, except in a very few instances when I couldn't remember a name. The excerpts from letters are accurate, except that I have made some corrections, and have done a little – not much -- editing when warranted.

The events described had their origin in World War II. Some would say that World War II had its origin in the harsh terms of the peace treaty and the humiliation imposed upon Germany after its defeat in World War I. No doubt after World War I German Army veterans felt betrayed, civilians were without direction and the nation was in a state of disorder. Within just a few years of Adolph Hitler's meteoric accession to power in 1933, he mobilized and rearmed Germany, occupied the Rhineland and a part of Czechoslovakia and annexed Austria, without opposition. Then, on September 1, 1939 the German army marched into Poland. England and France declared war. By the end of 1941, the United States and Russia were at war against Germany. In the meantime, France, Belgium, Holland, Norway, Denmark, the Balkan nations and Poland had fallen. For the next four years, Russia, Britain and the United States fought together to defeat the Axis powers, Germany, Italy and Japan. Russia did not enter the war against Japan until the final days of 1945, contributing little but taking much, including the establishment of North Korea as a communist state north of the 38th degree of latitude.

Not unexpectedly, disputes arose between Russia, Britain and the U. S. even before World War II ended. Germany surrendered on the 8th of May 1945. In anticipation of the end of the war, British Prime Minister Winston Churchill, American President Franklin Roosevelt and Russian Premier Josef Stalin met at Yalta on the Russian Black Sea for a week, in February, 1945. Roosevelt was sick (two months later he died) and Churchill was soon to face an election (he lost in July). Stalin was strong and his army seemed unstoppable.

Many believe that at Yalta Roosevelt "gave away the store." He promised to halt the American 3rd Army at the Elbe River and allow the Russian Army to occupy east Germany, to withdraw all U. S. troops from Europe within two years, and gave the USSR two extra seats at the United Nations. Russia was to have domination of Eastern Europe upon condition of conducting free elections. Russian domination occurred, but the elections never did. In addition, Russia's demand of twenty billion dollars in reparations from East Germany was accepted.

Roosevelt died on April 12, 1945 and Vice-president Harry Truman became President of the United States. Within two weeks Truman exchanged harsh words with Russian Ambassador Molotov.

In July 1945, two months after Germany surrendered, Truman, Stalin and Churchill met near Berlin, at Potsdam, where even more concessions were made to Russia; nine million Germans were forced to leave Poland and West Germany was compelled to give 25% of its industry to Russia as additional reparations.

After the Potsdam meeting, which had been strained, on February 9, 1946 Stalin delivered a speech asserting that communism and capitalism were incompatible. Less than two weeks later, U. S. Ambassador to Russia, George F. Kennan sent "the long telegram" to Truman arguing that the greatest danger to the free world was not the Russian Army but the spread of communism, the oppressive dictatorial form of Soviet government.

At Truman's invitation, Winston Churchill came to the United States and spoke about the Russian problem in what has become known as "The Iron Curtain speech." It was delivered on March 5, 1946 at Westminster College in Fulton, Missouri and set the tone of American-Russian relations for the next forty-six years. As Churchill described the situation:

From Stettin in the Baltic to Trieste in the Adriatic, an iron curtain has descended across the Continent. Behind that line lie all the capitals of the ancient states of Central and Eastern Europe. Warsaw, Berlin, Prague, Vienna, Budapest, Belgrade, Bucharest and Sofia, all these famous cities and the populations around them lie in what I must call the Soviet sphere, and all are subject in one form or another, not only to Soviet influence but to a very high and, in many cases, increasing measure of control from Moscow.

*   *   *

From what I have seen of our Russian friends and allies during the war, I am convinced that there is nothing they

16

admire so much as strength, and there is nothing for which they have less respect for than weakness, especially military weakness.

*   *   *

The situation did not improve. A peace conference was convened in Paris in April 1946, but after sporadic meetings throughout the summer, ended in October without agreement. In the meantime, the U. S. halted Russian reparation removal of industrial machinery from West Germany and sent war ships into the eastern Mediterranean Sea.

On May 12, 1947, President Truman spoke to Congress saying:

I believe that it must be the policy of the United States to support free peoples who are resisting attempted subjugation by armed minorities or by outside pressures.

The Marshall Plan, an ambitious American economic recovery program for Europe, was announced on June 5, 1947. It was described by Truman as "directed not against any country or doctrine but against hunger, poverty, desperation and chaos." Notwithstanding Truman's description, the Plan had the desired effect of arresting the overt spread of communism. Russia was invited to participate in the Plan, but declined.

Although the four Allied Powers agreed to rule Berlin jointly, because it lay in the Soviet sector, Russia controlled all access to the city except by air. The former German capital was stranded in the middle of the Soviet Zone, 110 miles from the areas of West Germany occupied by Britain, France and the U. S. From time to time, the Soviets interfered with Berlin supply convoys, but on June 24, 1948 they prohibited all rail and highway transportation, erecting barricades and cutting off the city entirely. The U. S. and Britain responded by establishing an airlift and for more than eleven months furnished Berliners with all essentials by air transport. Planes landed at five-minute intervals, twenty-four hours a day, in all kinds of weather. At length the Russians realized that their blockade was a failure and reopened overland supply.

Non-communist Western leaders thought action was necessary against Russia and its satellite nations, the communist states of Eastern Europe behind the "Iron Curtain." As a result, the North Atlantic Treaty Organization (NATO) was formed in April 1949. Russia and the Eastern Bloc responded by organizing the Warsaw Pact. Against this background, in July, American intelligence detected that a nuclear explosion had occurred in the USSR, clearly caused by a Russian atomic bomb. Russia confirmed that fact in September. As if the finish line were in sight, the pace of the arms race increased.

American physicists surpassed the Soviets in developing weaponry by exploding a vastly more powerful hydrogen bomb in 1950, but with the help of highly placed spies who stole the secrets of the H-bomb, the Russians quickly duplicated that accomplishment.

In the international contest for intellectual mastery, President Truman called for a campaign of truth to puncture the Russian "Big Lie." *Voice of America* radio broadcasts to Russia were increased and made more powerful in an effort to win the propaganda war and overcome Russia's attempt to jam freedom's radio signal.

The times were extremely tense. The French and British, occupying their zones of West Germany, marshaled their best air and ground units in the field and at home. The American 7th Army was in

Europe. It was a strong army comprising two corps, five divisions, four regimental combat teams and thousands of other troops in diversified units. The American Air Force, equipped with the somewhat outdated but well respected F-84 jet fighters, began to receive brand new F-86s at bases in West Germany, France and England. A strong U. S. Navy fleet was on patrol in the Mediterranean.

Occasionally the adversaries clashed and sometimes people were killed. Espionage and intelligence gathering was frenzied on both sides. Spies were identified, exposed, imprisoned and exchanged with some frequency. Military units remained on constant alert.

Because Soviet control of the people of Eastern Europe depended entirely on fearful oppressive force, in 1961 the Russians found it necessary to build the Berlin Wall, thus preventing East Germans from escaping to the West.

* * *

This story is a snapshot of the Cold War at a time when it was almost a "hot war." It is a narrative taken from three sources: remembrances, letters home and contextual history, designated here as "<u>THE TIMES</u>."

A word about the "letters home." I had lived away from home before: two summers working in California, three academic years in law school in East Tennessee. I kept in touch by mail in those days, too, but not nearly so frequently. Having decided not to keep a journal, instead, to share my experiences with my parents who had never been to Europe, I thought frequent and detailed letters home would be practical. Perhaps I would someday revisit the correspondence and do something with it. I asked my parents to keep the letters and they did. The Cold War times and events I witnessed were significant, and I knew it. I thought it was important to keep a record.

At the time I wrote the letters, messages in writing were traditional and the communication means of choice. Except for commercial telegrams, we had no electronic mail, nor any facsimile transfer. Long distance telephone calls were costly and, from overseas, unsatisfactory. Although time consuming in preparation and slow in delivery, letters had advantages. They were usually thoughtfully composed, sometimes enthusiastically received and, in this instance, lovingly preserved and now, romantically revisited.

This is also a story of the American civilian army, made up mostly of non-military citizens, who were called on to serve their country, did so and then returned to civilian life, many of them with never to be forgotten memories of their sojourn in the service. Some such citizen servicemen gave their lives, as did Sergeant Ed Kelley. Others, like Ed Fenig, had their professional careers disrupted by two wars and decided to remain in the military, rather than begin again. All of them exemplified the spirit of the last four letters of the designation "American,"— *I CAN*.

There are references here to incidents that occurred in World War II, but most of the story took place during the period 1952 – 1955, just seven years after the end of the war.

This is also the story of how a twenty-two year old law school graduate with no previous military training obtained a direct commission in the American Army and was metamorphosed from a happy-go-lucky, full time college fraternity president into a skillful and effective soldier and trial lawyer.

*   *   *

Throughout this narrative I have made use of designations of military rank employed at the time by the American Army. It might be helpful to indicate the order of rank. Commissioned officers, in ascending order, are: second lieutenant (2/Lt., one gold bar), first lieutenant (1/Lt., one silver bar), captain (Capt., double silver bars), major (Maj., gold oak leaf), lieutenant colonel (Lt/Col., silver oak leaf), colonel (Col., silver eagle), brigadier general (Brig. Gen., one silver star), major general (Maj. Gen., two silver stars), and lieutenant general (Lt. Gen., three silver stars). There were also four and five star generals, but I never saw any.

Enlisted personnel, in ascending order: private (Pvt., no insignia of rank), private first class (Pfc., one chevron), corporal (Cpl., two chevrons), sergeant (Sgt., three chevrons). Corporals and sergeants were non-commissioned officers; there were several grades of sergeant. All had three chevrons; up to three "rockers," below the chevrons were added as authority increased. There were also a relatively few warrant officers, who ranked between the commissioned and non-commissioned.

Enough of that.

PRELUDE TO THE COLD WAR

When World War II ended in 1945, I was fifteen years old and just finished my first year at Central High School in Memphis. A few of my older friends had gone off to war—and, except that my next door

21

neighbor, Joe Conard, participated in the D-Day invasion and was later killed in action in France—I didn't have much first-hand exposure to the hostilities. At the beginning of the war I volunteered to be a messenger in the civil defense corps and received an armband and identification card, but I never carried any messages. I was, however, an active messenger of a different sort. In those days when really important news occurred, one or both of the daily newspapers issued an "extra." I delivered the morning paper, so when *The Commercial Appeal* published an extra I was notified and picked up a bundle of papers to sell on the street. I picked a busy street corner, stood shouting, "Extra, extra, read all about it," and sold the paper announcing the end of the war and before that the one about the U. S., British and Canadian landings on the Normandy Beaches on "D-Day." It was a very exciting time.

The military draft, in effect since 1940, ended with the war. So, after 1945 there was no danger of being involuntarily inducted. However, on June 22, 1950, not quite five years after the end of World War II, 100,000 soldiers of the Communist Army of North Korea marched across its southern frontier at the 38th parallel of latitude and attacked its neighbor, South Korea.

By entering World War II just before it ended, the Russians had negotiated control and communist domination of Korean territory north of that arbitrarily selected boundary. This communist effort to consolidate the two countries by force caught the Western World by surprise.

Five months later the Chinese Army joined North Korea in the war. The North Korean and Chinese Communists were heavily supplied by the Soviets. By a quirk of fate, at the time of the invasion, Russia was boycotting the United Nations because Nationalist, rather than Communist China, had been admitted to membership. Consequently, Russia was not represented at the Security Council where it could have exercised its veto power. As a result, the United Nations voted to aid South Korea, sending a multinational force of mostly American soldiers, sailors and marines but also including military units from, England, Canada, Australia, Turkey, France, Italy and New Zealand. The Korean War was critical to American males of military age, eligible to be inducted under the reenacted draft laws. Ultimately, 109,958 Americans were casualties; killed, wounded or missing in the Korean War. Of that number nearly 30,000 were fatalities.

At the time, I had completed one year of law school. Those subject to the draft who were enrolled in college or graduate school could delay their time of induction into the military service so long as they were enrolled in an accredited institution and maintained passing grades. But after graduation, the draft board would get you if you didn't have a ROTC commission (Reserve Officers Training Corps) or could arrange some other way to fulfill your military obligation. Those who were drafted expected to be on active duty for two years. However, service as an enlisted man was often in uncomfortable circumstances. Those who applied for and received a commission served for a longer time, three or four years, but could usually look forward to a more pleasant experience. This was the dilemma facing me as I looked forward to my own graduation from law school in 1952.

Many of my friends had managed to get commissions in the Navy. That was the most glamorous prospect and I went for it -

applying for a commission as an ensign in Naval Intelligence. Although not officially accepted, I was advised by the Navy recruiter when I took my mental and physical exams in St. Louis early in 1952, that I should take extra courses so that I could graduate in March, rather than June, of that year. I did so and got my law degree -- but not my call from the Navy.

Classes over, twenty-two years old and law degree in hand, there was nothing for me to do but wait. At the time, I happened to be president (Eminent Archon) of SAE fraternity at the University of Tennessee in Knoxville and my term did not expire until the end of the semester, in June. So, while I waited for the Navy to tell me when and where to report, I became the only full-time (no classes) fraternity president on the campus; perhaps an all time unique achievement.

As weeks passed and I remained a civilian, my draft board began to turn up the heat. I was advised to volunteer for some military assignment else I would be drafted to perform military duties of the draft board's choice. If I wanted to avoid serving in the trenches as an enlisted man, I needed to get a commission from some branch of the service by the first of September 1952. Out went an application to the Coast Guard and a political inquiry on my behalf to the Navy from the office of Tennessee Senator K. D. McKellar. I learned that my Navy Commission was held up because of my physical exam — specifically, a skull fracture I had sustained in a motorcycle accident in California in 1949. The Navy wanted another exam, but in the meantime the Coast Guard responded favorably to my application. I was ordered to report to the Coast Guard Academy at New London, Connecticut, on August 25th.

I went to the library, checked out books on seamanship and navigation, notified my draft board that I had escaped their grasp and the Coast Guard that I was on the way! Then, one Friday early in August, I received a very significant telephone call from Harold Warner one of my favorite law school professors, a reserve colonel in the Army Judge Advocate General's Corps who happened to be on active duty at Fort McPherson (Atlanta) Georgia. Colonel Warner (we always called him that—even later when he was dean of UT Law School) reported that the Army had three vacancies in the JAG Corps and, if I could get down to Fort McPherson on the following Monday morning, he would arrange for me to take the necessary exams. I explained I was under orders from the Coast Guard, but he said I need not worry about that. The Coast Guard would have no jurisdiction over me if I were in the Army.

So it was that on Monday, August 11, I was at Fort McPherson taking written tests, undergoing physical exams, being interviewed, shuttling from one building to another, answering questions, standing around naked, coughing, being probed and otherwise subjected to the indignities usually associated with a livestock auction. Fortunately, Colonel Warner appeared from time to time to offer words of encouragement.

A little more than a week later, I received a letter dated 21 August 1952 signed by "L G CAUSEY, Colonel, AGC, Adjutant General, BY COMMAND OF MAJOR GENERAL BEIDERLINDEN" addressed to "First Lieutenant John Joseph Thomason, 01878077." The paragraphs in the letter were numbered. I was thunderstruck by the power of paragraph number one, which declared unequivocally that "The Secretary of the Army has directed that you be informed that, by

25

direction of the President, you are appointed in the ORC (Officers' Reserve Corps) as a Reserve Commissioned Officer in the AUS (Army of the United States) effective this date in the grade and with the service number shown in the address above."

WOW! I hadn't realized that President Truman was involved.

The letter went on to say that all I had to do to accept the commission was swear to an oath, provided in the letter, which could be administered by any notary public. Enclosed were additional orders (likewise, impressively, "By direction of the President") telling me that once sworn in, I was to report to Fort Jackson, South Carolina on August 27th.

That same day I took the oath becoming a first lieutenant, service number 01878077, in the Army of the United States, Judge Advocate General's Corps. E. W. Hale, Jr., the lawyer in whose office I worked while I waited for the results of the bar exam swore me in. Because of a physical disability Hale had never served in the military but he was a notary public. So, at my request, with just the two of us in his private office, he administered the oath, as unfamiliar to him as to me.

In the instant I solemnly swore to protect America from all its enemies, I was metamorphosed into an officer in the Army of the United States, commissioned by none other than the President, Harry S. Truman, himself. I would be on temporary duty at Fort Jackson, pending the start of the next class at The Judge Advocate General's School, to begin in October at the University of Virginia in Charlottesville.

I was nervous. Here I was, a commissioned army officer and the only thing I knew about the military was what little I had learned as a boy scout, plus four semesters as a private and then sergeant, training one hour a day, one day a week, in compulsory ROTC at Central High School.

By asking around, I discovered that enlisted men were issued uniforms when they reported for duty, but that officers had to provide uniforms for themselves. At that time there were some "Army Surplus Stores" on North Main Street in downtown Memphis where, I learned, one could purchase an army uniform and suitable insignia. I went to one of the stores to be outfitted as an army officer. The experience was less glamorous than expected.

The salesman sold me some khaki shirts, pants and matching socks, belt, a tie and one of those soft, folding "overseas" caps. He showed me where to pin the silver bar on my shirt collar and on the front of my cap and where to put the JAG Corps insignia, a polished brass wreath with crossed pen and arrow. He also suggested that I purchase a "B-4" bag (a sort of canvass two-suiter with side pockets) -- "Since all the officers have them." He then arranged for my name, rank, branch and service number to be stenciled on the side of my B-4 bag. I couldn't keep my eyes off that lettering. I was very, very proud.

The next stop was the public library where I checked out a copy of *The Officer's Guide*, a detailed and comprehensive how-to-do-it reference work which I had very little time to examine because I inadvertently left it in the seat pocket of the airplane I took from Memphis to Columbia, South Carolina. I had read enough of the *Officer's Guide* to know that my first stop at Fort Jackson was the headquarters building. The Columbia cab driver was familiar with my destination and took me there. It was early morning when I entered the building.

A sleepy sergeant sitting at a desk said, "Sign in over there," nodding toward a simple wooden lectern upon which was a sort-of guest book. This guest book, however, was different from any I had ever seen before. It had vertical columns headed by odd words and abbreviations and horizontal lines upon which, it appeared, one was to enter information. The problem was that I was the first one on the page - and the previous pages had been removed. I finally figured out the headings and inserted what I thought was required in all the columns but one - "authority"! I stared numbly at the page but no thought came. The clock was ticking. Soon someone would queue up behind me and I would have to turn away leaving "authority" blank (probably a court-martial offense) or confess that I did not know what "authority" meant.

I turned to the sleepy sergeant and asked -- with just a hint of exasperation – "I'm not familiar with this form of sign-in book. What does 'authority' mean?"

"The same as it does in every other sign-in book," he said. "That's where you put the number and date of your orders."

With great embarrassment, I wrote the required information, put on my cap and turned to leave. The sergeant, however, had yet a parting word. As I walked past him and reached the door I heard him say, "By the way lieutenant, your cap's on backward."

I reached up to touch the front of my cap where the silver bar should have been. I felt only cloth. The bright insignia of my esteemed commission was facing to the rear.

*　　　*　　　*

THE TIMES: On the day I reported for duty at Fort Jackson a presidential election campaign was in progress: Democrat Illinois Governor Adlai Stevenson versus Republican Dwight Eisenhower, retired, five star, General of the Army. That day, August 27, 1952, Stevenson faced a tough assignment. He was to speak to the National Convention of the American Legion on the subject of "Patriotism." The Legion was America's largest veteran's organization. Stevenson was a veteran and a well-spoken intellectual, but Eisenhower had been the victorious American commander in Europe in World War II and was the choice of most legionaries. Stevenson spoke eloquently on the meaning of patriotism:

I have no claim, as many of you do, to the honored title of old soldier. Nor have I risen to high rank in the armed services. The fact that a great general and I are competing candidates for the presidency will not diminish my warm respect for his military achievements. Nor will that respect keep me from using every honest effort to defeat him in November!

We talk a great deal about patriotism. What do we mean by "patriotism" in the context of our times? I venture to suggest that what we mean is a sense of national responsibility which will enable America to remain master of her power, to walk with it in serenity and wisdom, with self-respect and the respect of all mankind; a patriotism that puts country ahead of self; a patriotism which is not short, frenzied outbursts of emotion, but the tranquil and steady dedication of a lifetime.

*   *   *

Fort Jackson, South Carolina

Dear Mother and Dad   29 Aug 1952

I will try to make this an informative letter but I am very tired and weary after this hectic day of being "processed."

To start from the beginning, the trip to Knoxville was quite pleasant and my stay on the University of Tennessee campus at the SAE house there - though short - was most enjoyable. I was able to see quite a few people and get some addresses of buddies now stationed with the American military all over the world. Maybe I'll get to see some of them. The flight from Knoxville to Columbia was beautiful. I had never flown over the Smoky Mountains before and I thoroughly enjoyed the ride. I went directly from the plane to the hotel where I had planned to read the <u>Officer's Guide</u> I had brought with me but found I had left it on the plane. So, although I felt quite alone I settled down with a magazine and went to sleep early.

Fort Jackson is hot! At least it was today. Maybe the nonstop movement of my right arm overheated me. I must have saluted 10,000 times. I think I am getting good at it. I have learned that a salute does not involve just a simple movement of the arm; one must also venture a cheery greeting and a friendly smile, as in "Good Morning. Sir!"

Among the objects which I wish I had - but don't - are (1) a car; (2) a radio; (3) my record player; and (4) an alarm clock.

So far my uniforms have cost only about $30.00 - four sets of kakhis. Apparently that is all I will need in the near future.

Within 400 yards of my barracks is the laundry, officer's cafeteria, barbershop and the staff judge advocate office, where I work. I will not receive any formal training here. But a very exacting and meticulous Colonel Gross promises to make my time here as absorbing and difficult as he possibly can. After Colonel Gross, the worst thing about Fort Jackson is that everywhere one is surrounded by small black gnats called "no see 'ems" which persist in flying in and about one's eyes, ears and nose. They are inescapable.

INSPECTING THE MESS

A "transient" officer or enlisted man is one on his way from one post to another. At large installations, such as Fort Jackson, the Army sets aside special barracks and mess halls just for the transients - so that the officers and EM (Enlisted Men) regularly stationed there don't have to mingle with the transients. When I arrived, I was sent to a transient barracks since I am not permanently assigned to Fort Jackson – I am here only temporarily -- on my way to the Judge Advocate General's School in Charlottesville. As you might suspect, transients do not receive preferential treatment. Transients get what is left over. But the biggest problem for transients is that there is nothing for them to do except, from time to time, engage in some sort of "make work" detail.

So it was that I found myself in an assemblage of transient officers called together at the movie theater and advised that the next day each would be required to inspect one of the enlisted men's mess halls. I had never even *seen* an enlisted men's mess hall and needed a crash course in mess hall inspection. After supper I knocked on the door of a major of artillery whose billet is across the hall from mine and explained my problem. The major advised me that there was a lot more to inspecting a mess than simply looking around. Like most other things in the military, a protocol was involved.

"The mess sergeant," said the major, "is king of the world in his own mess hall. You will be given a long list of things to check and will be expected to evaluate the conditions that you find." The major continued. "But you don't just walk in the mess hall and start inspecting. First, the mess sergeant will have to inspect you, to determine whether you know anything about what you are doing. In order to demonstrate that you do know what you are doing, you must behave in a certain way. First, you enter the mess hall and announce to the mess sergeant who you are and that you are present for an inspection. The mess sergeant will pretend that he is delighted to see you - but in reality an inspection of his mess is the last thing he wants to have happen that day. You need to give the mess sergeant a little extra time to get things in order, so you say 'Before we begin the inspection, sergeant, I wonder if you have any hot coffee?'"

"'Yes sir, lieutenant,' he will say, 'in this mess we have the best coffee at Fort Jackson.'" (Actually there is no *best coffee* at Fort Jackson. There is not even any *good coffee.* Rumor has it that in 1917 when Fort Jackson was opened, a big pot of coffee was brewed to which, ever since, coffee and water have been periodically added.) The major continued, "While you are having coffee with the mess sergeant and everybody is scurrying around in the background trying to get ready for the inspection you might say 'Say, this is good coffee sergeant. Maybe I won't be so tough on you today. Maybe I won't probe behind the oven door hinge with the index finger of my white-gloved hand!'

"This comment," said the major, "is to inform the sergeant that you know how in the 'old army' they actually donned white gloves for such inspections and, also, that you are aware there is *always* grease behind the oven door hinge." After getting a few more inside tips from the major - (by this time we were sharing a bottle of his Scotch) - my confidence was high. Instead of fear and anxiety, I anticipated the next day's activity with certainty that the upcoming inspection of the enlisted men's mess was a challenge I would not fail to meet.

The Army likes to do things early in the morning and in alphabetical order. So, the next morning at 0700 hours (7 a.m.) the transient officers whose last names began with "A" through "M" were again assembled at the movie theater. Those transients whose last names began with a letter in the last half of the alphabet were expected fifteen minutes later. Even though my last name begins with a "T," I arrived at 0700. I did not want to be late for my first assignment and my military record to be blemished so early in my career. After about twenty minutes I received my check list, pencil and clipboard and was assigned a jeep and driver to take me to the particular enlisted men's mess I was to inspect.

We arrived after breakfast had been served. There were just a few soldiers present, hanging around, not doing anything in particular. I approached the first person I saw, a corporal, and after exchanging salutes said,

33

"Good morning, corporal. I'm Lieutenant Thomason. I'm here to inspect the mess. Would you please advise the mess sergeant."

"YES, SIR!" he shouted in reply, and scampered away.

In short order the sergeant appeared, saluted and said, "Good morning, lieutenant; how 'bout a cup of coffee?" There went the first few lines of my practiced repartee. I was forced to condense my well-rehearsed introductory lines to a simple response. "Fine." I said.

As we seated ourselves to enjoy our coffee and as I was about to embark upon my observations concerning white gloves and the old army, the mess sergeant innocently said,

"Lieutenant, that's a fine looking ring you're wearing; is that a class ring?"

"Yes it is," I said, not at all enthused about the direction in which this conversation was going.

"University of Tennessee," I added, proudly.

"What year?" asked the sergeant, with a look of absolute purity of heart upon his face. Everybody at the table knew what the answer would be.

"1952," I said, and all eyes shifted to the wall where a large calendar proclaimed the current month to be August, 1952.

"Is that so?" said the sergeant, not so much as a question, but a meaningful statement to all within hearing. It was also an unspoken declaration to the effect that now we all understood what the situation was at this time and place and that "nobody was fooling nobody," as they say.

I had been studying the inspection checklist on the way over. There were about forty items to inspect and rate. Then, there was a place for me to comment. Of the forty items, I recognized at least twenty, and thought I would be able to figure out the others as we went along. So, as I inspected I would say something like, "I'm eager to see the potato bin," and more often than not, someone with a gesture would volunteer, "It's right over here, sir." So, I would know where the potato bin was. As we walked through the inspection I was able to check off more and more items, except that there was something on my list called the "grease trap," about which I could not get a clue.

Finally, I had inspected everything but the grease trap. I worked the conversation around to include some general comments about grease traps and the necessity that they be frequently inspected, but got no hint as to what the grease trap was or where it might be located.

I found myself standing in a silent group - everyone obviously waiting for me to act. Following what I thought to be the procedure of countless military leaders before me when faced with uncertainty, I knew that the time had come to move. So, gathering my courage and assuming a look of determination, I turned to the sergeant and said, "Well, sergeant, I think it's time we took a look at the grease trap."

"Very well, lieutenant" he said. "Follow me."

Out the side door of the mess hall he went, followed by me, my driver and three or four others who had been participating in the inspection. We marched smartly to the end of the mess hall, turned the corner and stopped. I saw nothing. No one spoke. Everyone was obviously waiting for me to do something. Anticipation was palpable. Finally, I said - with perhaps a bit of apprehension in my voice that I hoped might be read as irritation –

"Well sergeant, I would like to see the grease trap!"

After a brief but dramatic pause the mess sergeant replied - in a kindly and understanding voice –

"You can see it, sir, if you will but look beneath your feet. Sir, you're standing on it."

What happened next is kind of vague. I do recall that I stepped away and requested that what appeared to be a concrete trap door be removed. I looked inside and saw a lot of grease and I think I said "h'mmm" and told them to put the lid back on, and gave the mess sergeant an excellent overall inspection grade.

The sergeant, who was about twice my age, told me not to worry, that now I knew where the grease trap was and would never have to concern myself about its location on future inspections. Thankfully, that information was never put to use, for not ever again was I called upon to inspect a mess hall.

THE JAG SCHOOL

The Judge Advocate General's School is located in the College of Law at the University of Virginia in Charlottesville, a lovely town in the foothills of the Blue Ridge Mountains about 100 miles southwest of Washington, DC. Thomas Jefferson was the founder of the university and his home, Monticello and burial place are nearby. At that time U. Va. had an all-male student body. The only female students on campus were in the school of nursing. However, many girls' colleges are close, for example Hollins College, Sweetbrier and Randolph Macon. Male undergraduate friends from Memphis at U. Va. and Washington and Lee always had good contacts at the girl's schools and were usually glad to share them.

JAG students differed from the regular students at the U. Va. Law School. We took our ten minute breaks after the hour and they, before; we wore uniforms to all school functions; they had about four classes a day, whereas we had eight; and we lived in a separate military dormitory. Of course, the class subjects were different. While the law students learned about torts and contracts we studied Military Justice, Military Affairs, International Law, Rules of Land Warfare, Procurement, Claims and such. Our professors were Army officers. We worked hard all week but were often free on the weekend and usually departed the campus.

Jim Linebaugh, a close UT Law School friend, who had been an enlisted man at Fort Jackson, had been accepted in the JAG school, commissioned a first lieutenant and was my classmate and roommate. His mother and stepfather were stationed at Quantico; a big Marine base nearby and we frequently visited them. At the entrance of that base I was pleased to see "Thomason Park" named for Colonel John W. Thomason, a well-known military writer, artist and historian. I would like to think we are related but can find no direct thread.

We also had a great contact and sometimes accommodations in Washington, DC, in that one of my classmates' uncle maintained an apartment there.

*   *   *

Dear Mother and Dad,   10 November 1952
    This week has been one of great interest to everybody. On Monday, four of the twenty of us (not including me) from the Third Army area (generally the southeast U. S.) got

orders after graduation to FECOM; that means Far East Command, in short, Korea. Then, on Tuesday, Lieutenant Verona from the Washington Headquarters of the staff judge advocate came down to talk with the rest us about our assignments. He had some rather important things to say, for example:

1. All category three officers will go overseas before they get out. I am a category three. 2. Twenty of the ninety-eight in this class will be assigned to the Pentagon - a place, now that I know something about it, I have come to dread. I don't want to go there. The prospect of spending my time in the military working for a large law firm in a big city, probably doing the same thing over and over, is not at all appealing. I would much prefer an adventure in a foreign country. 3.There will be no promotions for JAG officers other than those who go to Korea. 4. The assignment you ask for has a lot to do with what you get.

All this information has been important in my decision-making about what assignment I am going to seek..

After many lengthy barracks discussions and a good deal of considered thought I have made up my mind to put in an unqualified request for overseas duty - which probably means I will be sent to Korea! In deciding to do this the following factors were considered together with the ones listed above 1. I don't want to be assigned to the Pentagon. 2. I have about one chance in four of getting a good assignment in the third army area - there is no Army base close to Memphis. 3. It would be virtually impossible for me to get transferred outside *the army area. 4. I will have to go overseas if I am ever to make captain - and I would like to be promoted to the rank of captain before I get out. 5. I am likely to go to Camp Rucker, Alabama or Fort Jackson, South Carolina if I don't make an overseas request. Neither place would be much more than bearable. 6. So long as I am in the Army, I may as well see some of the world.*

So, it all boils down to the likelihood that I will go to Japan in about February or March, and then on to Korea after that. I will be back home in about a year and a half and I may get out sooner than I once thought. I hope you understand my conclusions and agree with my thinking. Of course, if I ask for overseas service I might get to go to Europe, but the chance of that is very slim. Very few-about five out of 120 -- will get that assignment. As I figure it, the odds are about 2 to 1 that I will go overseas and about 10 to 1 that it will be Korea.

We are in the midst of mid-term exams and although exams are never fun these are really not much to contend with. I plan to study about an hour tonight and let it go at that. My grades are consistently just above the halfway mark, which puts me in the middle third of the class, a good place to be if I am to get the kind of assignment I want. The top people will get Pentagon duty for sure.

We had a fine time in Richmond and will probably drive down to Sweetbrier College this weekend. The following weekend I will be on my way home and will probably know what my assignment will be. If I am sent overseas I should get some leave after graduation and before I ship out.

*   *   *

Dear Mother and Dad,   *14 December 1952*

I stayed in Charlottesville this weekend – not because I wanted to, but because there are a couple of infectious maladies running rampant though the dormitory to which I have fallen victim. None of these illnesses is serious, but it seems that germs just get passed around in such crowded living conditions. So, I am staying close to home in order that I might shake off a cold, athlete's foot and the pink eye! I expect to be well in the next day or so. I want to be healthy for the holidays. Maybe this will allow me to miss a few classes and get some packing done. Mid-term exams are over and I managed to stay slightly above the mid-class mark with a minimum of study. That has been my objective. So, I am satisfied. I expect this will be my last letter 'till I am home.

See you soon.

*   *   *

During the summer of 1952 while I was waiting to hear from my efforts to get a military commission, Bill Hale suggested I get involved in politics. Eighty-four year old Kenneth McKellar of Memphis was seeking reelection to the United States Senate. Congressman Albert Gore Sr. of Carthage, Tennessee opposed him. (Gore's son was later vice-president in the administration of President Clinton, 1992-2000). Because of his seniority, having served six terms in the senate - under every President from Wilson through Truman -

Senator McKellar had become *President Pro Tempore* of the Senate when, upon the death of President Roosevelt, Vice-President Truman had moved into the number one position.

A bus tour for Senator McKellar was organized and I made several speeches for him in small communities in West Tennessee. On the bus I became acquainted with the senator and members of his staff.

The Senator, who had never married, lived in a suite in the Mayflower Hotel, in Washington. It just so happened that for business reasons the uncle of Syd Keeble of Nashville, one of my classmates at the JAG School, maintained an apartment in Washington. Sometimes we would spend the weekend there and would use the apartment if it were available. Younger members of Senator McKellar's staff were good about arranging for us to have female companions for an evening on the town and occasionally the senator would loan me his limousine, which displayed U. S. Government license plate *number two!*

Occasionally I visited Senator McKellar in Washington. He had a quick mind and was a bottomless well of political recollections covering thirty-six years in the Senate. He told me once that when he was chairman of the Senate Appropriations Committee, President Roosevelt called him in and advised that he needed an appropriation in the amount of three billion dollars but that he couldn't disclose the purpose of the money -- only that it was necessary and important. McKellar said he would get the money, and did. It turned out that the funds were for the construction of the "Manhattan Project," – the atomic bomb. I later heard a variation of the story in which McKellar is said to have put a condition on securing the appropriation – that

41

the money be spent in Tennessee. Senator McKellar didn't mention that to me and I don't know if it is true. It is a fact, however, that much of the work on the atomic bomb was done in Oak Ridge, not far from Knoxville, and that a huge research facility and production plant was built there.

Another time the Senator challenged me to name all the counties in Tennessee. I named about twenty, jumping around the state in no particular order, as the county appellations popped into my head. When I gave up on the effort, beginning in the east at Bristol and working his way to the west, ending at Memphis, Senator McKellar quickly called out all ninety-six without pausing or omitting one.

After driving the Senator's limousine a couple of times I was beginning to think I was no longer one of the "mattress mites," as Washington insiders label outsiders. Maybe I was really *somebody*. While at the wheel, I scrupulously obeyed all the traffic ordinances as we tooled around the city. I didn't want the Senator to receive any complaints on my account. At the same time, I was pleased to accept premium parking places, frequently offered, and I suspect the ease with which I could line up a date during that interval was more likely related to my conspicuous and preeminent license plate number than to my sparkling personality and good looks.

ORDERS TO EUROPE

Home in Memphis for the holidays, I received the best Christmas present ever: orders to Europe! I was one of five in my class of one hundred twenty to be sent there. Army travel orders are written in a code difficult for a novice to read and I was still pretty much a novice when I received these:

DEPARTMENT OF THE ARMY

SPECIAL ORDERS NO. 255

Washington, D. C.   *24 December 1952*

    The fol named off is rel fr asg dy sta indicated and asg USA Europe, Bremerhaven, Germany. Wp Cp Kilmer Per Cen, New Brunswick, N. J. rept not later than date spec for trans through New York POE., Brooklyn, N. Y.

    1st LT JOHN J. THOMASON, 01878077, JAGC MOS 8101.From TDY, JAG Sch. University of Va., Charlottesville, Va., Eff upon comp present course a/o

    23 Jan 53.

BY ORDER OF THE SECRETARY OF THE ARMY

J. LAWTON COLLINS

Chief of Staff, United States Army

             *   *   *

This jargon means *"The following named officer is relieved from the assigned duty station indicated and assigned United States Army, Europe, Bremerhaven, Germany. You will proceed to Camp Kilmer Personnel Center, New Brunswick, New Jersey. Report not later than the date specified for transportation through New York Port of Embarkation, Brooklyn, New York:*

> *1st Lieutenant John J. Thomason, Service number 01878077, Military Occupational Specialty Number 8101, Judge Advocate General's Corps, is released from Temporary Duty at the Judge Advocate General's School University of Virginia, Charlottesville, Virginia, effective upon completion of the present course, on or about 23 January 1953."*

As a practical matter, it meant that when I finished the JAG School I would not return to Fort Jackson but would go home for a short leave and then report directly to a port of embarkation, to board a troop ship destined for Europe.

*   *   *

Sometimes the sequence of life's events is not only unexpected, but seemingly out of context, or irrelevant. So it was in the midst of my JAG School training when I was abruptly dealt a "wild card," having nothing to do with what I had just previously experienced, in what I was then involved or what I was planning for the immediate future. Nonetheless, it was a shock, an event with which I had to contend and to which I had to adjust.

On the 8th of January 1953, a few days after I had returned to JAG School from Christmas leave in Memphis, I was advised by a telegram from my father that his mother, my Grandmother Thomason, had died. At the moment of her death I had been visiting Monticello, the home of Thomas Jefferson. I returned to the Army dormitory at U. Va. to find Syd Keeble, a classmate from Nashville, watching for me. He had been advised of the telegram and had waited outside the dorm for a long time so that he could personally give me the news. It was an act of kindness I very much appreciated.

The news was a shock. I went to my room and wrote a letter to my father expressing my condolences. Grandmother Thomason, Theresa Berryman Thomason, was 82 when she died. She had been born in Fredricktown, Missouri, the granddaughter of Colonel William Newberry, also a lawyer. Newberry was born in Kentucky in 1800 and moved to Missouri when he was 19. I don't know why he was called "Colonel."

I remember Grandmother Thomason very well. For a while she stayed for part of the year with us when we lived at 109 Spring Avenue in Webster Groves, Missouri, occupying a small basement apartment. I was quite young - I think we moved away from Spring Avenue when I was four or five years old - and since I was not old enough to attend school - Grandmother Thomason and I spent a lot of time together. She was very quiet and frail, and always carried a supply of *Luden's Menthol Cough Drops*, although I don't remember her ever having a cough. She would give me a cough drop when I asked for one - which was frequently. They were sweet and tasted good. If you didn't chew them up they lasted for a long time.

Grandmother Thomason read <u>Uncle Wiggly</u> stories to me. I believe Uncle Wiggly appeared daily in the morning paper. She also read me fairy tales and told me stories about how things were when she was a child. She had two bachelor brothers, Uncle Jim and Uncle Joe, one of whom had lost a leg in a railroad accident. I think the only times she was impatient with me was when I would pester her to tell me about the night they brought Uncle Joe home from the train wreck.

Her hands were very soft on the palm side and bony on top. She seemed always to be sewing and wore a silver thimble on the fourth finger of her left hand. She was very kind to me and I loved her.

I think she grew weary of moving between our house and the homes of her two daughters, Carolyn in Oklahoma and Mary in Pennsylvania. So, as I grew older, I saw less and less of her. She never lived with us after we moved to Memphis in 1939. I hadn't seen her for several years prior to her death. I never knew her husband, my grandfather, Lewis R. Thomason, a St. Louis lawyer. He died in 1927, two years before I was born. Although my grandmother had not been physically present in my life for a long time, in a vague sort of way, the perception of her death caused a feeling of hollowness special to the loss of a loved one – a feeling that I experienced for many years after her death, and sometimes sense, even today.

THE CLOSE COMBAT AND INFILTRATION COURSES

In January, back at the JAG School we all talked excitedly about the orders each had received over the Christmas holidays. Eighteen of us were being sent overseas, five to Europe and thirteen either to Japan or Korea. Everybody else was being sent to some post, camp or station in the United States.

For those heading overseas there were unique activities in store. First came a series of shots, immunization injections, leaving both arms very sore for several days. These were administered at the University infirmary, a building we knew well because it was there we had previously "volunteered" to give blood every month or so. The discomfort resulting from the shots was somewhat offset by the fact that the trip to the infirmary allowed us to miss class. After three years of intensive study and required class attendance in law school and the more recent tedious classroom work at the JAG School, I was willing to undergo almost any travail if it meant I could avoid a classroom session.

Then, following the Army tradition of doing things early in the day, at four a.m. on a Wednesday in mid-January, the eighteen destined for overseas duty boarded a bus in Charlottesville bound for Fort Lee, Virginia. There we were to "P. O. R. Qualify" which was Army lingo for "Process, Overseas Replacement." This process, we were later to learn, involved completing the "Close Combat Course," the "Infiltration Course" and familiarizing ourselves with the combat weapon we might be called upon to use.

The first course - and to me the most fun - was close combat. The course, about seventy yards long, was in a swampy, wooded area. A carbine and thirty rounds of live ammunition were issued to each combatant. We formed a single rank, walking side by side - about ten feet apart - and started forward. As we walked along we encountered obstacles; maybe there would be a stream with a log thrown across for a bridge or a mud filled shell hole. From time to time an "enemy soldier" would jump out from behind a tree or up out of a ditch. The idea was for us to shoot as rapidly and accurately as possible at the "enemy soldier" target and not hit each other. The obstacles were not difficult; however, it seemed that it was always when we were in the midst of overcoming an impediment that the target would jump out. Army lawyers are not the most athletic or

47

agile and some of our group fell into the mud. But, thankfully, nobody got shot. The entire exercise lasted about thirty minutes and was like an amusement park experience but much more exhilarating. We were shooting real bullets!

Next came the carbine familiarization course. It would seem more logical for us to have become familiar with the carbine before we were required to use it in close combat but the Army has its own way. To learn how to use the carbine we fired eighty-four rounds, twenty-eight standing, twenty-eight kneeling and a like number in the prone position. We shot at a standard bull's eye target. I did pretty well. My shot groups were tightly bunched, but not on the bull's eye. The erroneous placement of the shot pattern I naturally attributed to incorrect sight adjustment on the carbine.

The infiltration course followed. We had heard about the infiltration course and most of us were looking forward to it with some degree of apprehension. To start, the group was required to form a rank in a sort of World War I type trench like the ones I'd seen in such movies as *All Quiet on the Western Front* and *What Price Glory*. When the command was given to go "over the top" we were to scramble from the trench with our rifles and packs, and move forward on our hands, feet and bellies - no knees or elbows - a distance of about fifty yards, keeping as low as possible. No incentive to keep low was required since several fifty-caliber machine guns in front of us fired bullets that whined a few feet over our heads. Strands of barbed wire about thirty inches overhead also served to keep us down. From time to time "artillery shells" exploded nearby, adding significantly to the war-like effect.

Having entered the trench behind two other groups, we waited while first one group and then the other crawled the fifty yards to the welcoming trench at the other end of the course.

As we tarried, I noticed several towers in which two or three men with a bird's eye view of the area were apparently setting off the artillery shell explosions by activating remote control switches. One of these towers was close by. As I was looking up, I saw one of its occupants, a sergeant, motion for me to come up. Aware we would be waiting for some time before our turn came, I made my way to the end of the trench and walked over to the tower where an access ladder extended from the tower to the ground. The enlisted men working in the tower gave me a friendly welcome and pointed out their panoramic view of the entire battle area.

The sergeant seemed to be genuinely interested in our group, explaining that it was unusual for him to encounter a unit consisting entirely of officers. When I commented that we were all lawyers and first lieutenants from the Judge Advocate General's School at the University of Virginia, he seemed pleased to have us at Fort Lee to experience the infiltration course, of which, I now perceived, he was in charge. In a gesture of friendliness, the sergeant pointed out how many areas of mud could be avoided if a crawling infiltrator knew where the dry areas were located. The sergeant suggested a trench position and route for me to take that would avoid the mud holes and allow me to traverse the entire area from trench to trench on a clear, arid and unobstructed path. After thanking him for his friendly assistance, I shook hands all round, descended from the tower, returned to the starting trench and made my way to the position I had been shown -- the beginning point of the dry pathway.

It wasn't long before the last man in the group ahead tumbled into the finishing trench and we were alerted to get ready to go "over the top." When the signal came, my comrades and I crawled out of the trench. I wormed my way along the dry route, which I had so carefully committed to memory while others, to my left and right, cursed the mud that they could not avoid. As I made my way across the dry ground to a point about halfway home, I looked up at the tower and waved a greeting to the sergeant, which he returned -- a smile on his face. Suddenly, there was a tremendous explosion just a few feet in front of me, an explosion so powerful that my entire body seemed to be lifted six or eight inches off the ground. Falling back with a thud and congratulating myself on having survived the experience, I was startled when mud began to fall; at first a sprinkle, then a torrent. The mud showered down for what seemed like several minutes. I was soon completely covered over with it. In astonishment I looked back up at the sergeant in the tower. His hand was on the explosion control switch and his smile had been replaced by a broad grin. Our eyes met and he laughed as he delivered to me an unusually smart salute.

* * *

Dear Mom and Dad,   *20 January, 1953*

I am to report to Camp Kilmer, New Jersey, on about the tenth of February, there to wait sea transportation to Germany. Camp Kilmer, I have heard, is a horrid place but I shouldn't be there very long. Troop ships depart fairly often from nearby New York City. I shall graduate from the JAG School on January 30th, a Friday. General J. Lawton Collins, chief of staff of the Army, will be here for the occasion. Then I will be home for a short leave about the first or second of February before departing for the port of debarkation. The baggage allowance is four hundred pounds, so I shall travel heavy; civilian clothes, record player, records, tennis racquet, ukulele and whatever else I can think of, including the 38-caliber snub nose revolver dad gave me to take along, "Just in case."

This is an exciting time for me.

*   *   *

THE TIMES: On February 2, 1953 President Eisenhower delivered his first State of the Union Address to Congress and said:

"Our country has come through a painful period of trial and disillusionment since the victory of 1945. We anticipated a world of peace and cooperation. The calculated pressures of aggressive communism have forced us, instead, to live in a world of turmoil.

"From this costly experience we have learned that the free world cannot indefinitely remain in a posture of paralyzed tension, leaving forever to the aggressor the choice of time and place and means to cause greatest hurt to us at least cost to himself."

Eisenhower then outlined a more aggressive policy against communism, In Europe and worldwide.

"The policy we embrace must be a coherent global policy. The freedom we cherish and defend in Europe and in the Americas is no different from the freedom that is imperiled in Asia."

*   *   *

ON THE WAY TO GERMANY

On the 6th day of February, 1953, my parents drove me to the Millington Naval Air station, just a few miles north of Memphis, where I had arranged to board a Navy flight to the New York City area near Camp Kilmer, New Jersey. There I would wait until a ship was ready to take me from the port of New York to Bremerhaven, Germany. Since I was a member of the military, I could ride free on a "space available" basis on any form of military transportation that happened to be going where I wanted to go. Having called the Navy base, I was advised there was an empty seat on this flight. As it turned out, I was the only Army person on a Navy DC-3, two-engine transport plane, filled with Navy aircraft mechanics, all seasoned enlisted men and non-commissioned officers. They were going to the Grumman aircraft factory on Long Island-- presumably for advanced training. Mom and dad were allowed to drive right out on the ramp close to the plane where I unloaded my B-4 bag, kissed my mother good-bye, shook hands with my father, and turned away to board the battleship gray painted Navy airliner. My parents and I knew it would be at least two years before we would see each other again. It turned out to be a little longer than that. The plane was just like the Chicago and Southern transport that took me from Memphis to St. Louis when I was eleven years old—my first airplane fight—except a little more Spartan in interior decor and, of course, without any attractive stewardesses on board.

When we had climbed to about 10,000 feet, I noticed that my fingernails were turning bluish. The plane was not pressurized. As the cabin became level, I was approached by a Navy chief petty officer with a clipboard.

"Lieutenant," he said respectfully, "it turns out you are the highest ranking person on the plane, so you have to sign for the airplane and everybody on board."

"What does that mean?" I inquired.

"Well," he said, "it means that if anything happens on this flight so that the plane is damaged or if anybody is injured or killed, you are responsible for it."

I was flabbergasted. "How could that be?" I asked. "I am just sitting here-I am only a passenger. The pilot should be the one to sign. He is the one who is flying the airplane!"

"The pilot is only a warrant officer; you are a first lieutenant. So, you will have to sign for everything or we will have to turn back and put you off the plane. Then the pilot will be the highest ranking officer and he can take responsibility," said the chief petty officer.

I thus became aware of one of the great differences between military and civilian life. Whereas, in civilian life only a few laws impact on an individual and little time is spent worrying about compliance, in the military everything is governed by rules or regulations and much time is devoted, rather wasted, in learning, complying with or avoiding them. What difference did it make who was "responsible" for the plane that took me on the first leg of my journey to Germany? If the plane had crashed, it could hardly have mattered who had signed for it. However, that expensive airliner was only the first of many items I was compelled to sign for before completing my incipient military career.

An unnerving thought occurs to me. Somewhere, in a dusty and remote military archive, there must be a record of Army clothing, supplies, and equipment including a Navy airplane for which I am to this day financially accountable. Perhaps sufficient time has elapsed so that prosecution is not probable, for I do not presently possess a single one of the many items for which I have accepted responsibility as acknowledged by my signature.

From the Beth Page, Long Island, Grumman airplane factory I journeyed by taxi, bus and train through New York City (my first visit) to Camp Kilmer in New Brunswick, New Jersey. Camp Kilmer was unpleasant but unremarkable. It has always been a place where soldiers wait to go overseas. There was nothing for me to do there except to check the bulletin board twice a day to see if I was on the list to ship out.

I did get to New York City a few times with new friends I met at the officer's club and enjoyed some memorable experiences in the city. Single tickets to New York shows were sometimes available at the last minute. Luckily, one evening I found one at the 46th Street Theater for the smash---hit, musical, *Guys and Dolls*. Seated in a box overlooking the stage, I waited for the show to begin. Suddenly, to my surprise a brass button from my dress uniform tunic popped off my chest. As I tried to catch it, the button went over the rail, striking the head of a lady seated below. Startled but unharmed, she retrieved the button and stood to inquire who its owner might be. Her investigation was of short duration for I was the only one above her in uniform. With great embarrassment I descended, apologized and recovered my button and, as I started back to my seat, was met in the aisle by a motherly woman who advised me she was the wardrobe mistress. She advised me that if I would accompany her back stage she would sew on my button. So, there I was, back stage at the most lavish New York musical of the season, surrounded by gorgeous chorus girls who, as word got around about had happened, were very attentive and gathered around to see the button being reattached. For a brief minute or so I was the star of the show!

Finally, after waiting for more than a week, on Sunday, February 15, 1953 orders were posted for me to act as compartment commander and a member of the advance party on the United States Military Sea Transport Ship *General W. G. Haan*, scheduled to leave the Port of New York the following day. The accommodations for the Army and Air Force enlisted men soon to board were uncomfortable. They were to sleep in bunks stacked five high with only 18 inches between. There were to be 179 enlisted men in my compartment, no portholes, stale air and very little space. I wasn't looking forward to the trip. At least, no one had asked me to sign for the ship.

Then thankfully, within just a few hours of getting the troops aboard, new orders came. Somebody realized that I was an Army lawyer--not a line officer--and reassigned me to the dual task of summary court martial and assistant special services officer. As summary court martial officer I would be in charge of any required military justice proceedings en route. Being assistant special services officer meant I would help provide recreation while at sea.

*   *   *

Dear Mother and Dad,   *16 February 1953*
We departed Brooklyn, New York at 1530 hours, on time.
As we sailed from the pier into the harbor I witnessed a sight

that has been seen by millions before me, but never before by me: the New York skyline and the Statue of Liberty.

So, with the memory of the Army band, which gave us a musical send off still in our minds, we were on our way.

*   *   *

Dear Mother and Dad,   *17 February 1953.*

It is quite dark now; but the stars and moon are bright. Our direction, reckoned by the North Star, appears to be NE. Our speed—I have heard – is 15 knots. We must be about 100 miles at sea. I have been walking on deck. The air is cold and fresh. The ship rolls, not much, but enough to make me constantly aware that we are sea. I am pleased to be where I am and excited to be on my way. I shall not see the shore again until we reach Southampton, England, and not set foot on land until I step onto the pier at Bremerhaven, Germany. Our estimated date of arrival there is February 28.

*   *   *

Dear Mother and Dad,   *20 February, 1953*

4th day out. We are perhaps 1300 miles east of New York. We expect to be in Southampton, England on February 26th and in Bremerhaven, Germany on the 28th if the weather holds. Since we left the mainland I have not seen another ship, or a plane, or anything but the sea.

This morning the ship collided with a twenty-five foot whale and killed it. There was no damage to the <u>Haan</u>. I *didn't actually see it, but wrote about the incident for the ship's newspaper The Haan Pipe. I am one of those responsible for publishing it. Nothing else of much note has occurred.*

Since a few hours after we left port we have been rolling and sometimes pitching. Most of the time the roll is about ten degrees but we have had a few rolls that were as much as thirty degrees, and every variation in between. This is, at the same time both frightening and fun. It is difficult to walk about without falling and difficult to eat. Much soup is spilled. I have not been sick. Few officers have, since we can get outside in the fresh air whenever we want. It is not the same with the enlisted men who mostly are required to stay in their crowded compartments where the air is hot and stale.

*   *   *

Dear Mother and Dad,   *21 February, 1953.*

5th day out.

Another day like the last four.

The vastness of the ocean is difficult to comprehend. We are only half way to Southampton yet we have been at sea for five days and have made good speed.. So much space and water bring on feelings that are difficult to describe, but personal insignificance comes to mind.

Besides the repeated reminders from the ship's regular compliment that we must conserve fresh water, there are other factors that keep us aware of our situation. The constant roll and pitch of the ship, the difficulty in making one's way down the passageways, the steel surroundings everywhere, all remind us we are at sea. Routine situations change at sea. For example, seeing a movie becomes a unique experience, as the ship rolls the chairs of the spectators crack and creak in unison. Occasionally the projector slips and the picture is momentarily shown on the bulkhead or ceiling rather than the screen. There is a constant strain to remain in your chair and not go crashing into another spectator. Getting a haircut becomes a hazardous activity since the chair may spin without warning or the barber slide away at an inopportune time.

*   *   *

My own accommodations aboard were not so bad. I shared a cabin with four other guys and although it was a bit crowded we couldn't complain. Our cabin was originally fitted out to accommodate nine persons. We were above the water line, cabin number 213 on "C" deck, so we had a porthole. My roommates were a Jewish chaplain, a dentist, a medical doctor and a medical administrator, all first lieutenants.

For those whose stomachs were up to it, the meals on the *Haan* were quite good. Officers and enlisted men were served the same food, with one basic difference. Officers received a printed menu and were served by stewards at tables with tablecloths and china, whereas the EM lined up for chow, served and waited on themselves and ate from compartmentalized metal trays. For illustration, the breakfast menu for Monday, 23 February offered the following choices: *chilled fresh tropical blended juice or fresh raspberries with* cream; hot oatmeal or assorted dry cereals with fresh milk; eggs to order, fried, boiled, scrambled or poached; sauté potatoes; grilled smoked American bacon; dry or buttered toast, raisin muffins; jam, jelly or peanut butter and tea, fresh milk or coffee. For lunch that day we were offered mixed sweet pickles or spring onions; English Beef Broth; fried Filet of Flounder with lemon butter, Old Fashioned Beef Stew with vegetables or "Fricandeau" of Veal with country butter; buttered parsnips, Green Beans "Au Buerre"; hot rolls; beet and onion salad with sweet and sour dressing and for desert Apple Brown Betty with sauce or pineapple in syrup followed by cheese and crackers. The supper selection featured celery and ripe olives; baked fresh Halibut with lemon, roast fresh ham with bacon gravy and applesauce or Salisbury Steak with onion sauce; buttered asparagus, mashed turnips and Snowflake Potatoes with an apple raisin and Mayonnaise salad, followed that day by a desert of Apricot Pie, ice cream or fresh fruit, and coffee or tea. As they say in Tennessee, I was eating "high on the hog."

When the *Haan* left New York with a civilian crew of 186, there was 220 tons of food on board, about 125 pounds per person for the thirteen-day trip. The ninety-one person steward's department, under Mr. Maury Silverman of Harrisburg, Pennsylvania, was responsible for storage, serving, handling and preparation of food for all messes. They did a good job.

My assignment as assistant special services officer required me to help produce and act as cartoonist for the ship's newspaper *The Haan Pipe*, a mimeographed six-page publication distributed every other day. As cartoonist I could draw whatever I chose to, but thought it best to limit my drawings to pictures of some event of general interest. For example I drew a cartoon of a ship hitting a whale when that occurred. My cartoons were more in lieu of photographs, which we couldn't reproduce, than satirical or political. Items in the *Haan Pipe* *included* the most recent ship's position and speed, "Lost and Found" notices, e.g., *Pvt. Lloyd Whitehead, RA51177319, lost his identification tags and some keys in the latrine. If found, please turn in to the Sergeant Major's Office.* There was also a religious column written by one of the chaplains, movie listings, a cross word puzzle, interviews by the "Roving Reporter" on what the interviewee expected to see and do in Europe and a summary of news stories gathered from world wide short wave radio broadcasts, for example:

BERLIN: - Red border guards, apparently acting on Soviet and Communist Party orders to shoot to kill, today fired on refugees from East Berlin attempting to flee to the West. West Berlin Police were quoted as saying that trigger-happy East German guards have, on at least four occasions in the past twenty-four hours, also opened fire at two vehicles making a dash across the partially barricaded streets separating the Russian Zone from the Allied Sectors of Berlin.

SEOUL: - U. N. warplanes blasted communist *targets all the way from the Korean battle lines to the Chinese Manchurian frontier before dawn today. U. S. Sabre jet pilots damaged two enemy MIGS and brought their week-long toll of the Red Jets to sixteen destroyed, five so severely damaged they probably crashed and seventeen less seriously damaged to a total of thirty-eight. B-29 Superforts opened a day of savage aerial attacks by hurling two hundred twenty thousand pounds of bombs on a sprawling Communist headquarters only five miles from the Yalu River.*

*   *   *

It was also my duty to systematically pass out the movie tickets In such a way that each of the troops got to see a film every other day and to produce, organize and act as master of ceremonies for a *Variety Show*.

Perhaps because I produced it, I thought the Variety Show was outstanding. The high level of talent that can be found among 2,700 young men is truly amazing. After placing a notice of the show in the newspaper, we conducted auditions and because of the excellent response, had to turn away some accomplished musicians, dancers, comedians and vocalists. The 45 minute show we put together was first class. Because we had such a relatively small space for our auditorium, the show was staged nine times in one day before enthusiastic audiences.

Church services were available each Sabbath, and one occasion I helped my Jewish Rabbi cabin mate conduct a Protestant Christian service. He was called upon to substitute for the regular Christian Chaplain who was seasick.

Although part of the crossing had been rough, thankfully, I had not been sick. One night when it was too rough for us to be outside on "C" deck (about 35 feet above the water) we had ventured out on "B" deck, (45 feet above the water) and were drenched when a wave broke over the rail. Sunshine was rare during the trip. By day the sea was always dark gray. At night it was sometimes so dark we could not make out the horizon – just black sea and sky – with no telling where one ended and the other began. The vast ocean surface was immense and seemed impenetrable, but the depth of the sea, which must have been enormous, was unrevealed. For five days we had not seen a bird, or light or ship or any other thing outside the *Haan*. Mostly, we were bored. Other than my special service duties, which kept me busy until the variety show was over, reading and eating were about our only activities.

After nine days at sea, on February 25, 1953, we arrived at the principal channel Port of Southampton, England, 3,426 miles east of New York City, where we debarked 700 Air Force officers and men who were to be stationed in the United Kingdom.

Utilizing the four-hour respite, I walked about the area near the ship. Possessing no papers that would allow me to clear customs, I couldn't go far. Anyhow, our ship was soon to depart for Bremerhaven. Southampton is the port from which the Mayflower, 333 years before, had sailed for Plymouth, Massachusetts; and a monument near our pier commemorated that event. The huge ocean liners plying the north Atlantic between England and the United States usually sail from Southampton, and we saw the vast and beautiful passenger ship *Queen Elizabeth* in port there. We departed at about 5:00p.m.on what we thought would be a three day trip, about 1100 miles across the English Channel and into the Bremerhaven estuary. Exiting the harbor we passed a British troop ship and exchanged greetings. The Brits were bound for Suez, Singapore and Hong Kong; some of them would be at sea a month.

*   *   *

The ship on which I journeyed to Europe, *General W. G. Haan*, was originally a Navy troop transport, 522 feet long, 72 feet wide and extending 24 feet below the water line (draft). She carried no armaments, had little distinguishing superstructure except for two tall loading cranes and a smokestack, aft, and eight very large lifeboats. Her speed was 16 knots, with a maximum capacity of 3,850 troops. She was launched on March 20, 1945, by the Kaiser Shipbuilding Co. in Richmond, California and commissioned by the Navy on August 2, 1945. She conducted shakedown training out of San Diego, departing about two weeks after the surrender of Japan for the southwest Pacific. There, *Haan* picked up homecoming veterans at Eniwetok, Leyte and Manila before returning to Seattle on October 22. Subsequently, the ship made two voyages to Japan and the Philippines, taking occupation troops out and bringing veterans back. She returned to San Francisco after her last passage, and departed April 30, 1946, for the East Coast via the Panama Canal, arriving in Baltimore May 25. The ship was decommissioned there on June 7, 1946 – less than a year after she had been commissioned. Alas, the waste of war!

The Cold War revived her. She was returned to service on March 1, 1950, and assigned to MSTS (Military Sea Transport Service) under a civilian crew. For three years, until 1953 she operated under the International Refugee Organization and carried displaced East Europeans from northern European ports to the United States. In 1952 the *General W. G. Haan* also made two support voyages to the American bases at Thule, Greenland, and Goose Bay, Labrador. Following this demanding duty, the ship made several voyages to Europe, including the one on which I was a passenger, in support of American units there. She continued this steaming schedule until March 1955 when she brought me home. Apparently that was her last voyage as a troop transport. She was then placed in reduced operational status at the port of New York. In December 1958 the *Haan* resumed duty as a refugee transport. Steaming from New York to Bremerhaven, Germany, she embarked refugees from the gallant, but ill-fated Hungarian Revolution, and brought them to America. On January 7, 1957, she was again placed in reduced operational status and on October 22, 1958, placed in the Atlantic Reserve Fleet and moved to Orange, Texas. She then entered the National Defense Reserve Fleet at nearby Beaumont, Texas where, I assume, she remains today, unless she has been scrapped.

George William Haan, for whom the ship was named, commanded the 32nd U. S. Infantry Division, *Le Terribles*, in World War I. The 32nd was the sixth American division to land in France and took part in several major battles including the Second Battle of the Marne and the Meuse-Argonne offensive, the final Allied offensive that ended the war.

General Haan, from Indiana, was a West Point graduate (1889) who served with artillery in Cuba and the Philippines during the Spanish-American war and afterwards in Panama and France. He retired from the Army in 1922 and was, for a time, associated with the *Milwaukee Journal*. He died in 1924 and is buried in Arlington National Cemetery.

After World War I ended, General Haan (the man, not the ship) remained for a while in Europe in charge of part of the American Army of Occupation. He commanded the VIIth Corps, the very same unit to which I was assigned thirty-five years later!

*   *   *

With the end of World War II, Germany was divided into two parts with the Russians taking the east. The west portion was divided by three. The British occupied the northern part, the Americans the middle, and the French the southwest. No difficulty was encountered in traveling through the Western zones. So, although Bremerhaven was in the British zone, it was the primary port for supplying the occupation needs of U. S. forces in Germany.

Fog settled in on the second day of our crossing to Bremerhaven. We lay at anchor, thirty miles from our destination, for three days. Most of us were critical of the ship's captain for being so cautious since the *Haan* carried modern navigational equipment, including radar. We were astonished when the sun finally broke through revealing no less than sixteen vessels anchored within a mile and a half of us. Among them was the large and famous Swedish *Gripsholm* no more than 300 yards off to port. There seemed to be a three-day party going on among the Swedes. When the fog lifted we could hear them plainly; before that we had not heard a sound. It was evident, our captain appreciated the danger of a blanketing fog.

We put in at the German port of Bremerhaven on the evening of Sunday, March 1, after thirteen days at sea. An American Army band was on the pier serenading the newly arrived troops as the tugs pushed the *Haan* into place and the ship was made secure. I'm sure one of the musical selections was a cause for concern among some of the soldiers on board. We all listened attentively as the military band played *I Wonder Who's Kissing Her Now*.

Cuxhaven and Bremerhaven, on Heligoland Bay, in the North Sea, respectively serve Germany's first and second ports, Hamburg and Bremen, which are about forty miles inland on navigable rivers. But, Bremerhaven is a large city and a bustling port in its own right.

The next day was spent packing and processing on board the ship, which included turning in all our American money. In exchange for "green backs" we received "Military Payment Certificates" ("MPCs" or "scrip") similar in appearance to the legal tender utilized in the game of *Monopoly*. Except by chance while on leave outside Germany, I would not see an American dollar again for two years.

By the time we arrived in Bremerhaven all the officers on board had received their orders but many, even after spending much time pouring over the available maps, couldn't find the locations of their ultimate destinations. My orders were to proceed to headquarters, 7th Army, located near Vaihingen, a suburb of the city of Stuttgart in the southwestern part of Germany, not far from France and Switzerland.

GERMANY

At 7:30p.m.on Monday, March 2, 1953, I stepped on board a very comfortable sleeper car attached to a slow south bound train and at 11:30 a.m. the next day, after a scenic journey through the cities and towns of the British and American zones, I arrived at the main railroad station, the "Hauptbahnhof," in Stuttgart the capital of Baden-Württemberg. The train had passed through Frankfurt at 7a.m. In daylight from that point on, the sights of this strange land had fascinated me. We rolled through Darmstadt, Heidelberg and Ludwigsburg, an area with which I was to become very familiar in the two years to come. On top of a high tower over the main entrance to the railroad station in Stuttgart is an immense Mercedes-Benz emblem in blue neon, the trilon star, Stuttgart being the home of that giant German auto manufacturer. Most of my baggage, which had been in the hold of the *Haan* but not in my immediate possession on the way over was waiting for me at the Stuttgart railroad station. I had been directed to temporary military accommodations just across the plaza from the railroad station, the Hotel Graf Zeppelin. After checking in and treating myself to a welcome shave, bath and haircut, I was advised to take a military bus which regularly made the thirty-five minute trip from the hotel to Patch Barracks, near Vaihingen where the 7th Army Headquarters was located.

Patch Barracks was the first German Kaserne (barracks) I saw. Built in the late 1930s as a German Army base, it is located ten miles southwest of Stuttgart. Having reported in at the staff judge advocate's office, I was welcomed and advised that I had been expected three days previously. Personnel of the J A section wondered what had happened to me. After I explained about the three day wait in the fog outside Bremerhaven my tardiness was brushed aside and I was told that I had been placed on detached duty and should report the next morning to VII Corps Headquarters at Kelley Barracks, ten miles to the east near the town of Möhringen. On March 4, after another short trip by Army bus from the Hotel Graf Zeppelin to Kelley Barracks, I reported to the staff judge advocate of VII Corps, Colonel Joseph Guimond.

Receiving a very friendly welcome and introductions to the other members of the staff, I was advised that the next day, at 1:00 PM, I would act as defense counsel in a general court-martial trial defending a soldier accused of larceny of secret radio frequency crystals. As a matter of fact, I was told, the accused was at that very

67

moment in a nearby conference room waiting to see me. That trial on March 5th was the first of fifteen general courts-martial trials in which I was defense counsel that month, my first month as an Army trial lawyer.

When I left Germany two years later, I had participated as prosecutor or defense counsel in 168 general courts martial trials, which, excluding leave and temporary duty time, averages about two trials a week. Sometimes we tried several cases in one day; sometimes trials took several days. Some weeks we might be in six or eight trials, other weeks, none. We worked long days and usually traveled on the week ends. When we weren't actually engaged in trial we would likely be preparing for trial, interviewing witnesses, examining exhibits and reviewing documents. We were busier than our counterparts in the States, but it was interesting, engaging and fun. I returned to Memphis a seasoned trial lawyer.

That first day Colonel Guimond advised me that I would be involved in trials at other VII Corps unit locations in the weeks ahead; Nürnberg the following week, Straubing the week after and then Munich. After that, it was thought I would return to and be permanently assigned to 7th Army.

Actually, in German "Munich" is "München." However, it is so frequently called "Munich," even in Germany, that I shall so designate it here.

*　　　*　　　*

THE TIMES: On Monday, March 2, 1953, the day I departed Bremerhaven and began my tour of duty in Germany, significant events were occurring elsewhere.

Thirteen hundred miles to the east, at a dacha just outside Moscow, seventy-three year old Josef Stalin, Chairman of the Council of Ministers of the USSR and Premier of Russia was found in a coma. He had been the undisputed leader of World Communism and Dictator of Russia for twenty years. Without regaining conscientiousness he died three days later and was succeeded by Georgy Malenkov.

On that same day, March 2, another incident directly connected to the Cold War but not then appreciated as such, took place. The Hanoi dictatorship of Ho Chi Minh instituted a Soviet inspired land reform program in Indochina by which farmers owning as little as two acres of rice land were declared to be landlords as distinguished from agricultural workers. As a result, approximately 15,000 "landlords" were declared to be enemies of the state and executed. The following year, on May 7, 1954, the French garrison at Dien Bien Phu surrendered to the communist Viet Minh and on July 21, 1954, at the Geneva Conference on Indochina, upon condition that unifying free elections would be held within two years, the country was partitioned at the 17th Parallel, creating North and South Viet Nam.

*   *   *

Since there were no vacancies in the bachelor officer's quarters at Patch Barracks, I remained for a while a resident at the Graf Zeppelin Hotel. Another officer and I shared a double room but the price (fifty cents a night) was a bargain and the hotel was in the center of downtown Stuttgart where there were many good restaurants. Not knowing the duration of my detached duty at VII

Corps – I guessed two weeks – I purchased 7th Army shoulder patches and had them sewn on my uniforms, replacing the 3rd Army patches appropriate in the ZI ("Zone of the Interior" – Army language for "the States").

Unpacking my hold baggage was comparable to a brief visit back home. Even the laundry tickets attached to my clean clothes brought on feelings of nostalgia. Nothing had been broken in the sea and rail passage. Eager to get my record player in operation, I lost no time in buying a voltage converter. However, problems remained. The local power was 220 volts and 50 cycles instead of the 110 volts and 60 cycles in the U. S. Consequently, not only was it necessary to use a transformer, but one also had to deal with the fact that American electric motors ran slower in Germany even after compensating for the change in the voltage. I could play the 33-RPM records at 45-RPM speed and the 45s at 78, but they sounded weird. Wrapping some wire around the motor spindle so as to change its diameter solved the problem – a solution well known to all record playing servicemen in Germany. When that was done all was well and for the next two years I greatly enjoyed the music I had brought from home along with additional records later sent to me by friends in Memphis.

During the month of March 1953, I wrote thirteen letters home. Airmail cost only six cents and since I was alone in the hotel most evenings or on a train going to courts-martial trial locations, I had plenty of time. But mostly, I think I wrote frequently because there was so much to tell about. Everything was new.

*   *   *

Dear Mother and Dad,   *4 March 1953*

Stuttgart is a lovely city. The population is about 250,000. It is set among mountains similar to those east of Knoxville, the Smokies. The difference is that Stuttgart is set right in the mountains so, there are many steep hills in the city itself. There is considerable artillery and bomb damage here, most of it, I think is in the downtown area. As I walk about the city I have regretfully noted that many of the larger, historically significant and consequential buildings are mere shells with sometimes only parts of the walls remaining. Such is the case with the Württemberg Palace in the heart of downtown Stuttgart. Although the walls remain the inside is gutted. Much new construction is in progress here but still, the war damage remains quite extensive.

*   *   *

READY FOR THE DEFENDANT

A lesson in how *not* to cross-examine a witness resulted from my first real-life courtroom experience. It is a lesson that I have passed on, by way of example, to many young trial lawyers since.

Electronic parts, called crystals, were used to change the frequencies of radio transmissions in the field. So, if the Russians could obtain a set of American radio crystals they could intercept our signals. Of course, some soldiers had access to the crystals. The crystals were valuable, especially to the Soviets. It was a serious offense for a soldier to appropriate a set of crystals because of the

71

potential for selling them to the enemy and the resulting harm to military security.

In my first general court-martial trial, I was to defend a soldier charged with having wrongfully appropriated a set of crystals and later having lied about the alleged theft when questioned by criminal investigators. There was little to work with in preparing the defense for the crystals had been found in the defendant's possession when his effects were searched.

The basis of such a trial are the charges and the specifications, the former being a general statement of the offense and the latter being the specific allegations of what is said to have happened. In this case, the accused was charged with wrongful appropriation and false swearing. The specification alleged that the soldier had wrongfully appropriated seventeen radio crystals and, upon interrogation, misrepresented that fact.

An agent of the CID (Criminal Investigation Division) testified that he had searched the possessions of the accused and had found the missing crystals. The investigator had possession of the crystals for "a second or two," then passed them to another agent who had returned to the ZI and was not available to testify. As I stood to cross-examine, I thought I might have an opening since the specification required proof of the exact number of stolen parts – seventeen. After a few preliminary questions, I began to bore in.

Q. You are saying that you found these crystals in the possession of the accused?

A. Yes, sir; with his things.

Q. How long did you say the crystals were in your possession before you passed them on?

A. Just a second or two.

Q. And you are testifying that there were exactly seventeen?

A. Yes, sir.

Q. After having them for a second or two you passed them on and didn't see them again, right?

A. That is correct, sir.

At this point I should have concluded that area of inquiry and switched to some other subject. Or I could have said "no more questions" and dismissed the witness. Then, in closing argument I could have made the point that having had the crystals in his possession for only "a second or two" it was impossible for the CID agent to have counted the crystals and known exactly how many there were – so, the specification that seventeen crystals were stolen was not proven beyond a reasonable doubt.

But, no, I was compelled to ask just one question more. It was fatal.

Q. Well, sergeant, if you only had the crystals in your possession for just a second or two how could you possibly know that there were exactly seventeen?

The agent looked at me suspiciously, as if either he or I was missing something. Then he replied.

A. Because, sir, the box held twenty and there were three missing.

*   *   *

Even so, things didn't turn out so badly. The maximum penalty on these charges was a dishonorable discharge and three years of confinement at hard labor. For whatever reason the court was

73

lenient. On the charge of false swearing, the accused was found not guilty. As for the charge of misappropriation, he was found guilty but sentenced to only five months. I didn't have much time to contemplate my blunder. The next day I was scheduled to defend another case.

During the two months I was at Fort Jackson I observed as many trials as I could and followed all the others, the charges, the defenses and the results -- all convictions. Accordingly, I was especially pleased that my second trial resulted in a finding of not guilty; the accused, a corporal, was returned to duty, his record intact.

In advance of my second effort as defense counsel I had visited a German luggage shop and for 65 Deutsche Mark (DM) – about $16.00 -- purchased a top grain cowhide briefcase, almost too beautiful to use. It went with me to my next trial. I hoped it would bring me luck. It did.

The defendant was charged with driving while intoxicated, reckless driving and leaving the scene of an accident. I described the outcome in a letter home:

Dear Mom and Dad,

What a pleasure it was to hear that verdict. My client, a big black corporal, was profuse in expressing his gratitude. He kept saying, "thank you" and grinned all over his face. Even now I'm not really sure whether he is guilty or not guilty, but he had a good story and apparently we were convincing for he is free tonight, and he still has his corporal stripes.

*   *   *

GETTING SETTLED

My roommate at the hotel had been in Germany for six months and had decided to take up oil painting. He suggested that I buy a small set of paints and associated art supplies. I did so but after a few desultory efforts, abandoned oil painting in favor of a sketch pad. The little wooden box and tubes of oil paint were in my possession for years. After moving the set from one place to another, one day, long afterward, I noted that all the paint tubes were hard, the paint dried beyond recovery. So, I threw it away, its noteworthy origin lost from memory until now.

My mailing address remained Judge Advocate Section, 7th Army Headquarters, APO (Army Post Office) 46 but my mail and military notices were forwarded to me at VII Corps, APO 107. On March 9, I received a letter from home – from my dad. It was the first mail I had received since I had departed Camp Kilmer in the middle of February. Dad noted that the cables I sent from Southampton and Bremerhaven to him and my mother had been delivered and suggested that I attempt to establish short wave radio contact through ham radio operators in Germany and Memphis. That was later unsuccessfully attempted. He also advised that he and mother were making plans to come to Europe while I was there. I encouraged them to do so but they never came. Meanwhile, I discovered Robinson Barracks and the main post exchange where, for fifty dollars, I bought a Swiss Hermes Rocket portable typewriter – the instrument used by me for most of the ensuing correspondence. Also in my mail, from the adjutant general of the 7th Army, I received a card which authorizing me to visit the British and French zones of

Germany and Austria. So, now I was free to travel throughout Europe, that is, anywhere west of the Russian occupation area.

About this time I was advised that my request for quarters would probably be filled the following week. That was good news for I had been living out of a suitcase for almost six weeks. I enjoyed, but was growing tired of the hotel. It had its advantages, especially since I was without an automobile and was dependent upon the military bus, the civilian public transportation system and my feet. There were plenty of German restaurants nearby and although I rarely knew what to expect when I made my selection from the German language menu, the food was always good. The hotel provided an American style restaurant, which I occasionally visited, and while it was always crowded I thought the offerings uninteresting.

At night, from my hotel room on an upper floor, I could look across the city and see the lights of Stuttgart on the surrounding hills. Some of the houses were far above the level of my room. It was a charming scene. On the streets I noted that small shops had been built in and in front of the ruins. Almost every building behind the shops had been bombed out. The walls were standing but there was nothing inside. Commercial signs, especially *Coca-Cola* and *Pepsi* as well as *Esso*, *Mobil* and *Shell* gasoline were a welcome reminder of home.

THE KASERNES

"Kaserne" is the German word for "barracks." Built during the thirties when Germany was rearming in preparation for what became

World War II, the three American military installations in the Stuttgart area, renamed by the Americans, Patch, Robinson and Kelley Barracks, had been occupied by the U. S. Army since the end of hostilities in 1945. Although the proper names of the American installations included the word "barracks," in the vernacular, speaking generically, we called them "Kasernes."

Located in the town of Möhringen ten miles southeast of Stuttgart, Kelley Barracks is surrounded by rich woods and fertile farmland. When the Kaserne was built in 1938, the German military made an unusual arrangement with Möhringen's local government. Because the new facilities were to replace highly cultivated nurseries, the military agreed to remove no more than twenty percent of the original trees, a compromise that gives the post its unmilitary character. Kelley is the home of the VII Corps headquarters, a signal battalion and a variety of miscellaneous support troops. The base has about twenty permanent buildings, a church, theater, a gas station, a recreation center and a bank. Kelley is the army installation closest to Echterdingen, the Stuttgart Army Airfield, located beside Stuttgart's commercial airport.

As described in a letter home:

A word about the Kasernes; these are the places where the Allied occupation forces have set up their military bases. They are not very large by American standards. Each Kaserne I have seen consists of about twenty permanent buildings both offices and housing. The buildings are either brick or stone and are about four stories high. They are painted a light yellow and are simple but distinctly European in design. They all have steep roofs and many gables,

*sometimes on different levels. As a place to work and to live,
I find them much more attractive and enjoyable than the army
installations I have seen in America.*

*   *   *

Kelley Barracks in Stuttgart-Möhringen was known by the German Army as Hellenen Kaserne. Shortly after the end of World War II, the Americans, in honor of Staff Sergeant Jonah E. Kelley, renamed it. Sergeant Kelley was posthumously awarded the *Medal of Honor* for actions at Kesternich, Germany, on 31 January 1945. Kesternich is about twenty-five kilometers south east of Aachen, Germany.

Kelley's citation reads:

KELLEY, JONAH E., Rank and organization: Staff Sergeant, U. S. Army, 311th Infantry, 78th Infantry Division. Place and date: Kesternich, Germany, 30 and 31 January 1945. Entered service at: Keyser, W. Va. Birth: Rada, W. Va.

Citation: In charge of the leading squad of Company E, he heroically spearheaded the attack in furious house-to-house fighting. Early on 30 January, he led his men through intense mortar and small arms fire in repeated assaults on barricaded houses. Although twice wounded, once when struck in the back, the second time when a mortar shell fragment passed through his left hand and rendered it practically useless, he refused to withdraw and continued to lead his squad after hasty dressings had been applied. His serious wounds forced him to fire his rifle with one hand, resting it on rubble or over his left forearm. To blast his way forward with hand grenades, he set aside his rifle to pull the pins with his teeth while grasping the missiles with his good hand. Despite these handicaps, he created tremendous havoc in the enemy ranks. He rushed one house, killing three of the enemy and clearing the way for his squad to advance. On approaching the next house, he was fired upon from an upstairs window. He killed the sniper with a single shot and similarly accounted for another enemy soldier who ran from the cellar of the house. As darkness came, he assigned his men to defensive positions, never leaving them to seek medical attention for himself. At dawn the next day, the squad resumed the attack, advancing to a point where heavy automatic and small arms fire stalled them. Despite his wounds, S/Sgt. Kelley moved out alone, located an enemy gunner dug in under a haystack and killed him with rifle fire. He returned to his men and found that a German machinegun, from a well-protected position in a neighboring house, still held up the advance. Ordering the squad to remain in comparatively safe positions, he valiantly dashed into the open and attacked the position single-handedly through a hail of bullets. He was hit several times and fell to his knees when within 25 yards of his objective; but he summoned his waning strength and emptied his rifle into the machinegun nest, silencing the weapon before he died. The superb courage, aggressiveness, and utter disregard for his own safety displayed by S/Sgt. Kelley inspired the men he led and enabled them to penetrate the last line of defense held by the enemy in the village of Kesternich .

*   *   *

The *Medal of Honor* is sometimes called "The Congressional Medal of Honor" because the President of the United States presents it "in the name of The Congress." The detached language of the citation doesn't really tell the story of Ed Kelley.

In June 1941, just six months before the Japanese attacked the American Pacific fleet at Pearl Harbor, precipitating America's entry into World War II, Jonah Edward Kelley, a deeply religious student athlete who worked hard and made good grades, graduated from Keyser High School in the mountains of northern West Virginia. He was then eighteen and destined for college. Under his graduation picture in the high school yearbook is his quote, *Today, I am a man.* He would not live to see his twenty-second birthday.

Kelley was in his second year at Potomac State College when he was drafted March 8, 1943 and was assigned to the 78th *Lightening* Division which had distinguished itself in World War I at the battles of St. Mihiel, Lorraine, and the Meuse-Argonne. Reactivated in World War II, the 78th trained at Fort Butler, North Carolina, where Kelley, 6 feet two and 175 pounds, became heavyweight boxing champion of the division. Barely 21, he was soon promoted to staff sergeant and squad leader, 1st Platoon, "E" Company, 2nd Battalion, 311th Infantry Regiment. When the division was ready for action it was sent to Europe, arriving in England October 26, 1944, made part of the VIIth Corps and was on the Western Front by December 1.

Allied armies confronting the Germans in the fall of 1944 had arrived on the European continent through two great invasions, Operation Overlord centered on the beaches of Normandy in June and Operation Dragoon on the southern coast of France in August. September found the Allied armies arrayed in strength on the doorstep of the Third Reich, from Antwerp, Belgium south to the Swiss frontier. Victory seemed within reach.

General Eisenhower's strategy was to attack on a broad front. Field Marshal Montgomery was to cross the Rhine River at Arnhem, Holland, the Americans were to advance primarily against the industrial Rhur north of Cologne and secondarily, south of Luxembourg and the Ardennes Forest toward the Saar. Although the German Army suffered a million casualties on all fronts in the summer of 1944, millions more remained in uniform. Additionally, the German defensive West Wall in the form of the Siegfried Line, stretching from the Netherlands to Switzerland was formidable, if not impregnable. In early September Hitler put the defense of the Western Front under the command of Field Marshal Gerd von Rundstedt, directing him to stop the Allies at the Siegfried Line long enough for the German Army to regroup for a massive counteroffensive.

The American Army VII Corps began its attack on the westernmost German City of Aachen on October 2, surrounded it on October 10 and demanded its surrender. Aachen, the birthplace of Charlemagne and a symbol of Nazi ideology, was ordered by Hitler to be held at all costs. The defenders of the city fought house-to-house for eleven days until finally the remnants of the garrison capitulated.

After the fall of Aachen, the Allied plan was to continue the fight throughout the winter, advancing at all points along the line. There was, however, a thorny problem, the Hürtgenwald - the Huertgen Forest. The crossroads town of Schmidt, eighteen miles southeast of Aachen, dominated the Huertgen area and the Roer dams; its capture was the linchpin of the winter operation.

As described in a brochure prepared in the U. S. Army Center of Military History, *Rhineland Campaign*, by Ted Ballard,

"The Huertgen Forest was a dense, primordial woods of tall fir trees, deep gorges, high ridges, and narrow trails; terrain ideally suited to the defense. The Germans had carefully augmented its natural obstacles with extensive minefields and carefully prepared positions because they realized something the Allies had not yet fully grasped- losing Schmidt exposed the Roer River dams to attack. So long as the Germans controlled the dams, they could flood the Roer River Valley, thereby destroying Allied tactical bridging and trapping any units that had crossed the river. These isolated forces could then be destroyed by German reserves. Consequently, the Germans were determined to hold Schmidt, knowing the almost impenetrable terrain of the Huertgen Forest would add depth to their defense and neutralize American superiority in aircraft, tanks and artillery."

*   *   *

The conquest of the town of Schmidt, just six miles east of the Belgian-German boundary, was assigned to the 28th Infantry Division, which launched its attack on November 2nd. For eleven days the 28th and three German divisions, one a panzer unit, slugged it out until finally, after suffering more than 6,000 casualties and losing almost fifty tanks and tank destroyers and vast numbers of trucks, guns and individual weapons, the battered 28th was withdrawn.

From November 13th through December 15th the Americans committed the 8th, 9th and 47th Infantry Divisions, 2nd Ranger Battalion and 46th Armored Infantry Battalion into the hell of Huertgen and sustained 21,500 additional casualties, but with little gain to show for its losses. On December 13, the newly arrived 78th "Lightening" Division, Ed Kelley's division, joined the battle, moving out from Lammersdorf, just across the German frontier, its objective - to seize Schmidt. However, its advance was halted three days later when the Germans began their counter offensive in the Ardennes.

In his chronicle of World War II, *Crusade in Europe*, General Eisenhower thus describes the Battle of Huertgen Forest:

"On November 16, Bradley renewed his offensive toward the Rhine... These attacks initially employed fourteen divisions, and the number was soon increased to seventeen. Nevertheless, progress was slow and the fighting intense. On the right flank ...the First Army got involved in the Hurtgen Forest, the scene of one of the most bitterly contested battles of the entire campaign. The enemy had all the advantages of strong defensive country, and the attacking Americans had to depend almost exclusively upon infantry weapons because of the thickness of the forest. The weather was abominable and the German garrison particularly stubborn, but Yankee doggedness finally won. ..."

On the other hand, General James Gavin, Commander, 82nd Airborne Division, observed,

"For us the Hurtgen was one of the most costly, most unproductive and most ill-advised battles that our army has ever fought."

German Field Marshall von Rundstedt launched the *Battle of the Bulge* on December 16, but the 78th held its position against violent German attacks throughout December and January. The action leading to Kelley's death and the posthumous award of America's highest military honor was described by his battalion commander, Lt.

Col. Richard W. Keyes, which description, slightly edited, reads as follows:

Since late November (1944) the Roer River (Dutch spelling; in German, Rur) had constituted a barrier to the Allied armies on the Western Front. The huge Schwammenauel Dam near Schmidt was a potent flood threat to any supply lines of Allied Forces attempting to operate east of the Roer. This threat had to be removed; Schmidt had to be taken.

Schmidt sat squarely astride the commanding ground and approaches to the dam. Earlier in the fall it had been occupied by elements of an American division, only to be forcibly and permanently ejected. Another American division had attempted to take Schmidt but was stopped cold in Bergstein, three miles to the north, but twice that far by a tortuous road. On 13 December 1944, the 78th "Lightening" Division launched an attack from the vicinity of Lammersdorf, eight miles east of the dam, pushed south east three miles through Rollesbroich, Simmerath, and into Kesternich against steadily increasing enemy resistance. There on the 16th and 17th of December 1944, the Germans counterattacked. They recaptured Kesternich, lost it and again retook it, this time to hold it. Elements of three American Infantry Battalions with supporting tanks and tank destroyers had been in Kesternich. The Germans had taken a heavy toll of Americans, including one battalion commanding officer, a battalion executive officer and virtually all the members of four rifle companies.

Kesternich had a triple strategic value. First, it was situated on high open ground, with excellent observation directly into the enemy's main defenses at Steckenborn and Strauch, two kilometers to the north.

Second, Kesternich controlled the approaches to Ruhrberg, four kilometers to the east on the western bank of the Roer River, and troops in Ruhrberg were in position to attack Wofflebach to the north, and out-flank the Steckenborn-Strauch defenses.

Third, and most important to the Germans, Kesternich provided observation of the important road from Simmerath on the west, to Schmidt on the north, and the assembly areas for a German counterattack against any allied effort toward Schmidt. Kesternich had to be controlled before the main effort against the Schwammenauel Dam could be launched.

*   *   *

On January 30, 1945, the terrain was heavily blanketed with snow, nearly knee deep in the open fields and, with drifts over a man's head in some places. A sunken road in Kesternich had drifted level full.

This heavy snow impeded rapid movement and furnished the enemy with a good background against which un-camouflaged figures were readily visible. Snow did aid the attackers in that the heavy anti-personnel mine fields of the Germans were rendered partially impotent, and artillery and mortar bursts were somewhat smothered.

This, then, was the situation before dawn at 0530 on January 30, 1945, when the 2nd Battalion, 311th Infantry … jumped off in the attack on Kesternich.

Each man carried a one pound block of dynamite, and each machine gun crew-member carried a twenty pound shape charge. The explosives were to be used to soften the frozen ground to aid in digging in. Improvised snowsuits had been made from bed sheets.

Snow, driven by a light northeast wind, was falling steadily as the attack jumped off on time. It was still dark and there was some confusion as the men floundered through the snow and drifts, over the fences, and through the hedgerows.

By 0600 it was getting light, and contact had been made with the enemy's main defenses. The men set about breaching the wire and anti-personnel mine fields. The enemy opened up with their protective line fires: 50 and 120 mm mortars and 105 mm artillery; Panzerfausts (one time, disposable, anti-tank rockets) *were fired at trees to get bursting effect on the troops, an SP 75* (self-propelled 75 mm cannon) *opened up on the tanks; machine guns and automatic weapons began to fire. (Later reconnaissance revealed that approximately 50 percent of the enemy weapons were automatic.)*

The attack bogged down and the (American) *tanks were called forward. Within five minutes their radio communication was out. Again, the attack stopped.*

*   *   *

For the remainder of the day the troops slogged forward, fell back, and regrouped, moving house to house further into Kesternich, encountering mortar and artillery, small arms and machine gun fire. In the cold, the automatic weapons began to freeze. Several tanks were knocked out and fifty-five casualties were sustained. Some German soldiers were captured and questioned. They advised that their orders were to hold Kesternich at all costs. During the night, the disabled American tanks were removed, the wounded evacuated and the units consolidated and reorganized. Enemy mortar and artillery bombardment continued through the dark hours.

After darkness fell, the Germans brought up reinforcements and laid new anti-personnel and anti-tank mines. Although it had stopped snowing, it was windy and bitterly cold. Very few of the men had any camouflage clothing left.

At 0830 the next morning, after a five-minute artillery barrage, the American attack began again. There had been a two hour delay so that replacement platoon and company commanders could comprehend their attack orders and "get a feel" for the terrain. The 1st platoon of "E" Company, Ed Kelley's platoon, was to attack on the east side of the main street and secure that part of the town, house by house. The sun emerged about noon and the snow began to melt. By 1400 the ground was slippery although there was still a six-inch blanket of snow over everything.

Continuing with Battalion Commander Keyes' description

*   *   *

"E" COMPANY HAD THE ROUGHEST FIGHT OF THE DAY.

...the enemy had organized positions about 150 yards from our front lines, furthermore, they did not withdraw from a single building they held.

The first platoon (Kelley's) *had to drive them from building 90 and the other buildings in its vicinity before they came against the main enemy positions.*

Three tanks supported the Americans with machine gun and cannon fire, as they slowly advanced through the prepared gaps in the minefields on the south. Through the coordinated action of the 1st and 3rd platoons and the tanks, the enemy position was penetrated.

The attack now became a slugging match. The enemy occupied reinforced sandbagged positions inside buildings, firing through embrasures which were formed by knocking out a foundation block. In at least two instances machine guns were fired in one building by personnel manipulating a wire from another building.

The advance was slow and tedious and was accomplished by having a tank fire at a building, breaching the wall, and permitting the men to enter and mop up. This continued all the way through Kesternich so that, at the end of the day, every building had been smashed and most of them burned.

Sgt. Jonah E. Kelley, squad leader of the 1st platoon, led his squad from building to building. He would establish a base of fire and under its cover, was the first to enter each building. Then he covered the advance of his squad and together, they mopped up. In one instance when his squad was held up by a machine gun, which a tank and hand grenades had failed to dislodge, Sergeant Kelley burst into the open, was hit by a German bullet and knocked down, but he killed four and wounded another before he died. His action in knocking out the German machine gun permitted his squad to advance.

*   *   *

"E" Company lost all its platoon leaders and platoon Sergeants, plus a good many squad leaders. The Company had received forty-

three additional casualties and an unknown number of dead. There were only eight of the fifteen tanks left.

*　　　*　　　*

That night the temperature dropped. Water froze in canteens and foxholes. First stages of trench foot, a disabling disease of the feet caused by exposure to cold and wet, began to appear. The men who had survived the battle were numb with cold and suffered from exposure. When the canteens froze solid they were forced to eat snow to get water. Fingers were so stiff that casualties were unable to take their wound tablets. Frostbite was prevalent and in some cases gloves froze to the men's hands. One hundred eighty-four enlisted men and six officers had been killed, wounded or were evacuated due to exposure, but Kesternich had fallen. The town of Schmidt was captured on the 8th of February and the Schwammenauel Dam the next day. A month later, on March 8th 1945, a unit of Kelley's 78th Division was the first Infantry to cross the Rhine River at the Ludendorf railroad bridge at Remagen, the sole remaining functional bridge over the Rhine, which the Germans had tried but failed to destroy.

*　　　*　　　*

General Arnold J. Funk, Commander of the Stuttgart Military Post, attended a special ceremony at Möhringen, Germany, on Thursday, September 29, 1949. The following day he wrote a letter to Ed Kelley's mother.

89

John J. Thomason

H E A D Q U A R T E R S
STUTTGART MILITARY POST
OFFICE OF THE COMMANDING GENERAL
APO 154   US ARMY

30 September 1949

Mrs. Rebecca Kelley
15 Sharpless Street
Keyser, West Virginia

Dear Mrs. Kelley:

I feel sure that you will be interested to learn that I have named one of the most important installations in my command in honor of your son, Staff Sergeant Jonah E. Kelley, who was awarded the Congressional Medal of Honor.

I am enclosing 5 photographs of the dedication ceremony and 2 copies of the Stuttgart Military Post News containing the public announcement of this dedication.

I trust that this action will not re-awaken in you the pain you must have felt when the War Department first announced your son's death. But, if this be the case, I hope you will find compensation in the thought that your son's heroic deeds are continuing to be an inspiration to the soldiers in the Army of Occupation, and that his memory is being kept alive in a part of the country where he gave up his life.

With kindest personal greetings, I remain,

Very truly yours,
ARNOLD J. FUNK
Brigadier General, U. S. Army
Commanding

90

*   *   *

On April 10, 2002, speaking at the fifty-seventh annual Keyser High School "J. Edward Kelley Award Assembly," Major General David C. Meade, U. S. Army, retired, suggested that the heroic actions of Sergeant Kelley on January 31, 1945 probably shortened the war in Europe by two months and may have altered the course of history. If the war had dragged on in the west and if the allied forces had not met the Russian army at the Elbe River, Austria and Denmark might well have been occupied and dominated by the Soviets. How that realignment would have affected the outcome of the Cold War is anybody's guess, but that altered political arrangement would surely have had a negative impact on the free world.

Today, there is a new high school in Keyser, West Virginia. The old one, from which Ed Kelley graduated in 1941 has become a business center, home to forty or so shops and offices. In the new high school, appropriately identified and prominently displayed in a glass case just inside the main entrance, is Staff Sergeant Kelley's Medal of Honor. His younger sister, Georgianna, gave it to the school in 1999, one year before she died. Ed Kelley is remembered in Keyser – not as a soldier – but as a smiling, tall and good-looking high school kid who loved sports, his church, his life, his town and the people there.

He is home again. His modestly marked grave, next to the graves of his parents and his sister, is on a hillside, overlooking the picturesque, rolling hills of West Virginia. And, in Stuttgart-Möringen, Germany, about 250 miles south east of the village where Ed Kelley was killed in action, still stands Kelley Barracks, one of the remaining outposts of the American Army in Germany. For almost fifty years it was an important American Army Corps headquarters, essential in our struggle against the Soviets to win the Cold War.

* * *

THE TIMES: On 5 March 1953 Polish defector Lt. Franciszek Jarecki flying from Slupsk Polish Air Force Base landed a Russian built MIG-15 jet fighter plane in Denmark.

Western air specialists thoroughly examined the aircraft and several days later the MIG was returned to Poland by ship. However, the pilot requested that he be allowed to enter the USA and that request was granted. It is believed that he provided American Intelligence with much important information about modern Soviet aircraft and air tactics.

NÜRNBERG

On Tuesday, March 10, 1953 I was ordered to proceed to Merrill Barracks in Nürnberg where the 2nd Armored Cavalry Regiment, another VII Corps unit was based. Engaged at the time in a trial at Kelley Barracks, I departed the next day and arrived in Nürnberg about noon. Trials there were scheduled for Thursday and Friday.

* * *

THE TIMES: On that same day, 10 March 1953, two USAF F-84G jet fighter planes based at the American air base at Fürstenfeldbruck near Munich, in West Germany, allegedly crossed into Czechoslovakian airspace and were intercepted by Russsian MIG-15s. One of the F-84s was shot down. Munich is the largest city in Bavaria; Nürnberg is the next. The situation was tense. Two days later a Royal Air Force AVRO Lincoln long-range bomber was shot down by Russian Migs over the Hamburg-Berlin air corridor. Six crewmen were killed and another was wounded. The U. S. and Britain lodged formal protests. In response to this attack, on Saturday, March 18, 1953, the 92nd U. S. Fighter-Interceptor Squadron stationed at Shepherd's Grove RAF base in England and equipped with the latest F-86 Sabre Jets was alerted and departed the next day for Fürstenfeldbruck, Germany. Its mission was to identify unknown aircraft violating the U S Occupation Zone in Germany. Its guns were "hot."

Upon arriving in Germany, the 92nd assigned twelve Sabres to alert status from ½ hour before sunrise to ½ hour after sunset -- four fighters were on the runway at all times for immediate "scramble" and eight more nearby on five minute availability. The remainder of the squadron was on fifteen-minute status. During the course of the day patrols of two or more Sabres directed by ground controlled interceptor radar were flown along the border.

*   *   *

The fighter pilots of the 92nd operated under strict "Rules of Engagement" by which they were forbidden to attack but could defend themselves if attacked. They were cautioned to stay clear of the border and fly parallel to rather than toward a Russian plane if one were sighted. Because it was known that some Eastern Bloc fighter pilots were defecting to the west, the Americans were warned to be heedful of that possibility. The American pilots were told to be slow to open fire should an adversary fighter turn toward them and cross the frontier.

*   *   *

The city of Nürnberg is almost 1,000 years old. According to tradition, around 1050 a German Emperor decided he needed a castle in the area where Nürnberg is now. His men looked around for a suitable place and found today's site. When the emperor saw the location he is said to have exclaimed, `But it is *ONLY A HILL!* ` (In German: `*NUR EN BERG*`), and that's how this little village got its name. Once the castle was built, a town grew up around it and soon the town rose in importance, especially since the old trading routes from east, west, north and south all met in Nürnberg (also spelled "Nuremberg"). The names of many German towns and cities end in "berg" (hill or mountain) or "burg" (castle or fortress).

When World War II began Nürnberg was a city of 400,000, famous for its toy production and the industry and genius of its citizens. It claimed to have invented the spring-powered clock and the first terrestrial globe and was the birthplace of Germany's greatest graphic artist, Albrecht Dürer. Because of its architectural importance with its high pitched roofs and half timbered medieval dwellings, its old walled central town, featuring turrets, towers, castles and cathedrals, it was known as the jewel box of Germany. Hitler chose it as the center for Nazi demonstrations and for the congress hall of an empire that was intended to last for 1,000 years. It was selected by the victorious Allies as the site of the trials of the Nazi war criminals and the place of execution of some who were convicted. One of the German cities most damaged by air raids, Nürnberg lost more than one-third of all its buildings and one-half of all its dwellings. During the War, 7,000 of its citizens were killed by American and British bombs. We were told that eighty percent of the buildings in the *Old Town* had been demolished but by 1953 much restoration had begun and some had been completed.

An annual Toy Trade Fair is held in Nürnberg each March. On Saturday, March 14, Dave Addis, my counterpart on the trial team, and I set out to do some sight seeing, shopping and visit the toy exhibits. We were disappointed to discover that the toy fair had closed the previous day, but we strolled around the area where the fair had been and chanced upon a school. In the playground were thirty or so seven and eight year old children who recognized us as American soldiers – we were required always to be in uniform – and swarmed around us. They all wanted chocolate or chewing gum and were disappointed that we had none. Despite our lack of candy, they stayed with us, jabbering and laughing. I was touched when a small boy came forward and presented me with what must have been a prized possession: an old, inoperative cigarette lighter.

We strolled into the Old Town and were shocked to see the destruction there. Many of the churches and larger buildings still standing were closed because they were structurally dangerous. The city wall was mostly intact. Built of large stones, it was originally thirty feet high and featured several eighty-foot towers and many smaller ones. There was a thirty-foot wide moat of equal depth outside the wall. On a hill inside the walls stood one of the Hohenzollern Castles; there were several in various locations in this part of Germany. We climbed the castle tower from which, we were told, one could see for forty miles. I believe it.

For lunch, we went to a restaurant where I ordered, but could not eat, *Blutwurst* or blood sausage. At first the wurst looked tempting but when I pierced the skin with my fork my plate filled with thick, clotted blood. That was the first time, and I think it was the last, that I turned away from German food.

The following day we departed for Straubing where we remained for a week to try four cases. In Straubing we were not in a town but in a Kaserne in the company of combat troops, the 6th Armored Cavalry Regiment, and about thirty miles from the Czech border and the Russian Army.

STRAUBING

The 6th Armored Cavalry Regiment, stationed at Mansfield Kaserne near Straubing, on the banks of the Danube River, was a tank combat unit equipped with the best and most modern weapons available. The whole regiment could be mobilized in forty-five minutes. I learned here that soldiers court-martialed in a combat unit were much more likely to be convicted and to receive harsher sentences than would likely be the case at a headquarters more engaged with administration than combat and farther from the frontier.

*   *   *

Dear Mother and Dad,   Thursday, 19 March 1953

This is being written from a place called Mansfield Kaserne where we have been since Monday trying four cases for the 6th Armored Cavalry. Here I encountered what I had long heard described but had not previously seen – a court whose members had apparently already made up their minds in advance of trial that the accused must be guilty because he had been charged. This is a bad situation – it's called "command influence." However, court reporters make a verbatim record of these trials and all convictions are automatically appealed. I hope that at corps level or before a board of review in Washington corrections can be made. I have had the blues since I got here. My efforts seem so futile. However, after talking with some of the court members at the officer's club I am convinced that these verdicts and severe sentences are not because of any lack of effort on my part but because this is a combat regiment which requires and enforces firm discipline.

Dave Addis and I requisitioned an Army vehicle this morning and drove to Regensburg to interview some German witnesses for a trial tomorrow. Regensburg is on the edge of a vast wild forest known as the <u>Bayrischer Wald</u> that stretches along the Czech frontier. A few miles east of Regensburg we chanced upon Walhalla, the German Hall of Fame, a replica of the Parthenon temple in Athens, just like the other copy in Nashville. This beautiful and classic structure stands high on

97

a hill overlooking the Danube. It is said to contain statues of famous German heroes and historic figures but we couldn't get in. It had just closed.

I regret that I don't have a camera. There are many scenes here I would like to photograph.

By a telephone call from VII Corps I was advised that I shall remain on detached service for a while longer – I don't know how much longer. I don't mind. The people I work with here are very friendly and able. The only problem is that I feel that I'm not actually settled anywhere. 7th Army headquarters is larger and the accommodations more comfortable than at VII Corps but I like both places and would be happy at either.

WHAT A DIFFERENCE A YEAR MAKES

On 20 March 1953 as drove along the autobahn from Munich to Stuttgart in an Army command car, an American sedan, it occurred to me that on exactly the same day, one year previously, I graduated from the College of Law at the University of Tennessee. Since then, I had passed the bar exam, began practicing law, worked on the reelection campaign of Senator McKellar, was commissioned in the Army and lived in Tennessee, South Carolina and Virginia, crossed the Atlantic Ocean and became a resident of Germany. Without any previous military training I was given a meaningful assignment and was performing duties important to our nation's security. This was a maturing time and experience for me. I was proud to be a part of this occupation force, in a sensitive location, helping to defend freedom against the threat of communism.

The next day back in my Stuttgart hotel I received a large collection of letters from home. I sorted them chronologically and occupied myself for the next two hours reading all the news from Memphis. Because my mail was sent first to 7th Army and then routed to VII Corps, it took a letter about six days to reach me but only four days for my letters to get home. Getting mail from home was very important to me and both my parents were good about writing. They expressed concern that I might be dangerously close to the Russian Zone, but from Stuttgart the Russian Army was almost 200 miles away. Nevertheless, the situation was always tense. Reminders of World War II were everywhere and the close presence of a large and hostile Soviet armed force was palpable and frightening.

Clearly there were differences between military service in the states and in Europe. We were required to be in uniform at all times -- and in dress uniform after seven p.m. As an officer I could leave the Kaserne whenever I wanted, but it was necessary that I leave information as to my whereabouts so that I could be reached at any time. At least once a month there was a surprise "alert." When that happened everyone had to report to a prearranged combat duty station, armed and ready to move out.

A midnight to five a.m. curfew was in effect for all military personnel throughout the American zone. During curfew hours we were prohibited from being in any public building or on the street. Penalties for curfew violations were severe. Because of the threat of disease, American military personnel were discouraged from eating anything uncooked. German dairy products were off limits. The army imported milk, cheese and butter from Denmark. We were told that a significant percentage of German cattle were infected with tuberculosis. However, on the positive side, restaurant meals were very good and surprisingly inexpensive. A delicious dinner in a fine restaurant might be bought for two or three dollars.

Finally, on 23 March, I was assigned a billet at Patch Barracks, 7th Army Bachelor Officer's Quarters (BOQ). My room (23 A) was in building 14, a four story post-war structure that resembled a college dormitory. My very comfortable, well-furnished accommodations were on the second floor. Although I shared a shower and toilet with the officer next door, I had my own lavatory, bed, table, desk, chest of drawers and closet. The view out my window was of a charming German forest, very clean, with tall, straight evergreen trees, which, I was certain, was home to at least a few elves. I was close to the officer's club where I could eat and the bus stop where each morning at 7:30 I boarded a military bus for Kelley Barracks. I was happy with my new situation, nevertheless, remaining at VII Corps was more and more appealing to me. Inquiries I made concerning my permanent duty station were not revealing. Nobody seemed to know anything about my ultimate fate.

*   *   *

Dear Mother and Dad,   *Sunday, 29 March 1953*

Last night Lt. Jack Crouchet and I went to the circus. Jack is stationed in the 7th Army JA Section, and is a resident of my BOQ,. Although the performers spoke German there was enough pantomime for us to follow what was going on. Besides it was a one ring rather than a three-ring circus so it was easier to concentrate; not everything was happening at once. We had good seats, close up, and had a great time. One of the acts featured some elaborately costumed "American Indians" who galloped their horses around the ring shouting to each other in German.. In the finale the band played "Waiting for the Robert E. Lee" which no one except me thought was out of place. Maybe I am the one who is out of place.

* * *

Afterward Jack and I decided to go to the Graf Zeppelin Hotel for a beer and happened to catch the floor show. The final event of the evening was a fencing act. Two protagonists took the stage and bared themselves to the waist. They wore no face protection or padding and after a few minutes of sparing around, attacking and retreating one of these fellows sustained a severe cut over his right eye. They kept at it and before long they were both pretty bloody. Even some of the spectators got spotted.

This was no fake. I was quite close enough to see what happened. The injured fencer was cut rather badly. I can't say that I enjoyed the demonstration very much; I think some others in the crowd shared my feelings.

Some other places I have been and enjoyed are the zoo in Nürnberg which is every bit as good as the one in St. Louis and the opera in Stuttgart, where I saw a production of <u>Carmen</u>. This Carmen weighed in at about two hundred *pounds. As she leaped about the stage I thought I could feel the impact of her landings vibrate through the bottom of my seat. Perhaps it was just my imagination.*

I have bought a camera, an Agfa. I shall soon be sending photographs.

*　　　*　　　*

On the 27th of March, I noted that I had completed seven months in the Army. Since arriving in Germany I had not experienced the humorous incidents I had encountered as a novice army officer in America. Things were more serious here. We were often reminded that the Russian Army – much larger than ours – was near at hand and we feared that if it attacked we might well be pushed into the sea.

The mission of an army is to fight. When there are no battles there is little for the soldiers to do. So, work is created. Many of the "make work" tasks are meaningless and boring. But I was not involved in "make work" activities. My duties were important and necessary. Military bureaucracy was troublesome, but I was learning to accommodate to the military style and was beginning to appreciate that in some situations there were reasons to do things the "Army Way."

Although I was not in command of troops, I was nevertheless required to issue orders and expect compliance. I was becoming comfortable with authority, my own and that of my superiors.

I found it easy to make friends and liked the way people addressed each other by rank rather than by name. It was easy and proper just to call someone "captain" or "major" or whatever. Each person's "name," i.e., his insignia of rank, was on his shoulder if he was wearing a coat or on his collar if he was not. I was proud to wear the uniform, especially the dress uniform "pinks and greens" (forest green tunic with bright brass buttons and gray trousers) and thought I looked pretty sharp in it. In some of my recent court cases my adversary had been a more accomplished officer of higher rank, yet I had won. Afterwards, I was pleased to hear, mostly facetious but maybe genuine, comments about how the young moose was knocking off the old moose. I was progressing, gaining respect and being accepted by the more experienced, seasoned officers. I was becoming a soldier – and a trial lawyer.

Dear Folks,   30 March 1953

Just time for a short note. Please observe that I have a new address. It is:

J A Sec., VII Corps

APO 107, c/o, Postmaster, N.Y., N.Y.

I have been permanently assigned to the VII Corps, which is what I wanted. I shall furnish details of my new assignment when time permits. Off go the old 7th Army shoulder patches, on come the new, VII Corps, a red seven pointed star with a blue and white "VII" in the middle.

<u>J A SECTION, VII CORPS HEADQUARTERS</u>

Nine years after I drove out the gate at Kelley Barracks for what I thought was the last time, I returned. This time I drove a Volkswagen that my wife and I had bought through a friend, and picked up in Hamburg at the beginning of a seven-week European vacation.

Stuttgart and Kelley Barracks, I insisted, were important points of interest on our tour. As the impeccably uniformed military police gate guard approached us he looked approvingly at our brand new red and white VW *Squareback* and asked for identification.

"Actually, I don't have any military identification," I said. "But, I was stationed here in the fifties and I would like to show my wife what the place looks like."

After checking my Tennessee driver's license and asking a few perfunctory questions about my military history he waved us in and with a friendly smile invited us to enjoy ourselves.

First, we stopped at the building housing the officer's club, which had also been the location of my BOQ. I lived there most of the time while I was in Germany. As one enters, the club is on the left, the BOQ on the right. It was mid-afternoon; no customers were present in the dinning room or the bar. At the entrance to the club a young man in a white jacket was watering the potted plants.

"Pardon me," I said utilizing the "street German" I had learned while stationed there, "do you by any chance know whatever happened to a VII Corps bartender named Hans Hölering?"

"Nothing happened to him," the attendant replied in English. "He's right over there, behind the bar, polishing glasses."

I was delighted.

Hans was a German Army veteran. He claimed to have fought on the eastern front against the Russians. Rarely would we encounter a German military veteran who would admit to having fought the Americans. Cynically, we wondered what had become of all those German soldiers who opposed us.

Shortly after the war ended, Hans began working for the U. S. military. He liked his job and was popular with his customers. His English was good, he could mix almost any cocktail, had a good sense of humor and was discreet. The officer's club was the favorite tavern for most of the officers stationed at corps headquarters, especially the bachelors and those whose wives were in the States. Almost nightly there would be a game of "liar's dice" providing free drinks for lucky players. Hans was the incorruptible scorekeeper.

We walked over to the bar, I introduced my wife and we had a beer. As always, Hans was affability personified. For a while we reminisced about the old times and "whatever happened to" whomever and how things still looked about the same. I wanted my wife to see the rest of the Kaserne so, at length we bid farewell to the Kelley Barracks officer's club, my old BOQ and to Hans Hölering, our never-to-be-forgotten bartender.

I certainly remembered him, but I'm really not sure he remembered me.

After my wife and I strolled through the Kaserne and I showed her the excellent stone two and three story buildings and all the places I had previously frequented, we returned to our VW and departed.

"Kelley Barracks absolutely doesn't look like an Army post to me," she said. "With those flowers in the window boxes and lovely shade trees everywhere, it looks more like a charming European town in a picture book of fairy tales."

And she was right.

*　　　*　　　*

Dear Mom and Dad,   *1 April 1953*

I work in the headquarters building of VII Corps. The commanding general, chief of staff, deputy commander and the staff offices of all the different sections: Intelligence, Supply, Engineers, Finance, Adjutant, etc., are located in this building. The building itself is imposing; three stories high, much wider than deep with a two lane roadway cut through the center. The entrance is to the right of the roadway. At the entrance stands a guard, one of those very sharply dressed no-nonsense armed military policemen wearing a white helmet circled with two wide blue stripes, white gloves, white scarf, white belt, white boot laces and mirror shined, cordovan colored, jump boots. He is a member of the elite security platoon, all of whom are tall, good-looking and well built.

Just inside the entrance and across the hall are the staff judge advocate's offices. Trial and defense counsel and some secretaries are in one room. Major Rosten and a secretary are in another and next to that is Colonel Guimond's private office. The rooms are not crowded because many of the officers are frequently out of town.

Joe Guimond is a "bird colonel," i.e., his insignia of rank is an eagle. If he were a lieutenant colonel it would be a silver oak leaf. He is a fine man. He wears his "Ike Jacket"_ open all day and doesn't care who else does. He is always friendly and, soon after I arrived, took the trouble to escort me upstairs and introduce me to the chief of staff and the deputy commander, both brigadier generals. I thought that an extraordinary thing for him to do. He is a short, stocky man, not exactly jolly but always affable. His office is invariably open to everyone. He doesn't seem to care when you do your work, or how you do it, or how messy your desk might be, just so you do your job and do it well. If I had the power to conjure up a section commander I couldn't improve on Colonel Guimond. He makes you feel relaxed and comfortable so that you can freely express yourself. When he asks for my opinion, which he sometimes does, he appears to value what I say. At least he acts that way. He is very much respected by all the officers, enlisted men and civilians on his staff.

I work with Major Rosten more than any other field grade officer. As I understand it, field grade is major and above; company grade is captain and below. (In a few places you will find field grade facilities, such as hotels and clubs in addition to Company Grade, which are not quite as nice. I once tried to register in a fancy hotel in Heidelberg and was told by the disdainful desk clerk that the hotel was "for colonels and generals only." So, sometimes even field grade is not high enough to get the nicest accommodations.)

Major Rosten usually acts as the judge in courts-martial trials, -- in military language he is the "law officer." Physically, he reminds me of dad. He is shorter than dad, but also somewhat stout. He is a naturally jolly person but not infrequently conceals that aspect of his personality in favor of gruffness, which I believe he thinks is more in keeping with his position. Major Rosten has advice for everybody on *everything. No matter what the subject, whether you are buying a car or a lunch, there is just one way to do it – the correct way -- the Rosten way. Major Rosten makes is clear that he does not want anyone to ask him for any sort of privilege – <u>ever.</u> If you have all your work done, he says, "Don't ask me if you can have the afternoon off. Just <u>take</u> the afternoon off." The problem is, I have been here almost a month and I have never had all my work done; so, no afternoon off. There is always more to do than can be done in the time available. I need to be more organized, or something.*

Captain McCartin, a troop commander in the 2nd Armored "Hell on Wheels" Division in the Second World War, takes every opportunity to wear his pistol and steel helmet, always wears his campaign ribbons and, in general, puts on a "War is Hell" presentation. Notwithstanding, he is a really nice guy, easy to get along with if you use a little subtle flattery now and then. He is not the sort with whom one is likely to become too familiar but he is very cordial, efficient, able and friendly. He adds to the pleasant environment of the office. The first time my efforts resulted in a victory for the defense, Captain McCartin was the prosecutor, but I have never reminded him of that trial.

Working with Captain Ed Fenig is a genuine pleasure. He is extremely bright, well versed in military law and a very capable trial lawyer. He is from New York City where he was establishing a practice when called up for World War II. After the war he once again began to practice law and once again he was mobilized for service in the Korean Conflict. I don't think he will try a third time. He will probably stay in the Army. Captain Fenig is rather shy and that impression is aided by his physical appearance; he is about five feet four inches tall and weighs around 140 pounds. He is a fine person, cooperative, helpful and good-natured. He has a subtle humor, which is contagious. He teases and doesn't mind being teased. Every morning he asks me "How many cups of coffee are you going to buy me today?" and then he usually ends up buying coffee for everyone. The second time a client I was defending was acquitted Captain Fenig was the prosecutor. He mentions my victory every couple of days together with some comment about my underhanded tactics. His friendliness, however, ends when we, as adversaries, step into the courtroom; which is, of course, as it should be.

I have mentioned my counterpart, Lt. Dave Addis before. He is from Chicago, a 1951 graduate of Loyola and a capable trial lawyer. He has a year more experience than I and has been a great help to me. We often travel together and generally have a good time. Dave has a certain indescribable pattern to his speech that suggests sarcasm and is wearying at times, but he is a good companion in many ways. He has a slight tendency to take advantage but doesn't press a personal point when opposed. He will admit it when he is wrong and doesn't rub it in when I am. Don't misunderstand me. I don't mean to picture him in a bad light. He is a fine person., Because I am with him more than any of the other judge advocate officers I am probably too critical of him. In fact, I like Dave very much and we get along quite well.

I almost forgot Captain Olney. Captain O. is slow, lazy and not too competent, withal, he is easy going, helpful, cordial and obliging. It is exasperating sometimes to have to do the work that was assigned to him, but everyone knows his shortcomings and somehow his work gets done. Captain Olney is easy to get along with, doesn't bother anybody, and when he feels like it, he works well enough to get by. His wife is on the way over and is expected to arrive next week. When she joins him I expect he will be even more pleasant.

When a trial is completed, the verbatim record is typed and reviewed for legality and correctness by the commanding general. Actually, that task is delegated by the general to a Department of the Army civilian lawyer who reviews the record and prepares a written report for the general's signature. In our office that lawyer and reviewer is John Tinnerello, a well built, intelligent and gifted ex-navy man from Texas. He sports a Clark Gable type mustache and is almost as handsome. John is agreeable and will treat you as you treat him. Dave Addis, John and I have lunch together almost every day when we are all in town so I have gotten to know him quite well. He is very knowledgeable on many subjects. I think he would be good law partner; he certainly fits well into this office.

We also have several enlisted men and two German stenographers assigned to our section. I will tell you about them some other time.

THE TIMES: The American Army in World War II was a segregated Army. Blacks, whites and asians were generally kept in separate units or in traditionally segregated jobs. Under the leadership of President Truman racial discrimination began to be eliminated after the war. The pace intensified under President Eisenhower. An order, not secret, but unpublicized, called for the integration of all Army units in Europe, except truck drivers, in two stages, with the first stage to be completed by April 1, 1953. On that date of 34,493 Negro enlisted men in USAREUR (US Army, Europe), 28,666 or 83 percent were serving in integrated units. Only a few years earlier none were.

USAREUR had not intended to conceal racial integration and, even if that had been intended, any attempt to hide the changing complexion of hundreds of military units involving many thousands of men would have been futile. On the other hand, publicity was so well avoided in the command that no official announcements were made to the public until the program was completed. The publication of this news in The Stars and Stripes on 31 October 1954 was the first public mention in USAREUR of the fact of integration.

In the course of implementing the integration program, USAREUR was interested in determining the degree of correlation between the progress of integration and the command crime rates. An analysis of 7th Army units showed that integration had not resulted in higher crime rates. The 6th Armored Cavalry Regiment, a VIIth Corps unit based near Straubing, reported that its integration in June 1952 had been highly successful in terms of maintenance of morale and operational efficiency. Many problems had been predicted but few actually occurred.

A JAG SCHOOL REUNION

Of the five in my class receiving orders to Europe, I was the first to arrive. Bill Bonwell from Wichita, Kansas, got to Stuttgart a month after I did. I met his train and showed him around town, but he moved on to Göppingen, about thirty miles to the east, where he was assigned to the 28th Infantry Division. Wick Anderson, Roanoke, Virginia, one of my closest friends at the JAG School, arrived in Stuttgart the day after Bill but only paused on his way to Augsburg and the JA Section of the 43rd Infantry Division.

As I was entering the revolving door at the Stuttgart Hotel Graf Zeppelin with Bill Bonwell I observed a male civilian leaving.

I thought, "That guy looks like George Kirby."

George Kirby was at the University of Tennessee with me, and was a good friend. I had no idea he was in Europe. The last I had heard, he was with the State Department in Washington.

I reentered the revolving door only to see George coming back the other way. He had recognized me! At length we were able to meet on the same side of the door. Indeed, this was in fact my old friend. George was still with the State Department, now in Frankfurt. We managed to get together in various places on several very enjoyable occasions during the year following that chance meeting.

Having friends from the JAG School in Europe gladdened my heart. Not being acquainted with anyone when I reached my destination had been a lonely experience. In addition, since I had no automobile I was required to use the military bus system. On the bus, I found, being an officer set me apart. I was usually the only officer on board and thus, slightly uncomfortable. The enlisted soldiers kept to themselves and, I thought, wanted me to do the same. It was an odd sort of arrangement. I was not accustomed to being aloof. I was much more a social type. The enlisted men would laugh and talk, but I was not a part of that.

Intuitively I felt that I should remain distant – otherwise, it seemed, I would lose their respect. I was unable to pinpoint the origin of that feeling. I was never actually taught that an officer shouldn't be sociable with enlisted men. As an American, I celebrated a classless society – but the reserved attitude was surely there. Maybe the old aphorism, *Familiarity breeds contempt,* governed my feelings. If I became familiar, perhaps the enlisted men would become contemptuous. At that point in my military career the officer-enlisted man relationship was troublesome. I was uneasy with the separate and unequal distinction that was always made. Perhaps many other American citizen/officers have perceived the issue. I wondered if the problem was more likely an American one. As time passed, I became more comfortable in my role.

My first few months in Europe had been a somewhat dreary time. A Corps headquarters is a "high headquarters," in that most of the officers stationed there are commanders of very large units, and consequently are older and hold high rank. Except for Dave Addis, the other officers in the JA section were married and usually went to their own quarters and their families after work. At Kelley Barracks, there were more old colonels than young lieutenants.

Now I had some JAG School friends in Europe. It was really wonderful to see them again and I am sure it was nice for them, upon arriving, to be greeted by a friend, a familiar face. I wish I had had that experience. I was later to take separate two-week leaves with both Bill Bonwell (England) and Wick Anderson (Italy).

Since I had to wear a dress uniform if I went out in the evening, I decided I needed another one. I bought a "dress uniform kit" at the Post Exchange. The kit contained everything needed for the uniform – everything, except a tailor. Major Rosten gave me the name and address of a tailor and after three fittings, I had a fine new outfit. The only negative aspect of the experience was that I was required to listen to an overbearing tailor, probably an ex-Nazi, rant about the inept American Army in Korea and how, if the German Army were there instead, the war would long since have been over. While being measured, in my mind, I composed clever responses and ripostes to his ravings but, apprehensive that winning an argument might result in a poorly fitting uniform, I kept my lips zipped.

THE UNSUCCESSFUL DEFENSE OF JAMES FRITTS

On page five of the 18 April 1953 edition of *Neues Volksblatt*, the "Independent Home Newspaper for Franconia," the area in Germany northwest of Bavaria, is a thrilling account of a gun battle between James Fritts, a thirty-four year old American soldier stationed in Bamberg and a large number of other soldiers and at least two military policemen (MP) from the area. The newspaper headline reads: "Fifty-five Years Prison for Mad Shooting Desperado."

Fritts was a member of the 2nd Battalion, 2nd Armored Cavalry, a VII Corps unit, and my client. Under arrest for the unlawful use of a government vehicle, Fritts managed to escape from the guard house, had stolen a weapon from his captors and taken four hostages. By threatening to kill the hostages, Fritts was able to pass through the Kaserne security gate. Once outside, he ran toward a taxicab stand and entered a cab, but was ordered out of the taxi with his hands up by one on the MPs. Fritts seemed to acquiesce but instead, came out firing, hitting the MP in the belly. Fritts then engaged in a running gun battle with the other MP, whom he also wounded. By this time the officer of the day arrived with a squad of guards. According to the *Neues Volksblatt* (translated)

Lieutenant Jackley, the Officer of the Day, led a group of the guards in the pursuit, encircling the desperado, who was wildly shooting around, and closing in on him near the water tower. Sergeant Martinez and Private Busker fired the shots that took Fritts out of the fight. He then threw his pistol away and gave up.

I defended Fritts in the ensuing court-martial at Nürnberg where he was charged with two counts of attempted murder. Luckily, both MPs had survived. Captain McCartin prosecuted.

When I met with Fritts before the trial, I noted that he had a superficial bullet wound in the throat. Although bandaged, he was able to speak. He was handcuffed and accompanied by four armed guards who waited outside the interview room while he and I planned his defense. He contributed little. Neither could I think of much to offer on his behalf.

According to the newspaper story, *Fritts' lawyer didn't have much to say.* I suspect that is an accurate report. The Court, however, was not so reticent and after hearing the witnesses presented by the prosecution and devoting only a few minutes to deliberations, found

Fritts guilty and sentenced him to fifty-five years imprisonment at hard labor.

As the four armed guards, present throughout the trial, removed Fritts from the courtroom, I told him I was sorry he had received such a harsh sentence. He paused and replied, with a smile,

"Don't worry, lieutenant. I'll be home before you will."

A BRAND NEW MORRIS MINOR CONVERTIBLE

When, on the first of May 1953, the Army discontinued bus service after 6 p.m. to, from and between all area Kasernes and downtown Stuttgart, my obtaining an automobile became a necessity. I shopped around and became convinced that the best buy would a Morris Minor, made in England by Morris Garages, the same company that made the classic MG sports car. I could get the Minor for about $1,200.00.   The very much-desired sport MG cost $1,600.00 ($2,200.00, in the States) but it was a much less practical vehicle and I didn't think I could afford it. My parents sent me a check, which I deposited in my bank, promising to repay them in monthly installments. In two weeks the check cleared and I was free to draw on the loan.

*   *   *

Dear Mother and Dad,   *May 1, 1953*
Today is May Day, widely celebrated by the communists. We are given to understand that there will be demonstrations in every city. Travel to Berlin has been halted and everyone is on the alert for some trouble. I saw a short parade in

Nürnberg this morning complete with anti-American signs and banners, but the turnout was pretty skimpy: about 200 participants. That's a poor showing for a city this size.

In the last two weeks I have tried eight cases, three as prosecutor and five as defense counsel.

The three cases I prosecuted resulted in convictions on all counts. Three of the cases I defended resulted in complete acquittals. The other two ended in convictions on some counts but very light sentences. Two of the acquittals were unexpected. I have heard that successful military defense lawyers are soon switched to the prosecution side. We'll see what happens.

VII Corps Headquarters has more colonels and generals than lieutenants. That is one of the reasons I like to get to Nürnberg where I am now and where there are many officers my own age and rank. Last night a group of us went out to supper at a small Italian restaurant and ended up at a gasthaus in the old part of the city, beneath the walls of the castle. Some students from the University of Nürnberg were there and were singing German songs. We started singing along, as best we could, and before long we were all at adjoining tables. We didn't know their songs, nor they ours, so we would alternate singing with them. They were better than we, for they had sung together before, but we were pretty good. Most of us knew some of the same college drinking songs and popular ballads. The Germans seemed to like Old Man River, best, but they also applauded You Are My Sunshine, Home on the Range and Show Me the Way to go

Home. I wish I had a recording of that songfest. I think I have not had more fun since I arrived.

I have recently received some letters from friends stationed in Korea. It takes a letter from there twelve days to get here.

The money situation here can cause difficulties. I get paid in military payment certificates, (MPCs or "scrip"), that cannot be used in German shops, or, as we say "on the German economy." It is not legal for Germans to possess scrip, so to buy things in German stores or purchase tickets or participate in any way in the Germany money system I must change the scrip to German Marks. The conversion can only be made at an American military installation.

On May third I completed all the necessary arrangements to buy a thirty horsepower, four cylinder, Morris Minor Convertible, Clarendon Gray with red leather upholstery. The dealership was in Cologne so it was necessary for me to get a couple of days leave, travel by rail, and then drive back to Stuttgart. One of the reasons I had selected a Morris was because most who owned them were so keen about them. Also, the Morris held an endurance record: 10,000 miles at 50 miles per hour, without stopping, except to refuel. I paid off my parents' loan in twelve monthly installments. Having an auto of my own resulted in a significant change in my life. It vastly improved my social life, my ability to get around and do some things otherwise not available to me and to establish some new friendships.

On the way to Cologne to pick up my car, I found I had insufficient German money to buy a train ticket. I had plenty of scrip but no place to change it. Finally, I found an American officer in the railroad station who would sell me enough German Marks to get to Cologne with a little extra to buy gas for my journey back.

The Old City of Cologne was almost completely demolished by Allied air raids during World War II. Although the area around it was leveled, the world famous twin towered, Gothic Cathedral miraculously survived untouched. I gave it a quick look, then hurried on to find the auto dealership which, I expected would resemble the car show rooms I was accustomed to in America. It did not. When I finally located the Morris sales office, it turned out to be in a large warehouse behind a gasoline service station. But there, inside, among three others, was my brand new car. It looked great!

At the car dealer I paid dock fees and filled the six-gallon (Imperial) gasoline tank, leaving me 85 pfennigs, about twenty cents. Traveling through the British and French zones offered no opportunity to get German money. At last, when I got to Frankfurt I was able to change some scrip, get something to eat and refill the gas tank; it required more than five gallons – I had less than a gallon remaining.

The next week I was sent back to Straubing to prosecute a case involving classified, secret information. This was a six-hour trip by train and a little too far for an easy drive. While I had the file in my possession it was necessary for me to be armed, so I carried the snub nose .38 caliber revolver my dad had given me.

The cases we handled infrequently involved classified information. If one did, it was necessary for us to arrange for appropriate security. The classifications were, "Restricted," "Confidential," "Secret" and "Top Secret." There were classifications higher than "Top Secret," but I don't know what they were called. I guess the classification names are secret, or conceivably, top secret.

*   *   *

The fact that Lt. Gen. Manton Eddy, commanding general of the 7th Army, was returned to the states on June 1, 1953, and was replaced by Lt. Gen. Charles Bolte probably meant nothing to most Americans but it was certainly important to us. As a result of this change, curfew was lifted and the dress uniform after 7 p.m. requirement, revoked. We still had to be in uniform at all times but we didn't necessarily have to pack a dress uniform when we traveled or change clothes just to go out to eat or run a night time errand. Lack of a curfew didn't mean that I would stay out all night, but it did mean that I could cease keeping one eye on the clock and the other on the lookout for the military police. Now I would not have to scurry home, like Cinderella, at the stroke of midnight. Off-duty British and French military personnel could wear civilian clothes in the zones they occupied, or anywhere else for that matter – not so the Americans. In the U. S. zone the uniform requirement remained in place.

THE TIMES: May 1953. Walter Ulbricht, leader of the Communist Party in East Germany, the "German Democratic Republic," faced economic shortfalls and production quota failures all over the Russian occupation zone. The lack of political freedom and scarcity of consumer goods combined in their negative impact on the country. The deep-seated economic, political and social crisis in East Germany was unmistakable. The East German leadership tried to combat the national economic problems by passing a law raising production quotas by 10.3 percent. In Moscow the Russian government urged the repeal of the quota increase viewing that action as the likely cause of an "extremely unsatisfactory situation" in East Germany. The concerns of the Russians were well founded for the unrest of the communist dominated East German people came to a climax the following month.

*   *   *

Stuttgart is near the Black Forest, *Schwarzwald*, which lies along the east bank of the Rhine River and extends from the Swiss border north as far as the city of Karlsruhe. It is called "black" because of the abundance of dark evergreen trees covering mountains similar to the Smokies in East Tennessee. The primary resort and spa of the Schwarzwald is Baden-Baden, the "favorite of kings." Queen Mary of England spent many a season there as did numerous "crowned heads" of Europe, when there was an abundance of royalty in Europe.

Several of us drove there for the day. Baden-Baden seemed to have escaped the war. We saw no damage anywhere. The largest and apparently the most important building was the Spielbank, or casino. I had never before seen such lavish surroundings. Red velvet and gilded woodcarvings were everywhere. The attendants, arrayed in 18th Century livery were quick to catch a cigarette ash or bring a drink. Roulette and baccarat were the games played. The minimum bet was two Deutsche Mark (DM) about half a U. S. dollar, the maximum, 2,300 DM. I bought and soon lost chips worth 20 DM, so spent the remainder of the evening watching the action.

Soon I noticed a crowd gathering around one of the baccarat tables and was surprised to see the Duke and Duchess of Windsor seated there.

The Duke had become King Edward VIII of England when his father George V died on January 20, 1936. However, Edward was notoriously involved with a divorced American woman, Wallis Warfield Simpson. He wanted to marry her and make her his queen. He sought the approval of his family, the Church of England and the political establishment to carry out his marital plans. Provoked by sensational publicity, the authorities became entrenched in their opposition and on December 10, 1936, Edward abdicated the throne so that he might marry "the woman I love." Edward became the Duke of Windsor and his brother became King George VI.

At first, there was no one else at the Windsor's table but the Casino attendants fanned out into the room visiting the other tables, speaking with one or two at each and directly established a game of high stakes players. I watched them play for a while. It was a silent game. Only the croupier spoke as he changed the positions of the bets, accepted tips from the winners and dealt cards from the shoe.

*   *   *

THE TIMES: On Tuesday, June 2nd 1953, following the 1952 death of her father, George VI, who had succeeded to the throne upon the abdication of his brother, Elizabeth Alexandra Mary Windsor, Elizabeth II, answered these questions propounded by the Archbishop at her Coronation in Westminster Abbey, London, England:

The Archbishop: Madam, is your Majesty willing to take the Oath?

The Queen: I am willing.

The Archbishop: Will you solemnly promise and swear to govern the Peoples of the United Kingdom of Great Britain and Northern Ireland, Canada, Australia, New Zealand, the Union of South Africa, Pakistan and Ceylon, and of your Possessions and other Territories to any of them belonging or pertaining, according to their respective laws and customs?

Queen: I solemnly promise so to do.

Archbishop: Will you to your power cause Law and Justice, in Mercy, to be executed in all your judgments?

Queen: I will.

Archbishop: Will you to the utmost of your power maintain the Laws of God and the true profession of the Gospel? Will you to the utmost of your power maintain in the United Kingdom the Protestant Reformed Religion established by law? Will you maintain and preserve inviolably the settlement of the Church of England, and the doctrine, worship, discipline, and government thereof, as by law established in England? And will you preserve unto the Bishops and Clergy of England, and to the Churches there committed to their charge, all such rights and privileges, as by law do or shall appertain to them or any of them?

Queen: All this I promise to do.

Queen (Kneeling at the altar with her hand on the Bible): The things which I have here promised, I will perform, and keep. So help me God.

*   *   *

Germany is much further north than Memphis. Kelley Barracks in southern Germany is on the same latitude as Newfoundland, Canada, further north than anyplace in America except Alaska. As a result the summers in Germany are seldom hot. It might get into the eighties for a week or so but that would be followed by a week in the sixties. In June, it got dark about 9:30 p.m.and was full light again at 4 a.m. In winter I went to work and returned home in the dark.

At 8:00 a.m. on June 9th, 1953 our trial team, a prosecuting attorney, defense attorney, law officer and court reporter needed to get to Straubing. Because of the long time required to go by rail we checked with the air section and learned that a plane was available. We drove the short distance to Echterdingen Airfield and an hour later we were in Straubing. It was a beautiful day. The clouds looked like those in a N. C. Wyeth painting.

After supper, about 9 p.m.I went for a walk in the fields near the Kaserne. To the northeast I could see the low mountains of Czechoslovakia. The temperature was perfect and the sunset magnificent. I felt like trying to outrun the huge jackrabbits that scurried away as I walked through the field.

ECHTERDINGEN AIRFIELD

The airport we used when flying on assignment out of Kelley Barracks was Echterdingen.

The field has an interesting history, according to documents recently prepared by the 6th Area Support Group, Stuttgart Army Airfield.

Aviation came early, unexpectedly, and dramatically to Echterdingen Airfield in the form of Count Ferdinand von Zeppelin's airship, LZ-4. While sailing over Stuttgart on August 5, 1908, LZ-4 lost power in one of her engines and Zeppelin was forced to land her. He had never landed one of his airships on solid ground before, since he considered it safer to use special floating platforms on lakes. He brought LZ-4 down safely, however, in the flat fields just southeast of the town, and a crowd quickly gathered to wonder at the unexpected visitor. Their excitement turned to dismay when a sudden thunderstorm blew the ship on its side, tore it from its moorings and carried it away. Instantly flames shot out from the hydrogen-filled craft, and within a few seconds it was completely destroyed. Fortunately, no one was killed.

Twenty-nine years later the German Zeppelin "Hindenberg," after crossing the Atlantic, exploded and crashed on May 6, 1937, while attempting to land at Lakehurst, New Jersey, resulting in 36 fatalities and ending the era of the hydrogen filled airship.

The more recent and happier history of aviation at Echterdingen started in 1936. As the city of Stuttgart expanded in the 1930's, it outgrew its two early airfields, one on the fairgrounds at Bad Cannstatt and the other in Böblingen. When the German air force, the Luftwaffe, decided to take over the Böblingen field, the Air Ministry and municipal officials made a study of the surrounding countryside in order to find a new airport site with room for expansion. They finally chose the present site near Echterdingen, and started construction in 1936. Stuttgart's new airport was designed with a grass landing field to handle such aircraft as fifteen-passenger Junkers JU-52, and with terminal facilities to service an estimated 150,000 passengers per year. The airport opened to commercial traffic in 1938, only a year before the start of World War II.

During the war the Luftwaffe based night fighters at Echterdingen, and shared the field with commercial operations. The fighters flew interceptions against the many Allied air attacks on Stuttgart and other targets in southern Germany. The Luftwaffe put down a concrete runway of 1,400 meters in 1943, but Allied bombers cratered it later in the war and eventually put the airfield out of commission.

The First French Army drove through Stuttgart in April 1945, and left behind a detachment to repair the runway at Echterdingen. American troops replaced the French Army in the early summer and put the airfield back into operation. When World War II ended and U. S. occupation began, Germany was ruled by the American military government, whose armed force was called "The Constabulary." The U. S. military government moved into Kurmärker Kaserne (now Patch Barracks) in 1946, and their small flight section operated from Echterdingen Airfield with L-5 liaison planes. In 1950, Headquarters, 7th Army was activated at Kurmärker Kaserne and their flight section replaced the disbanded Constabulary's at the airfield. The next year, headquarters, VII Corps moved into Hellenen Kaserne (now Kelley Barracks), and VII Corps aviation units joined the 7th Army section at Echterdingen.

In July 1954 Echterdingen Airfield was the scene of a near fatal aircraft accident in which I was involved. More about that later.

*   *   *

THE BERLIN RIOTS OF JUNE 17, 1953

Stalin's death brought about power struggles, not only in the USSR but also in the satellite states, including East Germany. Some of the measures taken after Stalin's death by East German party boss Walter Ulbricht were opposed by factions in Moscow, others were approved. At first no one knew who would be the communist leader. Malenkov, Beria and Molotov had been the only speakers at Stalin's funeral. Within weeks, however, Soviet Secret Police Chief Beria was under arrest and before the end of the year he was executed by a Russian firing squad.

In June 1953 Berlin, although divided into four zones, was easily traversed by public transportation; the S-Bahn (surface) and the U-Bahn (subway). East Germans who had the money could spend a night on the town in the West and buy whatever they wanted there. Tension was evident, however, because of the oppressive rule of the GDR (German Democratic Republic) in East Germany and the limited supplies of consumer goods available in the East.

Despite measures to compel attendance, the crowds that paraded through the streets of Berlin on May Day were thinner than usual. Later in May a GDR resolution issued by Ulbricht called for the work quotas to be raised by at least 10 percent. Workers were being asked to work ten percent harder and produce ten percent more, for the same pay. In the face of these new requirements, building workers decided to protest. They sent a letter to the ruling authorities demanding a meeting and threatening to strike if the increases in the norms were not rescinded.

An uprising began on June 17. Workers marched on the Council of Ministers Building, their banner proclaiming, "We demand lower quotas." As the march continued, it gathered new recruits, including many young people not in working clothes. Now, in addition to the demand for lower norms, there were chants of "Free Elections" and "We are not slaves" even "Death to Communism" and "Long Live Eisenhower." The government decided to capitulate, revoked the new quota requirements and informed the crowd. The response was triumphant. The successful demonstrators demanded more. There came new outcries, "Down with the Government" and "We want free elections."

Although the upheaval began in Berlin, it soon spread to more than 400 towns and villages throughout East Germany. In most towns industrial workers marched in orderly fashion to the city centers where they tore down posters picturing the party leaders and exhibiting official slogans and destroyed the communist banners. The protesters occupied town halls and various public party buildings, and tried to release political prisoners. Later on, the mood and emphasis changed as others -especially women and teenagers- joined the protests and enlarged the scope of the demands.

The Soviet leaders acted swiftly, declaring a state of emergency, sending in tanks and ordering troops to fire on the demonstrators. Events in Berlin were magnified because of the open border with West Berlin and the extra tension caused by the possibility of an armed East-West clash; conceivably the beginning of World War III.

All public transport in West Berlin was blocked in the areas near the border, while police and troops were used to prevent crowds gathering there. There was great concern among all governments involved that the situation in East Berlin might explode.

Within a few days, the uprising was quelled, but it had important consequences. Ulbricht's Stalinist policies won out and East Germany was ruled with an iron hand for the next thirty years. Moscow had established a pattern of suppressing by force any attempt on the part of the people to throw off the yoke of communist oppression. That pattern was continued until Mikhail Gorbachev, in 1989, repudiated violence as a means of stamping out dissent. Nonetheless, the Berlin riots of 1953 made clear the dictatorial nature and inherent weakness of communist rule. The subjugated peoples of Eastern Europe plainly wanted freedom, not oppression. Communism endured by force, not choice. The Berlin riots gave the West a positive vision that the Cold War might ultimately be won.

This was the first popular demonstration in opposition to what had been characterized as the "Workers' Paradise." For the first time, the "proletariat" had revolted against "the dictatorship of the proletariat." Other such revolts were soon to follow in Hungary, Czechoslovakia and Poland.

*   *   *

Dear Folks,   *19 June 1953*

The big news here is the Berlin riots. Of course, events of such great importance generate a lot of interest. Being so close to the border, we hear a hundred rumors. Many of my friends in armored units have been put on alert and are out on patrol. VII Corps headquarters went to alert status the night of the riots; I'm sure that wasn't coincidental. Luckily, I was out of town so I didn't have to don my combat clothes and go sleep on the concrete floor in the basement of the headquarters building which is what I usually do when an alert is called. Cots are issued according to rank, and I am presently the lowest ranking commissioned officer in the whole corps headquarters.

I have seen photographs in <u>The Stars and Stripes</u>, our European military newspaper, of East German civilians throwing stones at Russian tanks. I don't know how many have been killed; reports are that several hundred have been. I guess it would be fair to say that we are concerned – I can't think of a better word – about what is happening; but we are not afraid. I think that if we become involved in this we will have the East Germans on our side and the Russians will have to contend with adversaries on their front and in their rear.

I returned to Kelley Barracks last night. I shall leave again tomorrow; this time for Munich, then to Straubing, back to Munich and then back to Stuttgart. I should be "home" at Kelley Barracks on or about the first of July.

*   *   *

THE TIMES: 21 June 1953. At Sing-Sing Federal prison in New York state, Julius and Ethel Rosenberg, American citizens, convicted of treason for stealing the secrets of the atom bomb and delivering them to the Soviets were executed by electrocution after the expiration of a final stay previously granted by the United States Supreme Court.

*   *   *

My mother wrote in June 1953 to inquire if I could purchase some Meissen China for her. Regretfully, I informed her that the Meissen China factory was located in what had become the Russian Zone and was, therefore, no longer available.

SWITZERLAND

The first weekend in July five of us took the train from Stuttgart to Zurich and later went on to Luzern in the German speaking region of Switzerland. It was my first departure from Germany since my arrival. The trip was notable for the scenery—no war damage once we got to Switzerland—and the fact that I could wear civilian clothes for the first time in six months.

American soldiers could cross the Swiss-German frontier using either a passport or by showing a copy of appropriate orders. Subsequently I obtained a passport from the American Consulate in Stuttgart, but for this trip I intended to use a copy of my leave orders to cross the border.

I had my ukulele in Europe and sometimes played it and sang college drinking songs, ballads and hillbilly music. To facilitate the singing I had typed the words of some of my favorite songs in the form of a song sheet, copies of which I usually carried in my ukulele case. The songs on the sheet included such classics as Abdul

<u>Abulbul Ameer</u>, <u>Don't Make Me Go to Bed and I'll Be Good</u>, <u>On Top of Old Smoky</u>, etc. On this occasion five of us had taken over a six-passenger, second class, train compartment. I had distributed the song sheets and we were singing some time-honored country melodies when we arrived at the Swiss frontier.

The train stopped and in a few minutes the door to our compartment was flung open by a Swiss border guard who officiously proclaimed, "Passports," then observing that we were all in uniform, he supplemented his announcement: "or orders."

Lieutenant Addis was closest to the compartment door. Without a moments hesitation Addis handed the border patrolman his copy of the song sheet from which, just a few minutes earlier, he had been singing the tenor part to <u>Big Rock Candy Mountain</u>.

The Swiss sentinel studied the song sheet carefully. We sat, silently and solemnly, looking at the compartment floor or out the window or at the Swiss guard – but not at each other – for fear we would snigger, thus initiating some sort of serious international incident. At length the guard seemed satisfied with our papers, turned the song sheet over, stamped the reverse side with an official seal, signed it and turned to the next soldier, who also offered him a song sheet for transit. So it was with all five of us. Each song sheet was studied, stamped, sealed and signed. Nobody so much as smirked until the magisterial Swiss official completed his inspection, touched the bill of his cap as a salute and adieu, closed the compartment door and continued on his rounds. When he was out of ear shot we exploded in laughter. The only problem with our border passage was that afterwards no one would return the song sheets.

Everyone wanted to keep his, now impressed with the official Swiss seal and signature, as a souvenir.

In Switzerland, they say, everything is either compulsory or forbidden.

Walking about the city of Zurich, I was struck by the beauty of the lake and later, at the hotel, was intrigued by the bathtub in my room in which one sat, the water being up around one's neck. We went on to Luzern, enjoyed another lovely city by another beautiful lake, the famous lion statue carved into a stone hillside in the city center and were delighted to see signs promoting "Memphis," which turned out to be a brand of Austrian made cigarettes.

THE MEMPHIS BLUES

Memphis is known as the "Home of the Blues." W. C. Handy was a Memphian and the first songwriter to publish a blues composition: The Memphis Blues in 1909. That was soon followed by other Handy blues offerings including the St. Louis Blues and the Beale Street Blues. Handy ultimately moved to New York City, the core of the music publishing business, but Memphis was always his home.

Other luminaries of Memphis music, Beale Street and the blues include Furry Lewis, Muddy Waters, Albert King, Bobby "Blue" Bland, Alberta Hunter, B. B. King and Memphis Minnie McCoy. Elvis Presley made his first recording for the Sun label in Memphis in 1954 and began a trend which popularized the blues and what later became known as "Rock and Roll," but that was yet to come. In 1953, Elvis was a senior student at Memphis' Humes High School.

A few of my friends shared my enthusiasm for the blues and for Memphis jazz. Recordings of such music, however, were difficult to find at that time, even in Memphis. The only record shop of which I was aware where such music could be bought was "The Home of the Blues" record shop on Beale Street. I tried to find some good blues records in Germany but none were obtainable. So, on 6 July 1953 I wrote to Johnny Gordon, a Memphis friend who had a common appreciation for the kind of blues, jazz and spirituals that were available on Beale Street, sent him a money order for twenty dollars and asked him to pick out and send me some records. He did so. I thus became the source of the blues from Memphis in the Stuttgart area and perhaps am responsible for the popularity of that genre of music in the whole of Germany! Maybe I am the one who introduced the "blues" to Europe!

On many an evening after I had moved into the officer's club – BOQ at Kelley Barracks, I invited members of the German orchestra playing for dances at the club to come back to my room during their break. There, I would unveil my record player, select a platter and introduce them to the blues from Memphis. They were enraptured and I was delighted. I have always taken great pleasure in showing others the places and experiences that are especially important to me. The pleasure I felt by acquainting German friends with the music of my hometown was only exceeded by the appreciation I sometimes observed in them.

*   *   *

John J. Thomason

Dear Mother and Dad,   22 July 1953

We have a new lieutenant in the J A section! His name is Justin Albaugh and he is from St. Petersburg, Florida. He is several years my elder, but not as experienced as I in the courtroom. More importantly, his date of rank is more recent than mine. So, I have cast off the dubious honor and questionable distinction of being the lowest ranking commissioned officer in the corps headquarters. I am now the second lowest.

Several days ago I received a telephone call from Frank Liddell who is from Memphis, a slight acquaintance of mine and a very good friend of some very good friends. He is an exchange student at the local university here in Stuttgart. He said you had given his parents my name. We met for supper. Unfortunately he will be heading back in a few months but he has promised to introduce me to some of his female German university classmates.

Both of you and Ginger (my sister) have written, pointing out my failure to comment on the dating situation here. I am not trying to conceal anything. It simply did not occur to me to write on the subject. Since you are curious I shall address the matter.

I have dated both German and American girls. The Americans are schoolteachers in Army schools, daughters of older, high-ranking officers or civilian employees of the military. Moreover, I expect to get together with some Memphis and Knoxville girls I know who are planning to come *to Europe on vacation. Their visits will provide additional opportunities for female companionship.*

As for the German girls, Army officer friends introduced me to some; others I have met at parties. I dated a young lady employed as an aupairs by an American family. American students with civilian contacts, such as Frank Liddell, can be counted on to provide for meeting other young German ladies.

In addition, there is a novel system here that permits meeting a German Fräulein at a dance, but I have not found it to be a very good way to establish any sort of relationship. Not far from the Hotel Graf Zeppelin in downtown Stuttgart, is a very nice restaurant, the Hindenbergbrau, featuring good food and a dance orchestra. Singles, couples and groups are welcome and as the band begins to play it is considered perfectly proper for a male to approach a female to whom he has not been formally introduced and ask her for a dance. However, there are risks of embarrassment involved. The female may decline the invitation in which event the invitor must slink back to his table, having been publicly rebuffed. Several invitors may converge at the table of a particularly attractive prospect at the same time, humbling the one(s) not chosen. After the dance, it is expected that the female will be escorted back to her table, and that is that. An American soldier (remember, we are always in uniform) takes some extra risk by asking for a dance because the invitee or those in her group may not find acceptance on her part to be politic. I have heard that in Berlin, and perhaps other larger German cities, this same system is in place augmented by telephones on each table, which allow for follow-up conversations or private, less risky, dance invitations. However, we don't have anything like that in Stuttgart.

Many of the German girls I met are on their own. They come from smaller communities, usually nearby, and one or both parents may have been killed in the war or be missing. (One of the most popular television programs here, broadcast for an hour each evening, consists entirely of pictures and descriptions of missing persons, soliciting information about them. At dusk, crowds gather outside television stores to watch.)

I have invited out German girls who live with their parents but they have not permitted me to call for them at their homes, nor have I been introduced to their families. We meet at a restaurant or movie or some other public place. I suppose there yet remains a stigma attached to having a date with the enemy.

My German language skills are not nearly good enough for a complex social conversation, so I am limited to dating young women who speak English. Fortunately, that includes most of those whom I have met. English, taught as a second language in German schools for years, is frequently spoken and is the language of choice in international transactions.

Besides the language, another communication problem exists. Few German girls I have met have telephones. Consequently, when we are together we must make arrangements for a future rendezvous by agreement to meet someplace at a certain time and date. Usually that works out, but if I am required to go out of town or my date, for some reason, is unable to be at the place we have selected at the time and on the day chosen, the relationship may be unintentionally but permanently ended. Unfortunately, that has happened to me and I have been unable to reestablish communications.

To conclude my observations on this point, I must say, having an automobile at my disposal has notably improved my social life.

*   *   *

My 24th birthday celebration began at 3:30 in the morning of July 28, 1953 by the sounding of an alert. The alarm required me to dress in combat gear, go to the arms room for my weapon (a .45 caliber semi-automatic pistol) and report to the basement of the headquarters building, there to remain until the alert ended at about 8:30 a.m. How it is determined that an alert should be declared at an end, is unclear to me. Apparently the commanding general, satisfied that the troops have promptly assumed combat disposition, signals the "all clear," and everyone returns to his regular work. Later in the day the mail brought a birthday box of my favorite brownies from my mother and while they lasted they tasted as good as they ever had back home.

THE TIMES: Although the Berlin Riots of June 17 were over (125 men and women had been killed and thousands arrested) discontent was still rampant in East Germany. Food shortages became severe. Under the circumstances American officials thought a free food program was called for. Correspondence between President Eisenhower and West German Chancellor Adenaur was released on July 10, 1953 indicating the U. S. would deliver 15 million dollars worth of free food to East Germans if the Russians would agree. The Soviets rejected the idea the next day, but on July 27 the free distribution began anyway.

Over the next month or so hundreds of thousands of Eisenhower food packages were delivered through various check points in Berlin. East Germans flocked into Berlin from all over the GDR to collect the packages. Lines were long but the operation was extremely successful. By mid August, 2,598,202 packages had been distributed, far more than was originally proposed. Seventy-five percent of the population of East Berlin had received at least one package, moreover, two thirds of the parcels had gone to non-Berliners, many to East Germans who lived far away from the city. The program was finally halted because GDR officials stopped Berlin-bound trains and halted highway traffic. So much pressure was put on food recipients by East German Police that many were afraid to have the packages in their possession. In addition, the British and French, who had never been in favor of the plan for fear of destabilizing the political balance, prevailed on the Americans to stop the free food distribution.

In the meantime, the flood of refugees into West Berlin increased. A small airlift of refugees was established flying more than 1000 a day to the west.

After the death of Stalin, the West began to receive mixed signals from the Soviets as first one faction, then another came to power. On one hand, under Ulbricht, the East Germans were first ruled with an iron hand, then communist officials retreated in the face of the riots, soon afterward stronger steps were taken to quell resistance. Soviet – U. S. relations were also unpredictable. Molotov, the Russian Foreign Secretary made a surprising statement in July that all issues dividing the U S and Russia were negotiable. That led to talks about exchanging prisoners in Korea and finally to an armistice agreement ending the Korean War and reestablishing the 38th parallel as the border between North and South Korea.

*　　　*　　　*

With the lessening of tensions, the first week in August, the Army issued a directive that reserve officers, such as I, could apply for early release. Although I was thoroughly enjoying Europe, I wanted to get started practicing law in Memphis, so I applied for separation. My application was rejected.

*　　　*　　　*

Dear Mother and Dad,   *15 August 1953*

Major Rosten is gone having been replaced by Lieutenant Colonel Hodges, from Texas. Hodges seems to be a really nice person, although not very well versed in military justice. He comes to us from the Army patent office! It will be a while before he is up to speed. It won't take him long; he is a bright guy.

141

Enclosed is a picture of me and Dave Addis cooking spaghetti at the Tinnerello's house. Note that I have on civilian clothes. We think we can get by with being out of uniform because John is a civilian employee of the Army and the MPs are not likely to enter his home to check on identities. It is an immense relief to get out of uniform for a change.

Next week I shall drive to Freudenstadt in the Schwarzwald to meet Pat Hoshall and drive her to Luzern, Switzerland. She is on one of those grand tours of Europe sometimes given as a college graduation present. Remember her? She lived on Cowden Avenue, one block north of us when I was in high school. I dated her some.

My notes reveal that as of today I have participated in fifty-three general courts-martial trials since I arrived in Germany five and a half months ago. I have defended thirty-five and prosecuted eighteen.

<u>DACHAU</u>

About eleven miles north of Munich lies the pleasant old town of Dachau, now haplessly and perhaps permanently linked to the evil concentration camp east of the town. Before 1933, Dachau was known for its scenic beauty and was much visited by photographers and landscape artists.

The Dachau concentration camp was the first such facility constructed by the Nazis. It remained in operation for almost twelve full years. It is reported that 80,000 persons were executed there or died of overwork, starvation or torture. The prisoners were Jews, communists, physicians, lawyers, teachers; all manner of political opponents of the Nazis, as well as captured prisoners of war. The executions were carried out on the gallows, by pistol shot to the head or neck, firing squad or toxic gas. Some died by touching the electrified barbed wire that surrounded the camp. Bodies of the dead prisoners were buried or cremated in gas fired ovens designed and built especially for that purpose.

When the camp was liberated by General Patton's American Third Army on 29 April 1945, thirty-three thousand half starved prisoners were still inside.

Several members of our trial team, in Munich for VII Corps general courts-martial trials, visited the Dachau death camp on a sunny Sunday Afternoon. The visit was shocking.

We walked over the camp, which now, of course, is unoccupied, but still stands much as it was when in operation. At one place, marked by low concrete curbs, we saw a square plot about twenty-five feet on a side, on which had been erected a small metal sign announcing that it contained the ashes of 50,000 people! Inside an office we leafed through volume after volume of what looked like antiquated hotel register books, containing the names and brief descriptions of all the prisoners received there. The crematory ovens are still in place, six or eight of them, as I recall. Above each of the oven doors was an embossed metal nameplate prominently proclaiming the commercial name of the industrial furnace manufacturer.

We entered the gas chamber. It was a large tiled room with a low ceiling and what appeared to be built in shower heads above, spaced on four-foot centers. We were told that the prisoners were stripped naked, handed a bar of soap and told to enter the "shower room" for a bath. When the room was crowded with unsuspecting captives, the doors were shut, locked, and poisonous gas introduced through the "shower heads," until all occupants were asphyxiated.

I have seen photographs of the stacks of uncremated corpses heaped near the ovens, discovered by the liberating soldiers. Within days after the camp was emancipated, citizens of Dachau were required by the American Army to go to the camp to see for themselves what had been discovered. I have seen a photo of these well-dressed German civilians, turning their faces away from the ghastly sight, handkerchiefs to their noses in an effort to escape the overwhelming smell of death. They claimed not to have known what was going on at the camp, a doubtful assertion. Trainloads of prisoners arrived almost daily, but no trainloads of prisoners departed. The smoke from the ovens and the stench of burning cadavers surely must have been noticeable, especially over a period of twelve years.

But, upon reflection, who can reproach them for averting their eyes from that horrid spectacle? Would I have performed differently? Would I have investigated the activities of that camp, or would I have ignored it? What if I, a citizen of the town of Dachau, had scrutinized the operations of the concentration camp and had discovered the truth? What could I have done about it, except, perhaps to have objected, and most likely joined the ranks of those confined there?

No small number of highly principled Germans attempted to oppose Hitler and the Nazis. Few, if any, were successful. Notable examples are General Ludwig Beck, Colonel Claus von Stauffenberg and other high ranking German military officers who were executed or forced to commit suicide because of their efforts to remove Hitler and the Nazis from power. Even Army Group Commander General Erwin Rommel, the "Desert Fox," who was at the time of his death in charge of the German defense against the Allied invasion of Europe, was forced to take poison because of his suspected involvement in a plot to eliminate Hitler.

Others, like Dietrich Bonhoeffer protested against the Nazis on moral grounds and lost their lives but left a legacy of ethical courage.

As with any complex moral perplexity, the horrors of Dachau present questions more easily answered through hindsight.

*   *   *

Dear Mother and Dad,   20 August 1953

Colonel Conerly and Major Barry from 7th Army JA Section and Colonel Guimond the staff judge advocate of VII Corps have suggested that I apply for a regular army commission. Actually, they have all come to me separately and have attempted to convince me that I should become a career Army officer.

Presently I am a reserve officer on active duty. Regular Army officers are considered to be professional soldiers. Graduates of West Point are given regular Army commissions. You can't tell the difference from physical appearance, from the uniform or insignia, but as far as the other career officers are concerned, there is a big difference between a reserve and regular commission.

I must confess, the offer is tempting. This is not a bad life. It is really pretty easy. Once you figure out the system, you can get by without doing too much work. Promotions are to some extent guaranteed – up to a certain point. But they appear to be "lock step," in that everybody is likely to get promoted after the same length of time at a certain rank . If you get passed over twice you are out. I think once you get up to the rank of full colonel promotions are probably based more on merit – but I'm not sure. Politics plays a part.

On the other hand, the Army is a sort of "trap." It offers temporary security but nothing very permanent. My assignment here is great but there are many assignments elsewhere I would not want.

I know some officers who have committed to this life and now regret having chosen it. Others are afraid they are being forced out. They don't know what they could do in civilian life. Besides, the Army's methods, systems and bureaucracy are not to my liking. I don't like the petty politics, rules and regulations. On balance, my preference is to finish my military obligation and see what I can accomplish as a practicing lawyer in Memphis, Tennessee.

I don't think I shall apply.

*   *   *

A WEDDING IN FRANCE

On Wednesday, August 26, I departed Kelley Barracks about nine o'clock in the morning and drove 275 miles to Chaumont, France arriving about five thirty in the afternoon. Chaumont was accustomed to the presence of Americans. General John Joseph Pershing, Commander of the American Expeditionary Forces in World War I, and for whom my father named me, had his headquarters there. At the nearby U. S. Air Force base, I located my long time Memphis friend, Billy Cowan and his bride to be, Joan Morrell Adams. I brought with me what I thought to be a fine wedding present, a fancy carving set from Germany. They opened the gift and shared my excitement. We went to parties the next two nights and I got acquainted with Joannie.

On Friday, 28 August 1953, William C. and Joan Adams Cowan were married; I was best man. Actually, they were married twice. First, at noon, at a civil ceremony in the town of Smootier (pronounced by the French "Smoo-tee-yeh"; by the wedding participants "Smoo-chee")– all in French, conducted by the mayor of the town and witnessed by the local schoolmaster and me. When signaled to do so, Billy answered "Oui," but, since he doesn't speak French, I think he has no idea what promises he made. Joannie, who does speak the language, will probably remind him in future years what undertakings he unwittingly assumed.

Then, at seven-thirty that evening, there was a church ceremony on the base presided over by an Air Force chaplain and attended by all the members of Billy's jet fighter squadron, wives, friends and me. The evening service was attended by a standing-room-only crowd. In the time between ceremonies, courtesy of one of the pilots in the Billy's squadron, in the rear seat of a T-33, a two seat version of the F-80 jet fighter, I had flown to Paris, London, Brussels and Frankfurt. We had not landed but flew over the cities at a fairly low altitude, so I saw some of the sights I associate with those capitals.

147

Joannie is from Scottsdale, Arizona where she and Billy met when he was there taking flight training. Billy was one of my best friends in high school and at the University of Tennessee, in Knoxville; we were in the same high school and college fraternities. Joannie came to France on a tour, made a side trip to see Billy and after he proposed, decided to stay. Neither family was able to be present; as a matter of fact at the time of the wedding the Cowans had never even met Joannie. So, at Billy's request I drove over from Stuttgart to steady his nerves. Their wedding night was spent in nearby Nancy. I had roses sent to their hotel room. They did the same for me when I was married three years later. After their honeymoon, the newly wed Cowans settled down in the Beau Sejour Hotel, in Chaumont.

Joannie impressed me very favorably. I saw in her the qualities I would later seek and find in my own wife. As I write this forty-nine years later the four of us remain close.

On the way back to the Chaumont Base, between weddings, the pilot of the jet in which I was the rear seat passenger advised,

"We've got about thirty minutes of fuel left. Do you want to do some acrobatics?"

"Sure." I replied, "why not?"

With my assent, he proceeded to perform barrel rolls, loops, hammerheads and so forth. I found the stunt flying somewhat disconcerting since I didn't know what to expect before the maneuver began. However, I am blessed with a stable stomach and did not become ill. After a while the pilot inquired,

"How are you doing back there?"

"Fine." I replied, although that was a bit of an overstatement.

"Have you ever blacked-out?" the pilot asked.

I indicated I had not.

"Do you want to try it?" he wondered.

"I guess so" I said, without enthusiasm.

With that he put the jet into a steep dive coming out in abrupt climb. I guess the idea was to utilize gravitational and centripetal forces to push one's blood away from one's head down toward one's feet.

"Did you black-out?" asked the pilot.

I truthfully answered that I had not.

"No?" he said. "Well, we'll try it again"; and he did.

This time I experienced a very strange sensation. As we pulled out of an even steeper dive my vision began to lose color perception. I changed from color vision to black and white, then just to black, after a minute or so, back to black and white and finally back to color. At no time did I lose consciousness.

"Did you black out that time?" he questioned.

"Yeah," I said. "I sure did."

"I thought you would." he observed.

Afterwards it occurred to me that neither of us had on "G" suits that tend to keep your blood from leaving your brain when involved in such acrobatics. So, since I had blacked out, the pilot probably did too. I'm happy we both recovered.

Driving back to Stuttgart after the wedding, I tried out my college French at a small café. I thought I ordered a small portion of Brie Cheese and a glass of wine. The waiter brought me a whole bottle of wine and a huge round of Brie. Either I misspoke or business was slow that day!

Since Billy's parents, who were also friends of mine, had not been present at the wedding, on the day after my return I dispatched a long descriptive letter to them. The nuptial accounts I had seen in the local newspaper in Memphis seemed always to depict in great detail the bride's wedding gown, so, I tried my hand at that:

> *Billy wore his dark blue suit, as did I. Joan was beautiful in a newly completed white dress of a delicate material, with pearl buttons up the back. A pert hat of the same material complimented her wedding gown. The belt was of identical fabric. She wore white shoes and carried a lovely bouquet of pink roses which was accented by pink needle work on her white gloves. She was really lovely. There were no slip-ups and nobody dropped the ring or anything like that. The words of the ceremony were read from the book that you sent, which was later signed by all the guests. I'm sorry you could not have been there. You would have been very proud.*

*   *   *

Mr. and Mrs. Cowan later wrote thanking me for my portrayal of the wedding ritual and of the prior and subsequent marriage events. My letter had been the first account they had received.

*   *   *

Dear Mother and Dad   Monday night, 28 September 1953
> *I am on the train to Straubing, having departed Heidelberg at 3:15 this afternoon.*

> *It is now 9:15 and I have another hour and a half until I get to my destination, where I expect to be met by a Jeep and*

150

driver who will take me to the Kaserne. This has been a long ride and I am tired.

Seven trials in one week, that is what I have just completed; two on Monday, one on Tuesday, two on Wednesday and one each day on Thursday and Friday. It was a successful week for me. Of the four cases I prosecuted all resulted in convictions. Two of the three cases I defended were guilty pleas, the other resulted in an acquittal. I am very pleased at the outcome of the trials but also very fatigued. I hope I never have another week like that one.

*   *   *

In September I tried 18 cases which raised my total to more than 80. These were all general courts-martial, all criminal cases. The charges were diverse and the facts interesting. In advance of each trial we were furnished a packet of information about the case, including statements from witnesses, documents and exhibits. Most of the time, a day or so before the trial, witnesses were assembled so that both prosecution and defense could interview them. Occasionally, one or both counsel would require some additional investigation, which we would conduct ourselves or at our request would be undertaken by the military police or the Criminal Investigation Division. Because of the volume of cases and the serious nature of the charges, the work was hard and the trials stressful.

I brought my civilian clothes to Europe knowing that I could wear them while on leave outside the American Zone and in the hope that their off-duty use would be authorized sometime while I was in Germany. That wish came true in October when we were advised that civilian clothes would be allowed for off-duty wear beginning November 1. That was the good news. The bad news was that I was being evicted from the BOQ at Patch Barracks.

In my opinion, 7th Army Headquarters had the most comfortable BOQ in the American Zone. After living for several weeks at the Graf Zeppelin Hotel, I had been assigned quarters at Patch Barracks because my duty at VII Corps was thought to be temporary. When my assignment to Kelley Barracks was made permanent, I didn't bother to inform the housing authorities at 7th Army. I was very happy to remain in 7th Army quarters, and enjoy the privacy and convenience they afforded. However, bachelor quarters were scarce. I was, therefore, afraid I would be found out—and after eight months of "illicit" occupancy—I was. I received notice one day in October that I had one week to vacate my Patch Barracks BOQ room. By that time I had been at Kelley long enough to know people who could help me, so I was able to get a room next to Dave Addis' in the BOQ half of the Kelley Barracks officer's club. Dave and I decided to put our rooms together and completed our arrangement by sharing a sitting room and a bedroom. The bath was down the hall. It was not as splendid as Patch, but in many ways more convenient since I now lived where I worked, and I didn't feel like a fugitive anymore. Dave and I maintained that arrangement for about six months, then decided to split so that each of us could have more privacy.

THE TIMES: On 22 October 1953 American Intelligence Officers briefed a group of operatives from the British Secret

Intelligence Service with respect to their plan to dig a tunnel from West into East Berlin and intercept encrypted Russian military communications. Among the British agents advised of the plan was George Blake, a Russian KGB mole, who disclosed the existence of the tunnel project to Sergei Kondrashev, his KGB contact at a London meeting the following December.

The idea for the tunnel had emerged the previous year as East Berlin became the most important communications center in communist Eastern Europe for traffic between Moscow and the political capitals of the satellite states. The Soviets were switching from wireless radio communications to telephone lines since radio signals could be intercepted and wires could not except by physical connection, and thus were more secure. The wires were strung on poles or were underground. U. S. Intelligence thought underground cables offered a more suitable opportunity for a tap since the cables were not easily observed and the tap could remain in place without detection. The idea was tested in the spring of 1953 when an American intelligence agent was able to temporarily patch a line from an East Berlin telephone exchange into West Berlin in order to determine what sort of traffic might be intercepted. The results were gratifying and the project was approved at the highest level of the American government.

Although the Soviets knew of the creation of the tunnel before construction began, they did not wish to compromise their highly placed agent, Blake, so they did nothing to impede its progress. Work on the tunnel began in 1954. By early 1955 the taps were in place and functional. In 1956 the Soviets developed a plan whereby they could "accidentally" discover the tap and publicly remove it, without endangering the security of Blake. Before the interception was eliminated, however, 40,000 hours of telephone conversations were recorded and 6,000,000 hours of Teletype traffic copied.

Blake was arrested in 1961, convicted of treason and sentenced to imprisonment for forty-two years, one year for each of the forty-two British agents whose deaths he was said to have caused. Based on information obtained from him and from other intelligence sources it is felt that the data obtained from the tunnel tap was genuine. The Russians had been so afraid of jeopardizing Blake that they had not disclosed the existence of the tunnel to the East German Secret Police or even to their own agents in East Berlin. The most useful information obtained by the Americans had to do with Soviet and East German Army battle plans and troop dispositions and strengths, knowledge otherwise unobtainable before the development of reconnaissance satellites and other more sophisticated means of intelligence gathering.

In 1966, with help from a member of the Irish Republican Army, Blake escaped over the wall of Wormwood Scrubs, the British prison in West London where he was being held, and a year later surfaced in Moscow. He was awarded the Order of Lenin, married a Russian, fathered a son and still lives in Moscow where he goes by the Russian name Georgii Ivanovich.

*　　*　　*

Dear Folks,   *Friday, 29 October 1953*

I have over one hundred Christmas cards ready to mail! They are all in German, have German postage stamps affixed and will be sent by Deutschepost.

We have a new Lt. Col., Ernst Oeding, from New York City. He is a great guy. He will be assigned to VII Corps permanently. I am certain his presence will lighten the load on all of us. We couldn't have been assigned a more pleasant, well-informed or personable individual. Now, if we could only get rid of Lt. Albaugh, who has become a nuisance, everything would be great.

In the last two weeks I have secured two acquittals from Albaugh in cases that everyone expected him to win. As a result, my stock is up; his down. Consequently, I have been named as prosecutor on seven very serious cases: riot, attempted murder, etc. I shall also prosecute a case in which the defense counsel is of higher rank than I. That has not happened before..

Early Monday, Dave and I shall depart for a week of trials in Nürnberg. My baggage is much heavier than usual, containing both civilian clothes and uniforms. I hadn't thought there would be any disadvantage in being able to wear civilian clothes, but we travel so much, having to pack and carry two sets of clothes is inconvenient.

*   *   *

Early in October I was advised that there would be a corps headquarters Halloween Party at the officer's club. The JA section was to have a table. I decided to ask Annegret Hartmann, an attractive young German university student I met through Frank Liddell, to be my date. She also worked in the music department at the Süddeutscher Rundfunk, the South German Radio station with offices in downtown Stuttgart. As the party night approached it occurred to me that I had seen few, if any, German Nationals as guests at the Club. I decided to mention that I was planning to bring a German girl to the party so that no one would be surprised. So, I told Colonel Guimond, in passing, about Annegret and thought no more about it. A few days later Colonel Guimond called me to his office and advised me that the matter of my Halloween Party date had been taken up with the corps chief of staff, General Weyrauch, who, on behalf of the commanding general had given his approval that I might bring Annegret.

I had not previously appreciated the military significance of my social affairs or that the identity of my female companion was of such importance and concern to higher authority. I thought the exalted level of military involvement in my social affairs rather comical and so, next time I saw Annegret, I told her what had transpired and that she had been the subject of a high level command decision. She was not amused. As a matter of fact, she called me from the radio station several days later and advised that she would prefer not to attend the party and she did not. Furthermore, she said, having thought the matter over, she had decided that she would just as soon not have anything more to do with the American Army, including me.

Indeed, one might say that although we won the war, on Halloween, I lost the battle. I went to the party alone

It was never clear to me why bringing a German girl to the "O Club" was such a big deal. I thought for a while that perhaps the wives of the officers objected. I don't recall there being any female officer members of the club; so, objections could not have arisen from that quarter. I suspect the reaction to my inviting a German was more a matter of reflex than reflection. When, finally, I did bring a German, Gisela Luenig, to the club it was to the New Years' party in January 1954. Once again, I alerted everyone that my date for the evening would be a German. Gisela was an attractive and polished young lady who got along well with the entire group, including all the wives. Afterwards, once people got to know her, we were both invited many times by officers' wives to dinner parties at their homes and Gisela was welcomed, without fanfare, at the club. Perhaps it just took a while after the war ended for social relations to normalize.

GENERAL GAVIN

Seated at my desk one day in October 1953, I was surprised when a major I had not previously met appeared in my office and said,

"Lieutenant Thomason, General Gavin wants to see you."

My first thought was that the major was joking. Then, I saw that he wore the two star insignia of a major general's aide. There was only one major general at VII Corps headquarters, the corps commander, General James M. Gavin.

"Really," I said, flustered, "Does General Gavin really want to see me?"

"That's what he told me." The major replied calmly.

"Come with me. I'll take you upstairs to his office."

Major General James M. Gavin was the legendary World War II commander of America's first paratroop division, the 82nd Airborne, named the *All-America* division because its soldiers came from every state and known by its double "A" shoulder patch. Gavin was one of the most famous combat generals of World War II. Probably the most famous paratrooper, he was known as "Jumpin' Jim" because of many heroic combat jumps he made with American paratroopers.

The 82nd had been reactivated in 1941 under the command of General Omar Bradley. When Bradley was promoted, General Matthew B. Ridgeway took command; Gavin was assistant division commander. After participating in the invasion of North Africa, America's first World War II engagement with the German Army, the 82nd made combat jumps in Sicily and at Anzio in Italy. After that Ridgeway was promoted and Gavin became division commander. At age thirty-eight, Gavin was the youngest American Army major general since the Civil War promotion of Major General George Custer.

Born in New York City on March 22, 1907 and raised in Pennsylvania coal mining country, Gavin enlisted in the Army as a private at age seventeen. He had not completed high school. Because of obvious leadership potential he earned an appointment to the United States Military Academy at West Point, from which he graduated in 1929. Upon graduation he was commissioned as a second lieutenant in the Infantry, then, in 1941, qualified as a paratrooper. An outspoken advocate of airborne parachute attack, he wrote several books on the subject and shared in the development of the Army plans for tactical use of airborne troops.

Gavin lead American troops into Naples, Italy, in October, 1943, the first major European city to be liberated from Nazi control during World War II.

On D-Day, June 6, 1944 the main objective of the 82nd was to secure the roads and bridges behind Utah Beach, one of the principal attack points where American assault troops stormed the beaches. Gavin jumped with his men, 6,000 assault paratroopers and 4,000 glider borne combat infantrymen, behind enemy lines, to secure the essential area. As the D-Day invasion began, Gavin's division was the first to capture a French town, Sainte-Mere-Eglise. After D-Day, the 82nd remained in combat until July 8, thirty-three days without relief. During that period, no ground gained by the division was ever relinquished.

Gavin and the 82nd Airborne made its fourth successful combat jump in the Netherlands at Nijmegen, a leap-frog assault behind the German lines and later contributed to the rescue of the Americans surrounded at Bastogne in the Battle of the Bulge. When the war ended, Gavin was engaged in planning the airborne assault on the German capital, Berlin. Still in the vanguard, the 82nd met the Russian Army at the Elbe River not far from Berlin, and became the first American division to occupy that city.

By the end of World War II General Gavin was entitled to wear forty awards and decorations, including the Distinguished Service Cross for heroism in action at Bittoria, Italy, in July 1943 and an oak leaf cluster for his DSC for heroism in action at Le Motey, France in

June 1944. He received the Silver Star for gallantry in action in September, 1944, near Mook, Holland. He was also awarded the Distinguished Service Medal, an oak leaf cluster to his Silver Star, the Bronze Star Medal and a Purple Heart.

Gavin was promoted to the three star rank of lieutenant general in 1955. After retirement from the Army, he was appointed by President Kennedy as Ambassador to France. He died on 23 February 1990, aged 82, and is buried at the United States Military Academy Cemetery, at West Point, New York.

*   *   *

I followed the major to the second floor of our building. Rarely before had I visited this sanctified area of high command. We entered the reception room outside General Gavin's office where I was invited to have a seat. Nervously, I awaited the impending interview.

In a few minutes a secretary came out of the office and said,

"The general will see you now."

I walked through the door, halted at attention in front of the general's desk and saluted. There sat Major General Gavin, two gleaming silver stars on each shoulder and a wealth of combat ribbons, decorations, paratroopers' wings and infantry badges on his chest. I had seen him once or twice before, around the Kaserne, but had never been this close.

He returned my salute. "Stand at ease, lieutenant," said the general. (Easier said than done!)

"Have a seat." He motioned toward one of two chairs in front of his desk.

"Yes, sir," I said, and sat down—on the edge of the chair seat.

The general then proceeded to ask me a few questions about where I was from, how I liked my assignment and whether I had any complaints concerning my duties. We talked for a while -- just casual conversation. Then he got to the point.

"I understand you have applied for early release," he said.

"I wanted to find out if there is a problem. You're very well liked by your commanding officer; we'd like to keep you around for a while."

I was astounded. It had never occurred to me that General Gavin knew I existed, much less that he would be interested in my plans to get out of the Army. I was one of hundreds of lieutenants under his command.

I explained that I was very happy at VII Corps, that I liked my job and the people I worked with, but that my ambition was to get back to Memphis and practice law. He seemed interested in me. We chatted a little while longer. He observed that being a lawyer would be challenging and likely very gratifying and that he understood my desire to get started on my career. He might like being a lawyer himself, he said. He respected the many lawyers who worked for him in the corps and thought they did a good job.

At that point he stood and extended his hand.

"Thanks for coming up," he said.

"Yes, sir." I replied. "You're welcome."

Again, we exchanged salutes, I did an about face and departed, closing the door quietly behind me.

A little dazed, I walked back downstairs to my office and my work.

"Wow!" I thought. "What a leader!"

*   *   *

THE VII th CORPS

Smaller than an army but larger than a division, a corps is a tactical unit designed to fulfill its role as a combat headquarters and a link between the larger and smaller components. Its strength varies depending upon its mission at a given time and the units assigned to it. In the early 50s, the 7th Army in Europe consisted of two corps, the Vth, based in Frankfurt, and VIIth, in Stuttgart, five infantry divisions and numerous other specialty units.

There had been a VIIth Corps in the Union Army during the civil war and again in the Spanish-American war, but the modern concept was initiated in the American Army in France in August 1918. World War I ended three months after the VIIth Corps was created. After the armistice the VIIth Corps was, for a while, engaged in occupation duties in Germany and was then deactivated.

In preparation for the possibility of World War II, the VIIth Corps was reactivated in 1940 and trained in the United States. On June 6, 1944, the Corps led the assault on Hitler's Fortress Europe beginning at 1:30 a.m. when 800 transport planes dropped the 82nd and 101st Airborne Divisions on the French Cotentin Peninsula in preparation for the landing of its 4th Division (*"The Ivy Division,"* get it? IV) on Utah Beach. On June 26, the Corps broke through at St. Lo and on July 17 its 1st division (*"The Big Red One"*) fought its way to meet the British at the Falaise Gap. By September the Corps had crossed the Meuse River and in three places, penetrated the German Siegfried Line, a strongly fortified defensive wall. Temporarily delayed by a shortage of gasoline and by Von Rundstedt's December assault, the "Battle of the Bulge," VII Corps entered Cologne, Germany in February and crossed the Rhine River, Germany's strongest defense barrier, in March. In its race across Germany in the spring of 1945, the Corps captured 350,000 German soldiers before meeting the Russians at the Elbe River in April.

After performing occupation duties for a short time at the end of World War II, the Corps was again deactivated. As a result of worsening relations with Russia and a communist military build up in eastern Europe, VII Corps was reactivated. Just six years after the end of hostilities, in November 1951, some of its units arrived back in Europe. By 1952, it was deployed in force.

Its specific mission was to combat communist aggression anticipated from the east and to be ready at all times rapidly to assume its role as a combat headquarters for its artillery, regimental combat teams, infantry and armored divisions, in case of a Soviet attack.

The exact composition of VII Corps, when I was assigned to it, is unknown to me. I'm sure that information was highly classified at the time and I did not need to know it. However, from my own observations I knew we had two Infantry Divisions, the 28th and 43rd, two Armored Cavalry Regiments, the 2nd and the 6th, two Field Artillery Groups, an Engineer Combat Group, a Transportation Truck Battalion, a Signal Battalion, military police, a Medical Battalion and all the necessary assortment of appropriate support personnel. My guess is that there were about 50,000 men assigned to the Corps. The Infantry Divisions had their own staff judge advocates. So, our office probably had jurisdiction over about 20,000.

THE TIMES: As a direct result of the June uprisings in Berlin, the U.S. saw an opportunity to capitalize on the obvious unrest in Soviet occupied Eastern Europe and, fortunately, had a unit available to press the advantage.

The 10th Special Forces Group, later called the "Green Berets" was trained and in place at Fort Bragg, North Carolina. In November 1953, one-half of that unit was transferred to Europe, and stationed at Flint Kaserne, at Bad Tölz, near Munich, Germany, then relocated to Panzer Kaserne near Stuttgart. Its mission was to carry the fight behind Soviet lines by conducting sabotage and gathering intelligence information, operating in concert with partisan groups in eastern European countries.

The "Special Forces" designation derived from the OSS (Office of Strategic Services), the first true American Secret Service established in 1942 by William Donovan, a famous New York lawyer and patriot. OSS later evolved into the Central Intelligence Agency (CIA).

In the spring of 1952 the Army gave the job of organizing Special Forces to Colonel Aaron Bank, formerly of the OSS, and allocated 2,300 personnel slots for the unit. To the unit were then sent the best troops in the Army, former OSS officers, airborne troops, ex-rangers and combat veterans of World War II and Korea. They were an unusual lot, a motivated group looking for new challenges - the more difficult the better. Virtually all spoke at least two languages, had at least a sergeant's rank and were trained in infantry and parachute skills. They were all volunteers willing to work behind enemy lines, in civilian clothes if necessary.

Working in civilian clothes was no trifling matter. If caught, a soldier in civilian clothes was no longer protected by the Geneva Convention and would more than likely be shot. Many in the Special Forces had come from Eastern Europe where they had fled the tyranny of communist rule at the end of World War II. Many were not U.S. citizens.

As defined by the Army, the primary mission of the Special Forces was "to infiltrate by land, sea or air, deep into enemy-occupied territory and organize the resistance/guerrilla potential to conduct . . . operations, with emphasis on guerrilla warfare." There were secondary missions as well, including deep-penetration raids, intelligence missions and counterinsurgency operations.

The Rangers of World War II and Korea had been designed as light-infantry shock troops; their mission was to hit hard, hit fast, and get out, so larger and more heavily armed units could follow through. Special Forces, however, were designed to spend months, even years, deep within hostile territory. They were self-sustaining. They could speak the language of their target area. They knew how to survive on their own without extensive resupply from the outside.

*   *   *

An opportunity would be presented for me to work with some of these extraordinary intelligence agents when, in March 1954, I was sent to Berlin to investigate the circumstances surrounding the apparent defection and imprisonment of an American soldier in East Germany.

More about that in due course.

* * *

THE ANATOMY OF A COURT- MARTIAL
NÜRNBERG, GERMANY
10 November 1953

This fairly detailed description of an actual case will serve as an example of the 168 contested trials on pleas of not-guilty and hearings on guilty pleas in which I participated during my two years in Germany. My story begins with an account of the events that gave rise to the charges, continues with a portrayal the trial process, concluding with the verdict of the court. There is a later note about the post-trial review. This is the case of the *United States v. Proctor and Johnson,* a general court-martial conducted in Nürnberg on 10 November 1953.

The men of Battery "B", 690th Field Artillery Battalion attached to the VII Corps were usually stationed with their unit at Crailsheim, about fifty miles east of Stuttgart; half way between there and Nürnberg. In late October 1953, the 690th had been on temporary duty at the Army combat training area at Grafenwöhr. The events described here took place near Grafenwöhr, at the enlisted men's club in Vilseck.

Grafenwöhr was where the Army trained troops for combat in the field. This extensive training ground is about forty miles east of Nürnberg; twenty miles west of the Czech frontier. Soldiers on maneuvers there lived in simulated battle conditions, slept in foxholes, ate field rations, fired their weapons and tested their armored vehicles and tanks. It was not easy duty. Near this training area was the small town of Vilseck where servicemen with a pass could escape the field conditions and enjoy a modicum of leisure time at one of the Gasthauses or the enlisted men's club.

U.S. soldiers usually received their pay at the end of the month; the artillerymen from the 690th were paid on Wednesday, 30 September 1953. The next night, many of those men, just in from the field, went to the EM Club for some "rest and relaxation," after the rigorous combat exercises of the previous weeks. A German band was playing; and the club was packed. There was a big party in progress and naturally, a lot of drinking.

Confusion exists concerning exactly what occurred at the club at about 9:30 p.m. on the night of 1 October, but it is clear that two uniformed military policemen entered the club, attempted to quiet a disturbance and were forcibly disarmed and beaten by a group of about seven soldiers. One of the MPs said three soldiers threatened him with knives, whereupon he pulled his pistol and attempted to seat a cartridge in the firing chamber by pulling back the slide on his .45. He was then attacked from behind, hit over the head with a chair, his pistol taken from him and knocked to the floor. One of the assailants then pointed the pistol in the MP's face and pulled the trigger. The pistol did not fire. Meanwhile, the other MP was also attacked from behind, his pistol torn from its lanyard and his billy club taken. The first MP was kicked while down and both were beaten. The fight ended when the aggressors fled, after hearing that more police were on the way.

The next morning forty-five members of "B" Battery, 690th Field Artillery Battalion were formed into a "lineup". Moran and Delcour, the MPs involved, selected Corporals Proctor and Johnson out of the group, identifying them as the two primary assailants.

An investigation was ordered by the battery commander and completed within a few days. The investigating officer recommended that charges be preferred and the accused soldiers tried by general courts-martial. In total, four soldiers had been identified as having taken part in the riot. One was charged with having hidden the MPs' pistols after the fight (misappropriation) and was tried separately. Another was charged with having threatened one of the MPs with a knife. He was also tried separately. Proctor and Johnson faced more serious accusations: Proctor with assault to murder, Johnson with assault to do grievous bodily harm, and both with participating in a riot.

In terms of military law, a riot is a breach of the peace committed by three or more persons in furtherance of a common purpose by concerted action against any opposition. Riot is a serious offense similar to mutiny. Upon conviction of the charge of participating in a riot, the maximum punishment is a dishonorable discharge, loss of all pay and allowances and confinement at hard labor for ten years.

Proctor was charged with participating in a riot and with assault with the intent to commit murder, the maximum punishment for the aggravated assault to murder was an additional twenty years.

Johnson was charged with participating in a riot and aggravated assault with the intent to commit grievous bodily harm, which carried a possible additional five-year sentence.

The battery commander preferred charges, forwarded them to battalion headquarters where they were investigated, endorsed and sent to VII Corps where the staff judge advocate authorized a trial.

Orders were issued at VII Corps setting the time and place of the trial, naming the accused: Proctor and Johnson, the members of the court: eight officers, two majors, four captains, one first lieutenant and one second lieutenant, the law officer – judge: Lt. Col. Ernst Oeding, trial counsel: 1/Lt John Thomason and defense counsel: Capt. George McCartin. Charges and specifications were processed and served on each accused; the case was prepared for trial and the trial began – just forty days after the brawl.

The court-martial convened at 9:00 a.m. The law officer (judge) and trial counsel made standard preliminary statements to establish that the court was properly convened. Then each member of the court, the law officer and trial and defense counsel and the court reporter were sworn-in, whereafter the defense counsel entered pleas of "Not Guilty" for both defendants. Every word spoken was taken down in shorthand and later transcribed.

The procedure was generally the same as in a civilian criminal court. The trial counsel (prosecution) first called witnesses and questioned them. Each witness was subjected to cross-examination by the defense. After the prosecution completed its case and rested, the defense called witnesses subject to cross-examination by the trial counsel. When the defense had presented all its proof and rested, the prosecution had an opportunity to present rebuttal proof. Usually there would be none. Both counsel would then "sum up," commenting on the evidence and the inferences that each counsel asserted should be drawn from the evidence, in support of the position of each. Finally, the law officer would instruct the court as to the applicable military law. Then the court would deliberate and when agreement was reached the president of the court, acting the same as a civilian jury foreman, would announce the verdict.

Sergeant Charles W. Anderson, manager of the Vilseck Enlisted Men's Club, was the first witness. He identified a drawing prepared by the trial counsel as a reasonable representation of the club floor plan. Cross-examination of the club manager was lengthy. The dimensions of the room, position of light switches, number, location, weight and composition of tables were all subjects of detailed inquiry by the defense.

One of the military policemen, Private Robert E. Delcour, was next to testify. Delcour and his partner, fellow MP Thomas Moran, were on duty the night of October 1. Their duty was to make periodic checks at the gasthauses (taverns) in Vilseck and at the EM club. That night they were in Military Police uniform with appropriate insignia and brassards and were armed with billy clubs and pistols. Shortly after arriving at the club about 9 PM, they were requested by the club manager to clear from the bandstand several soldiers who were interfering with the German musicians. Proctor was identified as one of those soldiers. About ten minutes later, it was again necessary for them to clear the bandstand. For the third time soldiers took control of the bandstand, and for the third time the MPs moved in to clear them when a table near where the orchestra was playing, was thrown into the air. As both MPs moved toward the area where the table was thrown, Delcour was attacked from behind. While Delcour tried to free himself from a chokehold, his pistol and club were forcefully taken. Delcour couldn't see what had happened to Moran, but later observed him, in the hallway near the outside door, obviously having been beaten. Delcour was thrown to the floor, got back on his feet, retrieved his club and escaped from another soldier who had threatened him with a knife. He then, armed only with his Billy club, went to look for and assist Moran.

On cross-examination defense counsel established that the EM club was filled to capacity that night, Delcour couldn't be certain that someone had taken his pistol although it was secured to a lanyard that was somehow severed in the scuffle. Before the fight his holster had been closed and fastened. After the fight the pistol was nowhere to be found. Delcour admitted that an MP who loses his pistol "Has a lot of explaining to do," and that a previous statement in which he identified Proctor as the one who threw the table into the air was based on hearsay – in that Moran had told him that it was Proctor.

On re-direct examination by trial counsel, Delcour stated that he had never known a pistol to accidentally come off a lanyard or out of a holster and that the table had definitely been thrown; it had not fallen. He elaborated on Proctor's conduct saying that Proctor seemed to be the leader of a group all of whom, he thought, looked and acted like troublemakers.

Counsel grew irksome, voices were raised and several times the law officer felt compelled to admonish both trial lawyers concerning the vigor and noise level of the questioning. At length trial counsel objected to an aside from the defense, saying,

"I object to that. The ruling of the law officer does not warrant comment by the defense and I move that his remark be stricken."

The law officer responded wearily, "The remarks of both counsel will appear in the record and the court will take a recess."

Private Thomas J. Moran, Company B, 793rd Military Police Battalion, Grafenwöhr was called next. The principal witness for the prosecution, Moran testified that at the request of the club manager he cleared the bandstand on three occasions. He then returned to the bar area, turned around and saw Proctor throw a table into the air. He started toward Proctor intending to apprehend him but was met by Proctor and three other soldiers with drawn knives. In order to defend himself, Moran drew his .45 caliber pistol and pulled back the slide so that the hammer was cocked, a cartridge was transferred from the magazine to the firing chamber and the pistol was ready to shoot. At that point, someone "jumped" him from behind pinning his right (pistol) hand and arm to his side. Moran thought he had pulled the slide back far enough to seat a round in the chamber of the pistol and that it was ready to fire. Proctor lunged forward, seized the pistol and struggled with Moran for its possession. During the struggle, the other accused, Johnson picked up a wooden chair and moved toward Moran as if to hit him with it. Moran told Johnson to put down the chair, but Johnson replied, "Let go of the gun. Let go of the gun." and then hit Moran over the head with the chair

Question: (By the prosecution) "Now, this man you mentioned, Johnson, who hit you with the chair, if you saw him again would you recognize him?"

Answer: "Yes, sir."

"If you see him in the courtroom, please point to him.

Moran looked directly at Johnson and pointed to him.

Q. "What happened after Johnson hit you with the chair?"

A. "My hand relaxed on the .45 and I was stunned for a minute and fell. When I looked up from the floor, I saw Proctor had the .45 pointed at my face, and he pulled the trigger."

Q. "How far was the muzzle of the pistol from your face?"

A. "Eighteen inches, sir."

Q. "How do you know it was Proctor who held the pistol?"

A. "Because I was looking right at him – right into the .45."

Q. "If you see this man Proctor in the courtroom, the man who put the pistol in your face and pulled the trigger, please point to him."

A. "That's him there, sir. The one in the middle."

Proctor was seated between Captain McCartin and Corporal Johnson.

Q. "What happened after that?"

A. "After the snap of the hammer, I don't recall if he put the pistol in his belt or pocket, but he said, "Let's take this bastard outside and kill him.'"

Someone grabbed the shoulder strap on Moran's uniform while Proctor and others pushed and dragged him toward the door. There he was kicked in the face, sides and stomach until he heard someone shout, "Here comes the duty officer!" or "Here come more MPs!" or something like that.

When he got off the floor, Proctor and Johnson and the others had gone. Despite his injuries, Moran attended the line up the next day and identified Proctor and Johnson as two of his assailants.

Notwithstanding, a lengthy and meticulous cross-examination, Moran was unwavering.

About a week before trial Captain McCartin and I had been in the Nürnberg area to interview people who had seen this incident and prepare the case for trial. We had each been furnished with a copy of the investigation, including sworn statements of all potential witnesses. I knew there were numerous friends and battery mates of Proctor and Johnson who would swear neither was involved.

Nevertheless, three witnesses would be useful to the prosecution: Moran, Delcour and a Sergeant named Lane.

Moran could identify Proctor as the soldier who took his pistol and attempted to kill him and Johnson as the person who hit him with a chair. Delcour could identify Proctor as being nearby when the fight began and could describe the events. A third witness, Sergeant Lane, had been with the MPs and had at first identified Proctor – but later was uncertain. However, Lane could positively identify Johnson as the one who struck Moran with the chair.

I decided to gamble. Defendants in a criminal trial are not required to offer evidence, they are presumed to be innocent, and may not be called as witnesses against themselves. But, if they choose, they may offer evidence and they may voluntarily testify. It seemed to me that Proctor and Johnson would offer evidence that they were not involved in the fight and would take the witness stand and deny that they were guilty of the charges. If my expectation of the defense strategy was correct, I could call Sergeant Lane as a rebuttal witness. My evaluation of Lane was that he would be a convincing witness. The opportunity to present rebuttal proof would allow the prosecution to close the proof and have the last word before the court began its deliberations. Lane's evidence would provide a strong finish to the government's case. Of course, if the defendants, relying on the presumption of innocence to carry the day, presented no proof, there would be no evidence to rebut. Sergeant Lane would not be allowed to testify and the question of identification -- the crucial issue in the trial -- would be decided by the court based on the sole testimony of Moran. The trial would be a swearing contest: one witness against two, Moran against Proctor and Johnson.

I did not call Sergeant Lane as a witness for the government and the prosecution rested.

The defense called as its first witness Pfc. Johnnie Holley who testified that he was at the Vilseck EM club on the evening of October 1; that the troops had been in the field on training exercises and had been paid the day before. The club was packed and noisy. There was a lot of drinking going on.

Q. (By the defense) "Did you see an MP pull his gun that night?"

A. "Yes, sir, I did."

Q. "What were you doing before that?"

A. "Right before he pulled his gun, sir – I had – I accidentally turned the table over and after I started straightening it back up, I looked back down the aisle and seen this MP coming with a pistol in his hand."

As the pistol wielding MP approached, Holley swiftly departed the club, as did many others. As Holley was leaving the club he saw another MP entering.

Holley didn't see Proctor, or Johnson or a fight at the club that night. Only one table was overturned and that unintentionally by Holley himself.

Cross-examination established that Holley was attempting to climb on top of the table when it fell. Otherwise, Holley claimed not to have seen any of the events described by the MPs.

The next defense witness was Pfc Odyssey Murray, like Holley, a battery mate of Proctor and Johnson. Murray had been at the EM club on the night in question and had seen Johnson, but not Proctor.

When he entered the club a fight was in progress involving members of the 690th and two MPs. He placed the fight at a different location than the MPs did and said Johnson was not involved. He stayed at the club about twenty-five minutes; the fight was still in progress when he left. As he departed the club he saw Corporal Samuel Beck, also leaving, with a pistol in his belt and another in his hand. (Beck was convicted in a separate trial of misappropriation of government property, the pistols.)

When cross-examined, Murray elaborated on what he saw. One MP was sitting on a soldier who was on the floor. Beck pointed a pistol at that MP and said he would shoot, but did not. The MP didn't do anything when Beck pointed the pistol at him. The MP was choking the soldier who was down. There were many people around but they just "stood and looked." Beck pointed both pistols at the MP—and cocked the hammer on one with his thumb. Murray didn't see Proctor. Holley was walking around on a table after the fight started.

A member of a different battery, Battery "A", was next called by the defense. Pvt M. C. Hyman knew Proctor by sight, but not Johnson. Hyman was at the club and had seen the start of the fight.

Q. (By the defense) "How did it start?"

A. "I seen a guy climb up and walk on a table and I think the MPs came in and told him to get down, so, he got down. Some kind of dispute come up. I wasn't paying attention. I was just sitting at my table drinking. I looked around again and saw the MP bring his pistol up and I jumped up from the table."

Hyman saw Proctor at the scene but not in the fight and denied being uncertain about whether he had seen Proctor when interviewed by the trial counsel five days previously.

The defense called another soldier who had been at the club that night, Pfc. Harry L. Bryant.

When asked if anything unusual had occurred he answered, "Just a little raucous started."

Elaborating, he added, "From the part I seen, it was two soldiers got to arguing and the MPs went over to stop them." Then, fifteen or twenty soldiers gathered around the MPs one of whom drew his pistol. Bryant knew Proctor, Johnson and Beck and saw them there that night. They could have been involved in the fight or they could not have been.

Defense counsel was apparently unprepared for the answer to the next question. Upon hearing it he requested a fifteen-minute recess.

Q. (By the defense) "Did you see anybody drag the MP from where the fight was out into the hall?"

A. "Somebody pulled him out there, yes, sir."

When the trial resumed defense counsel claimed surprise and requested permission to cross-examine his own witness. The law officer, after being assured that the witness had given a different account of what he saw when previously questioned by the defense counsel, granted permission.

After questioning by both sides, it became clear that the witness had seen the defendants at the club but couldn't say if they were, or not, involved in the fight. Defense counsel had expected the witness to swear that they were not in the fight.

The defense next called Cpl. Luis Meza, "A" Battery. According to this witness there was a fight "with plenty of people around there." He didn't know how the fight started or who participated, but while it was going on he saw Proctor and Johnson, and they were not involved.

Cross-examination established that Meza was at the club when the fight began, while it was in progress and after it was over, but as he said, "We kept drinking all the time. We didn't pay any attention."

Next came Pfc. Milbert Brown who also saw the commencement of the affray. In essence, Brown saw the MP leave the bar. "Something had happened and he was going to stop it. As soon as he got over there, he pulled his pistol, and somebody grabbed him and everybody stood up."

Brown decided to get out of the EM Club and as he did so, saw Johnson standing in the doorway.

Battery "B" executive officer, 1st Lt. John J. George was then called by the defense.

He stated that he had known Proctor eight months and Johnson ten months. In his opinion both men were very good soldiers and each was of good character. Their reputations for "truth and veracity" was outstanding. He had never known either to tell a lie; if they were sworn to tell the truth, he believed they would tell the truth.

At this point, I asked one of those dumb questions that should go down in the annals of stupid queries propounded by lawyers during trial:

Q. (By the prosecution) "Have you ever seen them drinking off duty?"

A. "Yes, sir."

Q. "When was that?"

A. "During our battery parties."

Q. "Those parties were also attended by commissioned officers of the battery, isn't that right?"

A. "Yes, sir."

Q. "Have you ever seen them drinking off duty when no commissioned officers were present?"

A. "No, sir."

(It is difficult to conjecture how the witness, a commissioned officer, could have seen them drinking when a commissioned officer was not present, unless he was using a telescope.)

The question slipped by, without objection.

After some legal wrangling, Captain McCartin established through the witness that both Proctor and Johnson, having been confined after the lineup, were released from confinement by the battalion commander following a conversation the commander had with Corporal Beck. This testimony was apparently meant to suggest that the battalion commander, a lieutenant colonel, convinced of their innocence, had set Proctor and Johnson free.

Beck was the next defense witness. Beck had been found guilty of misappropriation of government property, the pistols, at an earlier trial and was under guard. Once again there was a squabble between the lawyers because the prosecutor had called both the witness and his guard into the courtroom.

DC (defense counsel) "Let the record reflect that at the insistence of the trial counsel, the guard who has Corporal Beck in custody came into the courtroom."

TC (trial counsel) "At the insistence of the trial counsel?"

DC "You called him."

TC "Let the record reflect the trial counsel went to the door and said "Guard", and that was all."

Defense counsel apparently thought the presence of the guard in the courtroom was an intimidating factor. However, the guard remained as the witness testified.

Beck was at the EM Club the night of the incident. Before the fight started, the German musical group had taken a break so one of the soldiers mounted the band stand and began to play the piano. Others soon joined him, picked up the idle instruments and began to play. Beck was on the bandstand playing the bass fiddle. A military policeman walked to the bandstand and told Beck to leave. About that time, Holley accidentally "tipped a table over." The "MP turned around and drew his pistol and backed into me." The MP was "fixing to eject a cartridge into the chamber and I grabbed him." Beck and the MP wrestled for the pistol, Beck took the pistol and put it in his pocket. Then he saw the other MP trying to get at his pistol while others held his hand away from the holster. Beck also joined that fight, got the other pistol out of the holster, off the lanyard; then took both pistols outside and hid them. The next morning, without having been charged with any offense, Beck returned the pistols to proper authorities and surrendered himself to his battery commander. He was later charged and convicted of participating in a riot and misappropriating two .45 caliber pistols. Beck testified Proctor and Johnson were at the club but were not involved in the fight. No one assisted Beck in getting the pistols away from the MPs. Beck described no efforts by the MPs to regain the pistols.

Sergeant First Class Jack Poole testified that he was chief of the fourth howitzer section of which Proctor was a member; that he knew Proctor, that Proctor had "shown every trait of a fine leader," and had a reputation for telling the truth. Next, the defense called Sergeant Stanley J. Bakaj, chief of Johnson's section, who testified that Johnson was not a trouble maker, had a good reputation, was a peaceable man and truthful, "As far as I know."

Then, although advised by his lawyer that he need not testify and that he could not be called as a witness, Proctor elected to take the witness stand in his own defense. According to Proctor, he had gone to the club to drink beer and listen to the band. He was standing near the bandstand. After about twenty minutes the German musicians stopped playing. Some soldiers took their places, one on the piano, Beck on the bass and "a big sergeant on the drums."

Proctor said, "we started hooting, hollering and singing in front of the bandstand." Holley tried to get onto a table but the table "flew over, toward - going toward the bar," where the MPs were standing. An MP started toward the bandstand and when he was about half way there he pulled his pistol. Proctor then left the club. He didn't touch the MP or his pistol.

On cross-examination Proctor stuck to his story but was vague about details. He didn't know why the MPs went to the bandstand, or how many times they went there; why the MP pulled his pistol; what the people around the MP were doing; what started the fight; how close he was to the MP; or the names of anyone else at the club that night.

One of the Court Members exercised his right to ask questions and elicited the additional fact that Proctor had seen Holley attempt to get up on a table and had tipped it over. After that the MP pulled his pistol.

The defense then called Johnson to the stand. His testimony was concise.

He had come to the club alone and stayed there about fifteen minutes. He saw the MPs start walking from the bar toward the bandstand and got out of there. He was in no fight, picked up no chair, saw no one he knew, except Proctor, and was never closer than fifteen feet to the MPs.

To some extent Johnson fleshed out his story on cross-examination. The MP pulled out his pistol and was coming toward Johnson's table. Johnson was frightened that he might be shot. Initially, he stated he left the club as soon as the fight started, later he said, "The fight was just about over when I left."

At that point in the proceedings, the defense rested.

My conjecture had proven correct. Proctor and Johnson offered proof that they had not been involved in the brawl, their own testimony was chiefly on that point. Consequently, the prosecution had an opportunity to offer rebuttal proof, and Sergeant Lane was called to the stand.

Raymond W. Lane, Sergeant, headquarters battery, was with the 979th Artillery Battalion stationed at Ansbach, about thirty miles east of Nürnberg. He had been on courtesy patrol with the MPs on the evening in question, which meant that he, although not an MP, was on duty at the EM club *with* the MPs. He observed two disturbances at the bandstand, beginning about 9:30 PM.

Q. (By the prosecution) "What happened after the last one?"

A. "The MP was walking back to the bar and this big corporal picked up a table and threw it into the air."

Q. "What happened after the corporal threw the table up?"

A. "The MP turned around to apprehend him."

Q. "What happened then?"

A. "Several guys had knives drawn and the MP drew his pistol."

Q. "Go on."

A. "Then a couple of guys jumped the MP from behind and this big corporal came forward and grabbed him by the arm and I started down to help the MP and this small corporal I know – Corporal Johnson – hit the MP on the head with a chair."

Q. "If you saw Johnson again would you recognize him?"

A. "Yes, sir."

Q. "Look around the courtroom and if you see him, point to him."

A. "Yes, sir."

Sergeant Lane looked at Corporal Johnson, seated at the Counsel table, raised his hand and pointed.

On cross-examination Captain McCartin concentrated on the fact that on the day after the fight, in connection with the investigation, Lane had given a sworn statement that "I also identified the big corporal who had assaulted the MP and who was fighting with the MP for the weapon." In court Lane said that he *thought* the big corporal was Corporal Proctor, but that he couldn't make a positive identification. Defense counsel made much of what he claimed was a prior inconsistent statement. Lane was steadfast. He had attended the lineup and picked out Proctor. He was asked if Proctor was the assailant and replied that he "thought so." The word "thought" was not in the sworn statement. The cross-examination on this point was lengthy. Many objections to repetitious questions were sustained. In essence, Lane was positive Johnson had hit the MP with a chair. He "thought" Proctor was the one who seized the pistol, but wasn't positive. My impression of Lane was that he had spoken truthfully and that the painstaking cross-examination had buttressed rather than diminished the effect of his testimony.

Sergeant Lane was excused. The prosecution had no further rebuttal proof and rested.

The summation for the prosecution centered on the strength of Moran's identification of Proctor, Lane's identification of Johnson, and the weakness of the defense, which had attacked all the evidence offered by the government but advanced no reasonable countervailing explanation of what had occurred. The defense concentrated on the lack of proof of a concert of purpose, the many defense witnesses who said Proctor and Johnson were not involved and the proof of their good character and reputation for truthfulness.

The government, having the burden of proving the charges "beyond a reasonable doubt," had the right to make the final argument. I directed the court to what I thought were the most persuasive, convincing and logical details in the record.

The prosecution:

"As for the identification of Johnson as the one who hit Moran with the chair, enabling Proctor to take the weapon, you have the positive statement of Lane as well as that of Moran.

Lane wouldn't swear it was Proctor, although he thought it was. But he swore it was Johnson.

He was positive. When he knew the truth, he told the truth. When he wasn't sure, he said so.

184

"Now let's consider Moran's identification of Johnson. Do you think, if you are fighting for your life, and you see a man raising a chair, apparently to strike you, that you will notice who is holding the chair? Certainly you would. The identification of Johnson is sure

"I concede, the identification of Proctor rests primarily on the testimony of Moran. So, you must ask yourself if Moran's positive statement that Proctor assaulted him is believable. Does Moran's testimony pass the test of reasonableness? Can Moran be certain his assailant was Proctor? Can you be certain that Moran is right? What facts establish Moran as a credible witness?

"First, Moran saw and talked with Proctor at the bandstand before any trouble began. Second, Moran saw Proctor at the table and saw him throw the table over, which was the beginning of the fight. Third, Proctor and Moran fought for the pistol – Moran thought he was fighting for his life; for the possession of a loaded pistol, a round in the chamber, ready to fire – do you think Moran would remember his adversary? Finally, and most significant, Moran saw Proctor standing over him with the pistol – the pistol eighteen inches from his face – and saw Proctor pull the trigger – and heard the snap as the hammer struck.

"Will Moran forget that face? Will Moran ever forget the face of Proctor? What do you think? Do you think Moran's identification of Proctor is unreliable? Surely, you must have no doubt that it was Proctor who pulled the trigger."

*   *   *

Following closing arguments, the law officer instructed the court as to the applicable law, the burden of proof, presumption of innocence, reasonable doubt, elements of the charges, definitions and such. The concluding charge was

"Each of you must impartially resolve the ultimate issue as to the guilt or innocence of the accused in accordance with the law, the evidence admitted in court, and your own conscience."

Deliberations began at 7:45 p.m. At 8:10 the court reconvened and the presiding officer announced that as to all charges both accused had been found guilty.

At that point the sentencing phase of the trial began. Trial counsel advised the court of any prior convictions. Proctor had been absent without leave twice, once for three days and once for several hours, while stationed at Fort Hood, Texas. Johnson had no prior convictions.

The defense called several additional witnesses who testified in extenuation and mitigation as to the good character and soldierly qualities of each accused. Most of their superior non-commissioned officers spoke for them. Lt. George, the battery executive officer, returned to the stand to say that both Proctor and Johnson were very good men, morale builders, among the best five or six in the battery. He wanted them back in his battery. He thought, despite being convicted, they would nevertheless continue to be good soldiers.

Corporal Johnson returned to the stand to give a sworn statement before sentencing. He stated that he had quit school in the seventh grade "to help his mother's situation." He had worked since then and had never before been in any trouble. He said he had two brothers and two sisters, but because he was the oldest he had joined the

Army when he was eighteen. He was now twenty. His father had been in the Army. He said he wanted to do his best and was sending money home from his Army pay to help his mother who is single.

There was no cross-examination.

Corporal Proctor chose to make an unsworn statement though defense counsel.

On behalf of Proctor Captain McCartin reminded the court that absence without leave, the prior convictions, were a minor offenses. Corporal Proctor, according to his counsel, was twenty-five years of age, married and had one child, he had a tenth grade education, and had never been in trouble as a civilian. To support his family, he sent money home from his Army pay. Both accused wanted to be professional soldiers and to make a career of the Army. Their battery wanted them back and they wanted to go back to their battery.

The court began sentencing deliberations on at 8:45 p.m., and reconvened an hour and ten minutes later. The Presiding Officer announced the sentences:

"Corporal Rossie L. Proctor, it is my duty as president of this court to inform you that the court, in closed session and upon secret written ballot, two-thirds of the members present at the time the vote was taken concurring, sentences you to be dishonorably discharged from the service, to forfeit all pay and allowances and to be confined at hard labor for ten years."

"Corporal Joseph L. Johnson, it is my duty as president of this court to inform you that the court, in closed session and upon secret written ballot, two-thirds of the members present at the time the vote was taken concurring, sentences you to be dishonorably discharged

from the service, to forfeit all pay and allowances and to be confined at hard labor for five years."

The court adjourned at ten minutes until ten, p.m. The trial, including deliberations, had lasted thirteen hours. It had been a long day.

*   *   *

Dear Mother and Dad,   Armistice Day, 11 Nov 1953

Dave Addis, Captain McCartin, Colonel Oeding and I have just returned to Stuttgart from Nürnberg where we have been for the better part of a week. Today is supposed to be a holiday; it has not been one for us.

Three of the four cases I prosecuted on this trip arose out of the same incident, a riot at the enlisted men's club at Vilseck, not far from Nürnberg. First I had to contend with Dave who was defending a soldier named Beck, charged with wrongfully appropriating two 45 caliber pistols. The prosecution was successful. Beck got one year. Next Dave defended a soldier named Thursby who was charged with assaulting an MP with a knife. Another win! Thursby got two years.

Then I took on Captain McCartin who was defending two soldiers, Proctor and Johnson, charged with participating in a riot and assault to murder. Another win! Proctor got ten years, Johnson, five. I felt sort of sorry for Johnson. He is only twenty and had a good record. On the other hand, he lied when he testified that he had not hit an MP with a chair when the MP was outnumbered and fighting off a gang of drunks, some of whom had knives.

The MP had a frightening experience. Proctor got the MPs' pistol after the MP thought he had seated a round in the chamber. The hammer was back. Proctor put the pistol in the MPs face and pulled the trigger. The pistol didn't fire. Apparently, the MP had not pulled the slide back far enough to seat a cartridge. Lucky for him!

Upon reflection, I think I would have defended the Proctor-Johnson case differently than Captain McCartin did. He attacked every aspect of the government's proof although some of the contentions of the prosecution were true beyond any doubt. For example, there is no question that there was a fight and that one of the MPs was beaten up and his pistol taken from him. Yet, the defense implied the MP was making up the story for fear of the consequences of losing his weapon. McCartin asserted that another witness should not be believed because he had identified Proctor in a statement, then reconsidered and voiced some uncertainty at the trial.

However, the defense never attacked the lineup identification. People who are asked to pick a lawbreaker out of a line up almost invariably identify <u>somebody</u>. I think if I had been defending I would have concentrated on the unreliability of the lineup being a means of verifying identity, and then argued that once the identification was made the prosecution witnesses, even though mistaken, felt they had to stick by their previous identification. Since both Proctor and Johnson were Corporals and had really good military records,

I think it would have easier for the court to accept the idea that the prosecution witnesses were mistaken than that were swearing falsely.

Of course, whether that would have made any difference in the outcome of the trial, I can't say.

THANKSGIVING 1953

A few days before Thanksgiving, I received a package from my grandparents, on my mother's side, Rufus and Mary Galyean, who lived in Corinth, Mississippi. My grandfather, a building contractor, employed a variety of tradesmen, including metal workers. Inside the package, obviously a Thanksgiving gift, was a galvanized steel cylinder about eight inches high and fifteen in diameter plainly labeled "Whiskey Cake." It attracted the attention of everyone in the JA office, as all of us were already caught up in the spirit of the oncoming holiday. The problem was that I couldn't open the sealed container.

The cake box was custom made. The cylinder itself was flanged at the top and bottom and the circular lid and base appeared to have been bent around the flange and *welded.* I tried using every tool I had in my desk, screwdriver, scissors, nail file, staple remover, letter opener—all to no avail. My unsuccessful efforts to obtain access to the Whiskey Cake attracted even more attention and an even larger crowd.

Everyone had a suggestion and many took a turn at attempting to uncover and reveal the contents of this obstinate miniature vault. As the gathering of onlookers increased so did the noise associated with the effort. At length — having heard the commotion from his office down the hall —Colonel Guimond appeared. His rank being the highest among those present required him to take command. First he grasped the cake container and repeated, without success, all the efforts and techniques hitherto employed by his predecessors. Next he retired to his office and returned with a hammer and pair of pliers. The pliers could not gain purchase and proved ineffective. None of the male subordinates objected when Colonel Guimond selected the hammer, but some of the female secretaries, perhaps not as indoctrinated in the prerogatives of military command, protested its use on the basis that hammer-blows might endanger the integrity of the cake itself.

Colonel Guimond stepped back, gathering his thoughts. The spectators stood in silent respect.

At last the colonel reached a decision and issued an order. "Call the corps engineer." He commanded and retired back to his office, noting as he departed, "Let me know when you get it open."

After a while, a sergeant with a toolbox appeared. Utilizing a special assortment of utensils and considerable exertion, the sergeant finally succeeded in opening the sturdy box. There, inside safe and sound was Grandmother Galyean's Whiskey Cake! Of course, I was the recipient of the first slice. It was just as good as the last time I tasted it on Thanksgiving Day in Corinth.

Colonel Guimond accepted serving number two and the sergeant engineer, number three. Then I served Whiskey Cake all around, and everybody got a piece – and, had the cake been larger, would gladly have taken another.

*   *   *

Of the three invitations I received for Thanksgiving Dinner, from Colonel and Mrs. Guimond, Colonel and Mrs. Hodges and our section civilian lawyer, John Tinnerello and his wife, I accepted the latter because I got it first. The VII Corps surely takes good care of its bachelor officers.

*   *   *

Dear Folks,   *10 December 1953*

For the second morning in three we have been "alerted." For me this procedure means I have had to get up in the middle of the night (actually, 3 a.m..) put on my field gear, collect my weapon, then sit around doing nothing until notified the alert is over. The alert is in force throughout the VII Corps command; not just here. I am sure the combat units are very busy demonstrating readiness. Thankfully, I am not included among them.

While am waiting for the "all clear," I shall drop you a line.

Speaking of weapons, my official "GI" (government issue) firearm is a Colt .45 caliber, semi-automatic pistol, Model 1911. It shoots very large bullets, has remarkable stopping power, almost jumps out of my hand when I fire it and makes a lot of noise. Oddly, it is a simple weapon, having relatively few parts. I can take it apart and put it back together very quickly, <u>even in the dark!</u>

For the pistol to be authorized as my weapon I have to qualify with it on the firing range every six months. Otherwise

I would have to carry a carbine, which is a rifle, heavier and more cumbersome than the pistol. I prefer the pistol. Yesterday I was due for another six-month pistol qualifying day. The experience had a humorous aspect.

The firing range is at Esslingen, not far from here. A jeep picked me up yesterday morning and took me over there.

The pistol range has ten positions where qualifying officers stand to shoot at the targets. There is a target in front of each position about twenty-five yards away. Ropes and pulleys control the targets themselves, so that before you shoot, the target is edge-wise, then, on loudspeaker command the targets are pulled broadside. You have about ten seconds to fire seven rounds and empty your pistol magazine into the target before it is pulled edge-wise again. It was pretty crowded. I had to wait before my turn came. I guess they qualify a lot of officers on the same day. Anyway, I was finally assigned to position seven.

I stepped up on the range and surveyed my target, at this time it was edge to me.

A guy with a bullhorn up in a tower controls everything. When he gave the command all the targets simultaneously turned broadside and everybody started shooting. At first the noise was deafening but then as everyone emptied his magazine it got quiet again. The tower guy gave another command and all the targets turned back edgewise -- all except mine.

"What's wrong with target number seven?" the tower guy bellowed over the loudspeaker.

"I don't know, sir." Somebody answered. "It won't turn."

"Well, go see." Said the tower guy.

With that, a soldier jumped out of a nearby pit and went scampering over to inspect my target. He took one look and yelled back to the tower -- to the amusement of everyone but me.

"This lieutenant has shot out all the ropes and pulleys from the bottom of the target!"

To make a long story short, the target was fixed and I was permitted to try again. The second time I did OK. While I was at the firing range I decided to do some practicing so I shot about a hundred more rounds. The people in charge of the firing range seemed to have an unlimited amount of ammunition.

So, now I am pistol qualified for another six months. It will probably take me that long to get my hearing back.

*　　　*　　　*

<u>THE TIMES</u>: December 1953. For his efforts to reinvigorate and rehabilitate Europe following the mass destruction of World War II through what became known as the "Marshall Plan," General George C. Marshall was awarded the Nobel Peace Prize, the first soldier ever so honored.

*　　　*　　　*

On Christmas Eve, the Russian people were advised of the execution for treason of Lavrenti Pavlovich Beria, previously head of the secret police, Minister of the Interior, Stalin's close advisor and only a few months before, one of only three Soviet officials who spoke at Stalin's funeral.

*   *   *

President Eisenhower addressing the United Nations in New York made a dramatic proposal for all nations to share in the peaceful use of atomic energy. His plan was outlined in a speech entitled "Atoms for Peace."

*   *   *

Senator Joseph McCarthy of Wisconsin who had charged but never proven that communists had infiltrated various branches of the U. S. Government, including the State Department and the Department of the Army was censured by the United States Senate.

*   *   *

CHRISTMAS AWAY FROM HOME

Bill Bullard, a JAG schoolmate from Houston, Texas, later a partner in the Baker – Botts law firm there, was assigned to the office of the staff judge advocate, 28th Infantry Division, Göppingen, about twenty-five miles east of Stuttgart, towards Munich. We decided a good plan for the Christmas holidays would be for each of us to get a three-day pass, meet in Munich on December 23rd and go to Salzburg, Austria, only about seventy miles away. I knew some VII Corps cases would be tried in Munich in late December, so I arranged to get myself put on the Munich trial team. That assignment put me in Munich at the time my pass was effective, just in time to meet Bill for Christmas in Austria.

After we finished our cases in the early afternoon of December 23rd, I went with the others on the trial team to the Munich railroad station and put them on the train to Stuttgart. Then I hastened back to the Excelsior Military Hotel to meet Bill.

He wasn't there. However, the desk clerk advised that I had a telegram. It was from Bill informing me that he had been assigned duty as officer of the day and his pass had been canceled.

Should I go back to Stuttgart? I pondered. The next train from Munich would get me into Stuttgart at a very late hour. Besides, I wasn't expected back. I had no Christmas plans in Stuttgart – in fact, I had turned down some invitations. Maybe I should go on to Salzburg by myself, or just stay in Munich. I didn't know anyone in either place, but at least I had a hotel room in Munich and although I been to Munich several times, I hadn't really seen the sights or enjoyed much recreational time there.

Munich it is, I decided. It turned out to be an astoundingly lucky choice.

After freshening up I walked across the street from the hotel over to Karlsplatz, then along Neuhauserstrasse to Marien Platz, looking into the shop windows filled with Christmas bounty. Green Loden suits for both men and women were featured in many of the apparel shops. Some were displayed on heavy-set, rather obese, mannequins such as I had not seen before. The Christmas decorations were like those at home except all the lights were of clear glass and Santa's fur trimmed coat extended all the way down to his shoe tops. Lots of sports equipment, mountain climbing gear and cold weather outerwear was on display as well as toys, weapons, radios and audio equipment. Munich was obviously a good place to shop.

I headed to the Hofbräuhaus, Platzl, because I had been there before, it was nearby and I knew the food was good. A brass band played in the beer hall below – where Hitler used to hold forth – but I wanted something a little nicer so I went to the restaurant upstairs. Following a good supper, Kalbshaxe and a salad plate, which cost me DM 6, I stepped outside onto the Platzl and noticed a small, intimate bar down the street to my right, inviting me for a nightcap. It was a cheerful refuge on a cold night, abundantly decorated in the spirit of the Yuletide season. There weren't many customers inside but an elderly piano player recognized me as an American, played "Jingle Bells" and gestured for me to join him by the piano. Then he played some familiar English language carols, inviting me to sing along. He joined in, also singing in English. I thought we sounded pretty good. I ordered a couple of cognacs and we toasted "a Merry Christmas." When he took a break, we began to talk.

Apparently his assessment of me was favorable, because after a while, he told me that his wife had instructed him to be on the lookout for a lonely soldier and, if he found one he thought was nice, invite him home for the celebration of Christmas Eve, the principal Christmas holiday in Germany. He then extended an invitation for me to join his family for Christmas Eve at his home and I accepted. The address he gave was across Plinganserstrasse from Sendlinger Church, not far from Sendlinger Tor, a busy intersection and one of the original gates into old Munich. It was an easy taxi ride from my hotel. As we parted he mentioned slyly, that when I arrived at his home the next evening his daughter would be there.

The events of Christmas Eve are described in a letter to my parents:

The dwelling to which I was directed was above the Schüntner Restaurant at number 10 Plinganserstrasse. On the way you go through Sendlinger Tor where there are two tall hexagonal towers and a wide archway marking the entrance through the old wall that once surrounded Munich. On the ground floor of the address I had been given was a busy restaurant in the rear of which was a pull down stair leading to a trap door in the ceiling and my host's apartment. The apartment was obviously in the attic: low overhead under the eves, where the beds were, and high in the center where everything else was, kitchen, dinning room and living room combined. A small Christmas tree decorated with little packages and alight with real candles was the focal point of the whole central area.

As instructed, I arrived about 4 PM, having made a stop at the Munich Post Exchange on the way where I purchased a bottle of very fine French Cognac (75 years old, according to the label), and two phials of perfume; one for the mother, one for the daughter.

It turned out that the piano player, Herr Barre', is a composer/conductor of some note here in Munich. The Barre' family had to leave their home in Berlin, so I was told, because of some trouble with the Russians. The wife is Latvian and, fortunately for me, has a particularly high regard for Americans. These are really very nice people. Although here in Munich and at this time they are quite poor, I am

198

certain that condition is temporary. They are all quite talented and will surely succeed in Munich, which is a thriving cultural center. We would be pleased to welcome them as guests in our home. It would be wonderful for us to have that opportunity, but unlikely that we ever shall.

There was another young man present, a Viennese film writer both of whose parents had been killed in the war. He is working here, the "Hollywood" of Germany, for a movie studio.

But the big surprise of the evening was the daughter, Gisa Barre', a twenty-two year old vocalist for a well-known and popular German dance orchestra and a bit player in the movies. Gisa also appears regularly on a "Bob Hope" type of radio show sponsored by a German brand of tooth paste. She is quite a beauty, speaks about five languages, has a terrific personality and is a charmer of the first magnitude.

I had a wonderful evening. At every turn some form of food was being thrust upon me: caviar, smoked ham, cheese, wurst, potato salad, white wine, red wine, champagne; the variety and quantity seemed endless. A novel custom to which I was introduced involved locking arms, sipping a beverage followed by a kiss on the cheek! The most memorable event of the evening was a rendition of "Silent Night" sung by all guests, simultaneously, in five different languages: Frau Barre' in Russian, Herr Barre' in Italian, Gisa in French, the film writer in German and me in English. Then we all joined in the preparation of a Christmas card for you, which I shall send later.

The party broke up about 2 a.m. when the film writer became overtly enthusiastic by virtue of an over indulgence in Christmas cheer. He began to pace around the room shouting comic excerpts from Shakespeare. After a while we all tired of that and I offered to take him home. He and I shared a cab to our respective destinations, caroling as we went.

What a remarkable occasion! Everyone had reason to be sad, especially Mr. And Mrs. Barre' who had lost a lifetime's accumulation of family treasures when they were forced to leave Berlin. Because we were all so eager to see to it that no one had a sad moment, the party was a constant laugh. There was a time or two when Frau Barre' became a little sentimental, but she soon perked up. One particular spirit booster was an original composition by Herr Barre' which he played on the accordion and which we all sang many times: "Johnnie ist Mein Rechtsanwalt," which means "Johnnie (that's me) is my lawyer."

The next day, Christmas, I went back to the Barre' apartment for a luncheon of roast duck, salad, potatoes and wine. Afterwards, Gisa, Frau Barre' and I took the trolley and then walked along Sendlingerstrasse to Marienplatz and next over to the Hofbräuhaus for a beer. At that point Gisa and I took Frau Barre' back to the apartment. The two of us were destined for the Haus der Kunst, at Prinzregentenstrasse 1, a massive stone Gallery originally built to house and display Nazi Art. The corner stone of this stark but imposing museum was laid by Adolph Hitler in 1937. Until 1945 it was the principal repository of graphic art glorifying the Nazi culture; now a large part of it is an American Army officer's club – probably the most lavish such facility in Europe. After dinner and dancing there we went to the nearby Intermezzo Bar, an elegant nightclub frequented by the Munich film colony. We had a delightful evening lasting until about 4:30 a.m. I was especially proud when, by popular demand, Gisa was called to the bandstand. She was asked to perform and selected the popular song "Moulin Rouge", which she sang in French to the delight of everyone. It appears that she is quite well known. Another part of the entertainment was a comic imitation of Adolph Hitler, which I could not follow, but which the audience seemed to enjoy.

Although I was the only American present, I was very well treated. No one showed any resentment that Gisa, obviously popular and quite likely an ascending young radio and film personality of star quality, was accompanied by an American soldier. Many people came to our table to greet Gisa, and of course, she introduced me to them. Almost all spoke some English, and every one of the Germans was very friendly and appeared to be quite prosperous.

Please write to the Barre's. They could not have been more gracious to me, nor more hospitable and generous. They certainly made my 1953 Christmas a memorable one.

*   *   *

The Christmas Eve card we had all prepared was sent to my parents along with the Barre's home address. My mother and father responded by letter with thanks for taking care of me on my first Christmas away from home. Later, my parents sent me a two page reply Gisa had written to them, in English, on behalf of all the Barre's, describing the evening and explaining

> *Maybe John enjoyed staying with us as he felt we could understand him so well, as many years in wartime our family would not be together on Christmas. Maybe John told you Munich is not our hometown (we used to live in Berlin) so we are strangers in Munich too and we enjoyed it so much to have John with us these Christmas days. We tried as well as we could to make it a bit easier for John to be so far away from home at Christmas.*

*   *   *

The snow finally arrived in Stuttgart a few days after New Years, 1954. It snowed for almost a week and by the 8th of January had reached a depth of nearly two feet. I hadn't seen such snow before; it was dry and powdery and blew around like dust. It was more like fine goose down than snow. I was told that such snow would be great for skiing; it was certainly worthless for snowballs or snowmen. The weather was disagreeably cold but the snow covered everything with an immaculate layer of white softness, beautifully rounding all outdoor straight lines and sharp corners.

<u>LIAR'S DICE</u>

One morning in December 1992, I was a little late arriving at my law office on the twenty-ninth floor of Commerce Square, overlooking the Mississippi River at Memphis. The mail had already arrived and was neatly stacked on my desk. On top was a letter, obviously from Germany, with seven colorful postage stamps and a blue and white label proclaiming "MIT LUFTPOST." The letter was clearly for me but the office address beneath my name was one I had not used for thirty-five years!

Some enterprising postman, or perhaps the present occupant of the office to which the letter had been sent – my former office, had located me and forwarded it.

For a long time I held and gazed at the envelope trying to guess the identity of the writer; there was no name or return address. The letter looked like a Christmas card and was postmarked *München*, German for Munich. It must be from someone I met in the service, I thought. But it wasn't.

Upon opening the envelope I found that, indeed it contained a Christmas card, but also, folded inside was a copy of a letter I had written thirty-seven years previously, in August 1955, together with some photographs and a hand written explanation.

The author was Gina Murphy, the widow of Dan Murphy, "Murph," whom I had known at Kelley Barracks. Murph had died in January 1988, Gina wrote, and searching through old letters she had found this forgotten one from me. Although Gina and I had never met, she remembered that Murph and I had been great friends. He had spoken of me often, she said. Murph and Gina had married in 1960, and had one son. Murph had lived the rest of his life in Germany. In the letter I wrote to Murph I had requested that he use some German money I had left with him to buy and send me a pair of Lederhosen (leather shorts); she wrote to say she would send them if Murph had not. He had.

Although an American working with the Army, Murph was not in the Army. He was a civilian electronics technician employed by an

American company but assigned to Kelley Barracks because a signal communications battalion was stationed there. Like me, he lived in the BOQ section of the officer's club and was a frequent and animated participant in the almost nightly games of "liar's dice."

The equipment necessary to play liar's dice consists of a dice cup, five dice and three to about eight players. I would say it's best to have at least five. To start, each player rolls a die, the one with the highest number begins.

The beginning player rolls all the dice under the cup. Holding it so no one else can see, he peeks under the cup to note the result of his roll, then without disturbing the dice, passes the cup to the next or receiving player, announcing but not disclosing what he has rolled. He may tell the truth, or he may lie. Each player must pass the cup announcing a higher poker hand than was specified when he received the cup. The passing player may actually have a better hand than he calls, but he must have at least as good a hand as he announces. If a receiving player believes that the passing player has at least what he has announced, he accepts the cup, rolls some or all of the dice and passes the cup on, announcing a higher hand. If the next receiving player does not believe the passing player actually has a hand equal to or better than what he says he has, the receiving player challenges, by lifting the cup for all to see. If the challenge is valid, that is, the passing player was not telling the truth, the passing player must give each of the other players a marker. If the challenge is invalid, that is, the passing player had a hand equal to or better than what he called, the challenger must give each of the other players a marker. The fun of the game lies not so much in getting the best poker hand, but in fooling the other players.

For example, let us say the beginning player rolls three fours, a five and a one. He might pass the cup saying, "I have two pairs, sixes and five's."

That would <u>not</u> be a lie, because what he actually has, three of a kind, is better than two pairs. If the next player accepts the cup, he might peep under, leave the three fours hidden and openly roll the other two dice. Let's say he openly rolls a four and a three. Now he has four fours and a three, but only he and the previous player know that. With a look of pleased astonishment he might pass the cup saying, enthusiastically, "I have three aces and a pair of twos."

The next player would likely be baffled. Neither an ace nor a two is showing, and neither number was previously called. The receiving player might well challenge. Lifting the cup, he would be shocked to see four of a kind (fours) which is better than the call, a full house. So, the challenger would lose and would pass out the markers.

There are many ramifications to this game, as varied as the personalities of the players. Murph was a lively player. Invariably he would look under the cup and then, with a combined exclamation of shock, disbelief and astonishment say,

"Can you believe it?"

"Can you believe it?"

"Can you believe it?"

"Three threes, a five and a one, in one roll!"

"C A N   Y O U   B E L I E V E   I T?"

If you picked up the cup you might find he had nothing, or you might discover five sixes.

The way we played, each person began with a supply of markers of a certain color. If you lost, you distributed a marker to each of the other players, your color if you had no other, or if you had won and had received another's marker, someone else's. When someone else lost, you received a marker. When it was time to order a beer, you would give the marker of another player (if you had one) to Hans, the bartender, and he would collect payment for the beer from the player whose markers matched that color. If you were lucky you could play all night and have a beer whenever you liked without ever paying. Murph was usually lucky and always skilled. At the end of the evening we would settle up and Murph usually took some money back to his room.

When I left Kelley Barracks in February 1955, I gave my German money to Murph saying I would probably want him to send me something, sometime. He agreed. In the meantime he was to use the fund as his liar's dice grubstake.

In his memory, I here quote the final paragraph of my 1955 letter to Murph, the letter that Gina had returned to me thirty-seven years later. Murph had died four years earlier, yet I clearly remembered then and can recall today, his matchless enthusiasm, at play in liar's dice, and in the joyful way he totally experienced life.

*   *   *

Let me hear from you soon, Murph, and if you can, roll something to beat this!

Four sixes, Murph! On the first roll, Murph! Can you believe it?

FOUR SIXES, Murph! CAN YOU BELIEVE IT?

Wait Murph! Don't pick up that cup! Don't do it, Murph. Wait Murph!

*   *   *

But Murph, it was there. I told you Murph. See; five five's on one roll. That beats four sixes! You should have believed me, Murph. You should have believed your old buddy.

*   *   *

I'll have a Dinkelacker, Hans.

*   *   *

<u>THE TIMES</u>: In January, 1954, America launched its first nuclear submarine, The <u>Nautilus</u>.

*   *   *

Secretary of State John Foster Dulles announced that the U. S. had adopted a new policy which he called "Massive Retaliation" whereby America would meet any major Soviet attack with a massive nuclear response. The Intercontinental ballistic missile, utilizing inertial guidance systems and booster engines for multi-stage rockets was developed in support of that policy. Establishing the Cold War atmosphere for the next four decades, both the United States and Russia developed the ICBM, armed with a powerful nuclear warhead and capable of destroying a target 5,000 miles distant.

*   *   *

The <u>New York Times</u> published the account of three repatriated American prisoners of war to the effect that in 1954 the Soviets and Chinese were holding more than 5,000 Americans in prisons and slave labor camps. Those imprisoned included soldiers, civilians, women and children. Many had been residents of eastern European countries caught in the communist advance after World War II, others had been deported to Russia from German prisoner of war camps near the end of the war, and some were simply kidnapped.

*   *   *

Dear Mother and Dad,   9 February 1954
   Arrived back in Stuttgart last night after three weeks in Nürnberg, Straubing and Munich in connection with corps GCM activities. At this very moment I am filled with pride and an acute sense of importance inasmuch as I am temporarily the VIIth Corps staff judge advocate. That happens when every other officer in our section is away. A little while ago Colonel Guimond went to the bahnhof, Colonel Oeding and Dave went to the PX and everybody else is in Nürnberg. So I am in command! I hope General Gavin doesn't suddenly require the answer to some involved legal question..

   Being the SJA reminds me of a story told by WWII veterans of the Third Army about General George S. "Blood and Guts" Patton, the blunt, gruff and decisive tank commander whose armored columns were sweeping across southern Germany in the closing days of the war. It seems that American military vehicles were taking advantage of the autobahns, those fine four lane, divided highways networked all over Germany, by speeding – "pedal to the medal" – as they say, everywhere they went. There had been several serious accidents so General Patton had signs erected on the autobahns setting speed limits and giving notice of specific fines that would be levied by the military authorities in case of violation.

The story goes that the staff judge advocate of the Third Army thought the signs were unlawful because the military code required that punishments be imposed in the discretion of the judicial officer, not in accord with some predetermined agenda set by a unit commander. He went to General Patton and voiced his concern.

After impatiently hearing out his SJA, General Patton is said to have gruffly inquired, "Are you telling me that my road signs aren't legal?"

"Yes, sir," the Colonel replied. "It's not legal for you to set punishments before an offense has been committed, and before due process of law has resulted in a conviction followed by punishment determined through the exercise of judicial discretion by the hearing officer."

*"Well," said General Patton, characteristically, "if it's not legal, **<u>make it legal</u>**."*

Whereupon the General turned his attention to matters he considered to be more significant..

*   *   *

While in Munich I had a wonderful time participating in what is called "Fasching," It is a big carnival type celebration, party after party – some private, some public – every day and lasting several months. Fasching ends just prior to Ash Wednesday. It is observed all over Germany but some places celebrate more than others do. February is the big festival month and Munich is a great place for revelry. The party I went to Saturday night was still going strong when I left at 5 a. m. on Sunday morning. I shall make an effort to get back to Munich before it is all over. Fasching is also celebrated in Stuttgart but not nearly to the same extent as in Munich.

*　　*　　*

THE TIMES: The Soviet delegation at the Berlin Four Power Foreign Ministers' Conference in January and February 1954, for the first time seemed willing to accept the concept of collective European security rather than the reunification of East and West Germany under terms and conditions favorable to the Soviet Union. Over the next year and a half it became obvious that the Kremlin's Germany policy now rested on the assumption that there would be two independent German states for the foreseeable future. Apparently Molotov and the Soviet foreign ministry began to think along these lines soon after Josef Stalin's death on March 5, 1953.

*　　*　　*

Work began on the Berlin espionage tunnel in February 1954, using the construction of an Air Force radar site and warehouse as a cover. The tunnel itself was completed a year later, at the end of February 1955, and the taps were in place and operating shortly thereafter.

210

*   *   *

The United States tested nuclear devices at Bikini Atoll in the Marshall Islands in the Pacific. During Operation Crossroads, the United States exploded two atomic devices-one above the water on July 1, 1953, and the other below the water on July 25 -- to test the effects of atomic weapons against naval vessels.

The 162 inhabitants of Bikini Atoll were relocated to Rongerik Atoll, 128 miles east of Bikini, and eventually moved to Kili Island. Approximately 70 ships and submarines, "manned" only by test animals, were anchored in the lagoon of Bikini Atoll for each test. The above water blast sank five ships; the below water test sank nine. Both tests used atomic devices like the one dropped on Nagasaki, Japan. Forty-two thousand servicemen witnessed the tests from the decks of ships anchored outside Bikini Atoll.

*   *   *

Four days after the last test, the bikini swimsuit debuted at a French fashion show.

*   *   *

The United States used Bikini Atoll again for its largest atomic test ever, code-named Bravo, in February 1954. The explosion from the Bravo test was three to four times greater than anticipated, equal to that of 15 million tons of TNT. The fallout area was also three to four times greater than anticipated. Fallout from the test contaminated an area 300 miles downwind from the explosion and 40 miles wide. Inhabitants of Rongelap Island, 120 miles from the test, and Utrik Island, 300 miles away, were hurriedly evacuated days after the explosion.

*   *   *

Russia announced it would reject an Austrian Peace Treaty unless the west agreed to bar Austria from NATO and the European Defense Community.

*   *   *

President Eisenhower told reporters he bitterly opposed involving the U. S. in a shooting war in Indochina saying such a step would be a great tragedy.

SKIING WITH THE COWANS IN KANDERSTEG

Billy and Joannie Cowan and some other pilots and friends from the Chaumont Air Force Base, including some young ladies who worked there for American Express, planned a skiing trip to Switzerland and invited me to join. Skiing was completely new to me –Memphis being flat and usually hot.

Since I expected the weather in the Swiss Alps to be cold, and I had no ski clothes, I checked out my army winter field gear: fur cap, mittens, wool shirt, wool pants, field jacket, etc. Dave Addis, Ed Killorin and I boarded the train in Stuttgart bound for Zurich where I would change trains, continuing on alone to my skiing destination.

Lieutenant Killorin, from Savannah, Georgia, was stationed in Nürnberg with the 2nd Armored Cavalry Regiment. When I was in

212

Nürnberg, Killorin and I would bum around together. Ed had a girlfriend who lived in Zurich. We had supper at her apartment where I was introduced to Swiss Fondue.

There are many kinds of fondue, I learned. This night we were served little pieces of steak, which we stabbed with a long fork and immersed in hot oil until the meat was cooked to our satisfaction. The instructions given me did not include a caveat to change forks before eating the steak. As a result, I foolishly put the hot fork in my mouth and burned the hell out of my lower lip, immediately raising two unattractive, painful and inconvenient white blisters, one for each of the fork tines. I have enjoyed fondue many times since, but I can assure the reader that I have never repeated that agonizing tasting maneuver.

Next morning, I departed for Bern and after changing trains there started the final leg to Kandersteg, not a very large place and with infrequent railroad service. It occurred to me that the Cowans and their friends from France might be on the same train, and sure enough, they were.

We had lunch together, although my food intake was limited to small, painful bites, and arrived at the resort, a winter wonderland, where we were met by a horse drawn sleigh taxi attached to which was a smaller sleigh for the luggage.

As it turned out, the weather was quite warm, in spite of the fact that there was a deep covering of snow everywhere. The army winter field gear I had brought was inappropriate but satisfactory. While I was on the slopes most of army clothing remained in my hotel room.

First I tried the "beginner's slope," to the top of which I was towed by a sort of wooden circular seat attached to a moving cable. The cable went between one's legs and the seat against one's bottom. Managing to get to the summit without a spill, I deftly stepped off the seat lift and was poised to begin my descent – but uncertain how to go about it. Not many were using the beginner's slope, so I stood there, on the ski lift exit point, for a time, unsure and hesitant. Abruptly, I became aware that another skier, approaching from below, was shouting for me to move on so that he could get off the lift. At least, I though that was what he wanted. I couldn't understand what he was saying or even identify the language.

I had to get out of the way. I gave a mighty shove on my ski poles and fell flat on my face. While I had paused at the top of the hill my skis had become frozen in the snow.

That was the first of about 485 falls I experienced during the following three days. However, no injuries were sustained, save some skinned knuckles, a slightly twisted knee and much snow down the backside. I even managed to get a little sun tan in the bargain and my lip got well.

Of course, it was great being with the Cowans. They were a link with home. Billy and I know all the same people. We were in the same high school and college fraternities, so we talked endlessly about our friends at home so that Joannie would know who was who when she and Billy got out of the Air Force and back to Memphis. We had a lot of fun together taking midnight sleigh rides, going up and down the cable cars, and drinking hot toddies and grogs after many hours playing in the snow.

The Cowans visited me at Kelley Barracks a few weeks later. They had bought a Springer Spaniel puppy in Munich and were taking it back home to France. I knew Billy had owned Springer Spaniels in Memphis, most recently one named "Tawn."

I was waiting for the Cowans at the Kelley Barracks officer's club to which I had directed them. As they parked their car in the "O club" parking lot I noted that they were accompanied by another Air Force officer, whom, I presumed, I had met at the wedding, but did not recognize. Billy, smiling, with the puppy in his arms and the unfamiliar officer by his side, walked toward me and exclaimed,

"You remember 'Tawn,' don't you?"

Thinking he meant the officer, and not associating the puppy with the Memphis dog, I assumed my most friendly expression, extended my hand to the officer and said to him with assurance,

"Sure I do, Tawn. I met you at the wedding."

*   *   *

The Cowans visit also undid a life change I had been attempting to achieve.

Although my given name is "John," since childhood my nick name in Memphis has always been "Buddy" or "Bud." Upon graduating from law school I had thought it unfitting for an attorney at law to be known as "Buddy," so I decided to change my appellation to the more dignified "John."

The Army, I thought, would provide me with the necessary anonymity to effect the change, but I was wrong. Everywhere the army sent me I would always encounter someone from Memphis who would call me "Buddy," which would invariably defeat my effort to become known by a more distinguished name.

When the Army sent me Europe where I knew no one, I was certain I was being provided the perfect opportunity to become "John." By introducing myself as "John" on every occasion, for almost a year I was completely successful in effecting the transition. Then the Cowans arrived.

Dinner at the VII Corps officer's club afforded me a chance to introduce my Air Force friends to the Army officers with whom I worked during the day and dined and played liar's dice in the evenings. Soon, Billy was referring to me as "Buddy," and not much later, picking up the nick name used so comfortably by my hometown friends, so were my Kelley Barracks acquaintances. So, my cover was blown. Once again "John" became "Buddy," my attempt to achieve dignity was destroyed and it has pretty much been "Buddy" ever since.

I NEED A LAWYER!

At about 0445 hours on Sunday, February 28, I was eastbound on Pleiningerstrasse on my way back to Kelley Barracks. The streets were icy and the road was slick. Two hundred yards west of the entrance to the Kaserne I saw an oncoming automobile begin to skid sideways, into my path, presenting its left side rear, to my left front. As investigating traffic police like to say, "A collision ensued."

The impact was powerful, throwing the other driver from his vehicle, extensively damaging the left front of my Morris Minor and resulting in a laceration to my forehead that required five stitches to close. I did not mention any of this in my letters home.

Remaining at the scene until the investigation by the military and German Police was completed, I observed that the other car was a 1941 Chevrolet coupe, like my vehicle, exhibiting license plates bearing the legend "US Forces, Germany" and learned that it was owned by Master Sergeant Roger P. Slater, who was a passenger, asleep in the vehicle when the accident occurred, and driven by Sergeant Hugh Moreland. Apparently Moreland had dozed at the wheel. Suddenly becoming aware of my oncoming lights, I surmised, he had abruptly applied his brakes—not a good idea under the icy conditions--causing his vehicle to slide sideways into mine. Although no one was seriously injured, I was losing a lot of blood.

After the police told me I could leave and I arranged for my car to be moved into the parking lot at the officers club, I went to the VIIth Corps Dispensary. Lt. Peters, of the medical corps, sewed me up and diagnosed my injuries as a deep laceration of the scalp, contusions and abrasions of both knees and a sprained right thumb.

Wurttembergische Feuerversicherung, a German liability insurance company in Stuttgart insured Sgt. Slater's Chevrolet. My telephone call to their claim office on the following Monday did not result in a very helpful response. It was obvious that Sgt. Slater had not reported the accident.

Without much difficulty I traced Sgts. Slater and Moreland to the 7th Army machine records unit at Patch Barracks in Vaihingen and telephoned Slater, requesting his cooperation in the processing of my claim against his insurance company. He promised action but did not perform.

Although my Morris was being repaired, the cost was in excess of 2,000 DM and I didn't have that kind of money.

Repeatedly telephoning Sgt. Slater didn't accomplish much. He assured me he would get Sgt. Moreland's statement and send an accident report to his insurance company but evidently didn't want the accident on his record and thought if he ignored me, I would go away. I phoned him several times without satisfactory results.

Then one day Lottie Klein, one of the German secretaries in Colonel Guimond's office, stuck her head in at my door and said,

"Lieutenant Thomason. You have a telephone call on the SJA's phone."

I walked down the hall to pick up the phone. It was just outside the colonel's office door, which was ajar.

The caller was a Captain Milbranch in the machine records unit at Patch Barracks, and he was angry.

"Are you the guy who has been calling Sergeant Slater in my office?" he demanded.

"Yes, sir," I began, "I'm trying to get him to..."

"I don't give a damn what you're trying to do," interrupted the captain. "Haven't you ever heard of the 'chain of command'?"

"Yes, sir, I have," I replied," but this has nothing to do with the chain of command. Sergeant Moreland was driving Sergeant Slater's car, and ..."

"I know all about the accident," Captain Milbranch broke in again. "I don't want you calling Slater. If you want to talk to Slater, you call me, his commanding officer, <u>Captain</u> Milbranch. Do you understand that, <u>lieutenant</u>."

"But, sir..." I began to protest, when Colonel Guimond stepped out of his office and asked quietly, "What's going on?"

I put my hand over the telephone mouthpiece. "This is a Captain Milbranch over at Patch Barracks," I said. "He is the commanding officer of the sergeant involved in the accident with me. I'm trying to get the sergeant to make an accident report to his insurance company and this captain is chewing me out and giving me hell for calling the sergeant directly instead of going through him, Slater's commanding officer."

"Give me the phone," said Colonel Guimond.

"<u>Captain</u> Milbranch, this is <u>Colonel</u> Guimond. I am the staff judge advocate of the VIIth Corps. Lieutenant Thomason is a member of my command."

He paused. Apparently, Captain Milbranch did not respond.

"In the future," Colonel Guimond calmly continued, "if you wish to speak with Lieutenant Thomason, you will first call me, his commanding officer. Do you understand that?"

It appeared that Captain Milbranch understood. Colonel Guimond said "thank you'" and hung up the phone.

*   *   *

Sgts. Slater and Moreland completed the necessary reports but Wurttembergische Feuerversicherung remained recalcitrant. Concluding that it would be necessary for me to file suit against Sgts. Slater and Moreland in a civilian court, I embarked upon the necessary legal action.

The American occupation forces were at that time legally regulated and operating under laws promulgated by the office of the

United States High Commissioner for Germany. In order for me to avail myself of the only civil tribunal capable of resolving a dispute between two American soldiers involved in an automobile accident on a German highway, it was necessary for me to obtain authorization from the High Commissioner, office of the general counsel in Bad Godesburg. Only then could the German courts exercise jurisdiction over an American soldier. My request for such authorization had to be approved by the staff judge advocate of the United States Army, Europe, with headquarters in Heidelberg.

Once begun, the process moved swiftly. On 22 March 1954 the Commander in Chief of the United States Army, Europe, through Colonel E. H. Snodgrass, Judge Advocate, granted permission "*to First Lieutenant John J. Thomason, a person subject to the military laws of the United States, to be a party to judicial proceedings in the appropriate German courts in the United States Zone of Germany for the limited purpose of instituting civil proceedings against Master Sergeant Roger P. Slater and Sergeant Hugh C. Moreland for damages allegedly resulting from an automobile accident on 28 February 1954.*"

Four days later the chief of the legal affairs division of the office of the United States High Commissioner for Germany pursuant to Article 3 of Law number 35 issued the required authorization.

Presented with these documents, Wurttembergische Feuerversicherung agreed to a settlement conference. Accompanied by a female German civilian lawyer from 7th Army headquarters, I met with the insurance company representatives in their conference room in a downtown Stuttgart office building.

"Let me do the talking," my German lawyer said on the way downtown.

I did. Most of the discussion was in German, but occasionally my lawyer would turn to me to ask a question in English. Once or twice she became plainly offended when a suggestion was made that I compromise the damages in some way she thought beneath the dignity of an American Army officer. At length we reached a settlement, entirely satisfactory to me.

The restoration of my Morris to "like new" condition was promised. In addition, I was adequately compensated for my injuries, pain and suffering, loss of use of my car and "inconvenience."

Everyone smiled and hands were shaken all round. On the way home I asked "my lawyer" to stop and I bought her a case of wine. Come to think of it, although I had possessed my law degree almost two years at that time and had experienced more than a hundred military trials, I paid a legal fee before I ever received one!

*   *   *

In March a letter from Gisa Barre' arrived. Her family in Munich had received gifts from my family in Memphis thanking them for taking care of me at Christmas. Gisa had written a thank you letter to my parents also describing the recent progression of her singing career. I knew she was very busy because the last two times I had been in Munich when I tried to reach her, Mrs. Barre' told me Gisa was not at home and because of her busy schedule, it was not clear when she would be. My parents forwarded the letter to me. Her report of the development of her career made me suspect that I was not likely to see much more of her, and I was correct.

221

"I have started a new engagement in the American Officers' Club "Haus der Kunst" here in Munich as a singer for American songs. As I haven't sung for a long time for American people I have much to learn, how to keep in mind the words to songs not written in my native language. I have to run to find the few German people who know American music to copy it. I had also on last Thursday an A. F. N. (Armed Forces Network – American Radio in Europe) performance at 2300 O'clock. So you see, I have much work to do. But I like to sing in American or French language, even if it isn't too easy for me."

* * *

Reading that account of what she was doing made me realize that she would likely be working when I was free and that it would be only coincidental if we should be in the same place at the same time. It was not surprising that she was so sought after. She was a beautiful, talented young woman with an effervescent personality and enchanting presence. I hated to lose contact with her, but, after all, hadn't General George Washington advised Americans to "avoid foreign entanglements?"

Concerning Gisa, however, I would have disregarded General Washington's admonition, if possible for me to do so.

<u>BERLIN</u>

Dear Mother and Dad,   March 1954, 2045 hours

* If you have difficulty reading this it is because it is being written on a train. In a few hours I shall be speeding through the Soviet sector of Germany. When we reach the frontier the doors of the train will be locked and the windows sealed so that we can't see outside. At about 0730 tomorrow morning we shall be in Berlin. Dave and I left Stuttgart at 1600 hours this afternoon on a trip I didn't even know I was going to make until about noon. We are doing some work on a case that has so far proven to be the most interesting one I have yet handled. I am not sure just how much I am allowed to say about it, so I shall say nothing. Someday it will make a fascinating story.*

* * *

Initially, the case seemed simple enough; the accused was charged with desertion. I was prosecuting; Dave Addis was defending. Trials for "desertion with the intent to remain away permanently" were probably the most common charges in the States. However, such cases were rare in Germany. Actually, the most common military offense, everywhere, was absence without leave (AWOL), but those charges were considered minor and were generally dealt with in the lower courts: summary or special courts-martial. We never handled AWOL cases except when combined with another, more serious offense.

In the U. S. it was commonplace for a soldier to be charged and punished for being absent from his unit without leave. If the absence was short, the punishment was light and rarely involved confinement. Being late back from a pass or overstaying leave a day or so was not unusual either in Germany or in the States. In America, however, a homesick soldier on leave with his family or girlfriend might overstay his authorized absence a few days and then decide *not* to return to his military assignment. If he was caught and it could be proven that he intended to remain away permanently, he could be tried and found guilty of desertion. That happened a lot. Many soldiers, drafted involuntarily into the service, didn't adjust to military discipline and wanted out. In the U. S., effectively removing oneself from military control was not too difficult. America is a big country and it is easy to travel about since there are no border guards at state lines. Many deserters were never apprehended. In Germany, however, there was really no place to desert to. Most American soldiers couldn't speak another language, didn't have a passport and couldn't get across the border. So, those of us concerned with military justice in Germany saw few indictments for desertion with the intent to remain away permanently.

The case at hand involved a soldier of Mexican decent who, facing criminal charges and awaiting trial for larceny, had disappeared from his VIIth Corps unit posted near the Czech border. After many months he had been apprehended in Berlin and sent back to his unit where he was to stand trial for desertion. I thought the case was pretty clear cut. It seemed to me that the long duration of his absence, the fact that he was confronting a court-martial trial when he disappeared and because he had, when apprehended, denied his true identity, justified the inference that he didn't intend to return. The accused's expected assertion that he had been detained against his will and always intended to return was not, in my opinion, believable.

After interviewing his client in the stockade, about noon one day, Dave came into my office and said,

"We've got to go to Berlin."

"Why?" I asked.

"Because there are witnesses there who can prove that this guy in the desertion case was held in East Germany involuntarily. He was kidnapped by the Russians, held prisoner at some place called 'Bautzen' and finally, with the help of American secret agents who live in, or move in and out of East Germany, escaped to West Berlin," Dave explained.

We went to see Colonel Guimond who listened patiently and then observed,

"Well, if these people are really necessary witnesses for the defense, I guess you'll have to go talk with them, and maybe take their depositions, but it's going to be complicated."

"When is this case set for trial?" asked the Colonel.

"Next week," we answered, "and everything except the defense proof is ready. The litigation will be in Straubing. Travel arrangements for the trial team have been made; the court members have been appointed. We've arranged for all the other witnesses to be present, and some of them are scheduled to rotate back to the ZI in about ten days."

"OK, we'd better get busy," said the Colonel.

"I'll get the adjutant general to cut some orders for you to make the trip. I think the orders have to be in Russian."

Although military personnel might seem to be slow-moving and frequently action is, at best, unhurried, when the Army needs to move, it can do so. In about two hours we had our orders (in Russian), travel from Stuttgart to Frankfurt to Berlin was laid on, arrangement for necessary security clearance, for the witness interviews and for us to be met in Berlin by agents of the CIC (counter intelligence corps) were made. We hurriedly packed and by 1600 hours, just four hours after Dave had said, "We've got to go to Berlin," we were on our way.

The train from Stuttgart to Frankfurt was part of the regular German railway system, but the one from Frankfurt to Berlin, was different. It was *The Military Duty Train.* At the Soviet sector frontier Russian soldiers boarded, sealed the windows, locked the doors and carefully inspected all travel documents, including our translated orders. Some of the Soviet soldiers stayed on the train, to be sure, I guess, we didn't peep out the window. I don't know what it was that we were not supposed to see. Whatever it was, we didn't see it. Anyway, it was dark outside; we couldn't have seen much even if the windows had not been sealed.

Early the next morning, we were met at the station in Berlin by a young man in civilian clothes who spoke German and motioned us toward a small four-door sedan parked in a restricted zone. I asked him to open the trunk so that we could stow our luggage. He smiled and did so. It was jam packed full of radio equipment--no room for suitcases. The "German" who greeted us wasn't German at all. When he spoke to us in English he sounded like he might be from

Kansas City. Thus, were we introduced to the Berlin theater of espionage.

The witnesses we were to interview were a Spaniard who was with Dave's client when they were arrested at the same time and place in Berlin, and several CIC agents who were knowledgeable about the prisoners and the prison at Bautzen. Dave hoped these persons would establish that his client had been held against his will and had always intended to return to his American military unit; however, the evidence didn't turn out that way.

We talked with the Spaniard, separately, through an interpreter. He made no bones about the fact that he was a communist and a deserter from the Spanish Army. He had made his way to East Germany to enjoy the anticipated contentment of living in a communist state. Things had not evolved as he thought they would.

After weeks of interrogation and confinement, he was sent to the East German town of Bautzen where he was put to work at very low wages in a glass factory. He wasn't exactly in prison, but he couldn't leave the area of the town. His travel pass was not valid elsewhere in East Germany. He said that East Germany was divided into sectors and that people with a pass valid in one sector, couldn't use it in another.

In the Bautzen prison he met Dave's client, who was also working in the glass factory and had taken an East German wife. Initially both soldiers had been content in Bautzen, but after a while they grew tired of their monotonous lives in this "Utopian Garden of Communism" and decided to pretend that they were both Argentineans, escape back to the west and hopefully, South America. To do that they needed to get in touch with a network of underground agents who could provide them with necessary travel documents and transport them to East Berlin, from which they could get to West Berlin by public transportation. They hadn't figured out how they would get from West Berlin, through the Russian Zone to West Germany.

They found out that there were "people" in the prison who could help them escape. Contact was made and the escape was arranged. As they made their way north, they were moved forward by the "people" from one sector to another until finally they arrived in Berlin. Unbeknownst to the escapees, however, these East German "people" were American agents of the CIC. When the deserters arrived in the Allied part of Berlin, instead of being free, they were correctly identified by their real names and arrested. The American, Dave's client, was flown to Stuttgart to be tried later as a deserter at his military base in Straubing. The Spaniard was given a short non-renewable visa to remain in confinement in West Berlin until he could make arrangements to immigrate elsewhere, but the visa was about to expire.

The interview complete, I offered the Spaniard a cigarette and inquired,

"What are you going to do now?"

"I don't know," he said.

He was about five feet four, very thin, with a dark complexion. Clean-shaven but with the potential for a heavy beard, he exhibited a sorrowful countenance except once or twice when the interpreter had made a humorous error in translation, then he flashed a quick and engaging smile. He was a very agreeable sort and I liked him.

228

"Why don't you go back to Spain, turn yourself in, serve your time and start over," I suggested, assuming my legal assistance officer alter ego.

"I can't," he said, matter–of--factly, without bitterness.

"General Franco has issued a decree that anyone in Spain can shoot a deserter from the Spanish Army on sight and collect a big reward. If I go back to Spain I am a dead man."

"Well, then," I continued, in my naiveté, "you ought to apply for a visa to some other country."

"I have," he said. "To about fifteen. They all have rejected me. I have no passport, and since I am a deserter, no citizenship."

"What about West Germany," I proposed. "Have you thought about that?"

"It's the same as West Berlin." He sighed, gloomily. "They won't extend my visa."

I continued my advice, but with noticeably less confidence. "Maybe they'll let you stay in West Berlin after your visa runs out."

"No," he said, taking a long drag on his cigarette. "The West Berlin authorities say that when my visa expires I will have to go back to East Germany."

"What will happen to you there?" I inquired, not especially wanting to know.

He responded promptly. "Because I escaped from the prison, they will kill me." He said.

I had run out of questions and proposals. I felt acute compassion for this man but I was powerless to help him.

He turned toward me and looked deeply and sadly into my eyes. "May I have another cigarette?" he asked.

229

"Sure," I said, "take the pack."

*   *   *

Since that conversation I have often wondered whatever became of the melancholy Spaniard. He was an idealist, a dreamer, impractical, probably the cause of problems for his family, but not an evil person. He was simply seeking a better life. In another place, at another time he might have found it. Many have in America. As I suspect things turned out, he became a casualty of the Cold War, one among thousands.

*   *   *

Later in the day Dave encountered additional problems in preparing for the defense of his client when we interviewed the CIC agents. They avoided using the first person in their accounts of Bautzen Prison and descriptions of personnel there, but they told us about the prison in astounding detail; where it was, who worked there, who was confined there and why. They showed us photographs of the prison commandant, his wife, his children, his mistress, his wife and mistress *together,* and the members of his staff. Many of the photographs had obviously been taken by telephoto lens.

We were shown itemized lists of prisoners with particulars as to nationality, date of entry, physical and photographic descriptions and commentary, including the two prisoners we were investigating. The CIC information made it clear that Dave's client had voluntarily surrendered to the East Germans after crossing the Czech border and had given his interrogators all the information about the

American Army he possessed, although they wanted a great deal more than he could provide. After the Soviets were satisfied the information well was dry, they had transferred him to Bautzen and initiated his glass-making career.

Surprisingly, he was not an American citizen at all, but an illegal immigrant who had crossed the Rio Grande into Texas, somehow enlisted in the American Army and was sent overseas to Germany. Having been charged with larceny of a barrack mate's property, he had decided to flee to the east where he became the temporary guest of the Bautzen prison authorities. After our trip to Berlin failed to produce any exculpatory evidence, Dave's client entered a plea of guilty at the Straubing trial, was given a fairly light sentence which he served in America. Afterwards, he was deported back to Mexico.

Back in Berlin, we were astounded by the amount of particularized information the intelligence agents had accumulated. Although we didn't ask directly, we were convinced that these American agents with whom we spoke were making regular and frequent trips in and out of East Germany, and Lord knows where else. They told us that Dave's client was being tried in Straubing instead of Berlin, where he had been captured, because there had been a similar trial in Berlin a year or so before, which, although the entire proceeding was conducted secretly, had resulted in the disappearance of six underground agents previously operating in East Germany. Apparently assassinated, those agents had also assisted an American deserter escape from Bautzen. Somehow, the Soviets had infiltrated the secret proceedings, learned the identity of the strategically placed agents and eliminated them. Our impression was that the agents were Americans posing as East Germans. It had taken a long time, they said, for the agents to be replaced—but ultimately they had been.

*   *   *

The Bautzen Prison had been in place for a long time and had an extensive history that pre dated its use by the communists by many years.   Before arriving in America, Bruno Richard Hauptman, the convicted kidnapper and murderer of the two year old son of Charles and Anne Morrow Lindbergh in 1932, was confined there from 1919 until 1923 for armed robbery, burglary, larceny, and possession of stolen goods.

In 1989, after the Soviets relinquished control of the area, horrifying discoveries were made in the Bautzen prison complex. Investigators unearthed the largest mass grave created in post– World War II Germany. It contained the remains of more than 17,000 political prisoners of the Soviet occupation era.

*   *   *

After working on the case all day on Friday and Saturday, we took Sunday off. The Transient BOQ next to the CIC headquarters had served as our hotel. It was within walking distance to the city center. Dave decided to visit some Berlin friends I did not know, so I took a walk around the city.

When I saw Munich I had thought no viable city could be more devastated; Berlin was far worse.   The almost incessant Allied bombing during the last year of the war and the massive artillery assault mounted by the Russians immediately prior to its capture, had left Berlin in shambles.   I walked for almost four hours, approaching and all through the city center without seeing a habitable building. The destruction was awesome.

I also visited the impressive Russian Military Cemetery where thousands of Soviet soldiers, killed in the street fighting that characterized the final assault of the city, are buried in mass graves beneath colossal red granite sculptures of Russian flags and mourning fellow soldiers. At the far end of the burial ground is another triumphant gigantic bronze figure of a Russian soldier, a sword in his right hand, a small child in his left and a broken swastika at his feet. At the other end is a statue of Mother Russia, mourning for her fallen sons.

Arrangements had been made for us to take a military flight back to Frankfurt. When we arrived at Tempelhof Aerodrome we paused to admire the towering tridentate monument dedicated to the memory of the 31 Americans, 39 British and 9 German civilians who, just six years before, lost their lives maintaining the Berlin Airlift. Then we boarded our air transport home.

*   *   *

Dear Mother and Dad,   *29 April 1954*

I can't remember when I last wrote but I know it has been a long time. This letter won't be very lengthy either. I just want you to know that I am safely back from my two-week leave. Wick Anderson and I drove 2400 miles through Germany, Austria, Italy and Switzerland and had an absolutely marvelous time. So that you can get a better understanding of where we went and what we did, I will mail you the journal I kept. However, I will mention here one funny thing that happened on the trip that is not in the journal.

Wick and I were having supper in a restaurant in Florence, Italy, when in walked two very attractive young ladies, obviously American, in airline stewardess uniforms. I was elected to attempt communication; so, adopting my most suave bearing, I approached their table and said with what I hoped was an engaging smile,

"I see by your uniforms that you young ladies are Americans. My friend - there at the table across the room – and I are also Americans. Have you been to Florence before?"

"No," the taller one replied, "This is our first trip."

"Well," I said knowingly, "We are very familiar with the Florence area; perhaps we could show you around."

The tall stewardess spoke again, "Buddy Thomason, I went to Central High School with you. You don't know Florence Italy any better than I do!"

It was Anne Holmes. She was at Central in the class behind mine. I hadn't recognized her. Anyhow, the four of us had a great time exploring Florence together.

*   *   *

Here in the JA Office we are all quite interested in the Army-McCarthy hearings. I believe the Senator has gone too far in his attack on the Army. The Army has its faults, but basically it is a good organization made up of conscientious people trying – and usually succeeding – in doing a competent job. I sincerely hope that this is the beginning of the end for Senator McCarthy and I think it is.

*   *   *

It was. Most accounts I have read assert that the turning point in McCarthy's unproductive investigation to find communists in the Army was Lawyer Joseph Welch's unanswered rhetorical question, not to a witness, but to Senator McCarthy himself. From that moment McCarthy's political career spiraled downward ending in his premature alcoholic death at age 49.

McCarthy charged that the Army was riddled with communists in high places. Televised hearings were conducted before a Senate subcommittee and droned on into the month of June, with McCarthy making countless accusations but offering only innuendoes and insinuations in support of his allegations. Boston lawyer Joseph Welch who had been assisted by a young associate in his firm, Fred Fisher, defended the Army. McCarthy found out that Fisher, while in law school at Harvard, had once attended a single meeting of an organization whose purpose was reportedly sympathetic to the communists. McCarthy viciously attacked young Fisher at the beginning of one of the nationally televised sessions, naming him as a communist and otherwise, without any basis in fact, discrediting his good character.

Welch listened quietly to McCarthy's tirade. Then, when he finally had the floor, before setting the record straight concerning Fisher, Welch looked directly at McCarthy and asked, rhetorically, "Have you no decency left, sir?"

McCarthy's sulky, scowling, angry glare answered for him. He had no decency to begin with, and his lack of that quality was apparent for all to see.

With his sly hint of a smile and a quick wit, lawyer Welch became a popular personality. He later appeared in the role of the trial judge in the movie, *Anatomy of a Murder*.

Fred Fisher, the young associate who had been the target of McCarthy's scorn, later became active in the American Bar Association and one year was chairman of the 17,000 member General Practice Section. I was subsequently elected to the same position. Fred and I became great friends. Little did I guess when I suggested to my parents that McCarthy might have stubbed his political toe by so ruthlessly assailing the Army and Fisher, that one day Fred Fisher and I would be friends.

Small world.

*　　　*　　　*

Dear Folks,　　　　　　　　　　　　*26 May 1954*

John Tinnerello and his wife are in France for a week so Colonel Oeding and I have moved into their house. You simply can't imagine how wonderful it is living in a house again – it has been sixteen months since I have had that experience. I can actually walk ten steps without colliding with a wall. We have been having a wonderful time, although I am going to be pretty tired when the week is over because we have been partying every night.

Day before yesterday we had quite a surprise. U. S. military personnel, throughout Germany, were notified at six

A. M. that all military payment certificates had to be exchanged for a new issue, completely changed in appearance, by noon that day. After the deadline the old MPCs were not valid. We use MPCs for all cash transactions on military installations, including the post exchange. There are no coins; everything is paper, even nickels and dimes. There are no pennies. It is illegal for German nationals to possess scrip, but some do. I understand that Germans were trying to sell ten-dollar script notes for 3 DM on the morning of the changeover. In other words they were willing to trade something worth ten dollars yesterday for about seventy-five cents today. All details of the exchange were kept quite secret. I don't know anyone who was aware of the transition before it happened. The net worth of some Germans who trade with Americans on the black market is likely to have evaporated. The change was made so quickly that I doubt anyone illegally holding scrip could get rid of it.

A CHANGE IN COMMAND

General Gavin completed his tour of duty as commander of VII Corps in the spring of 1954 and was replaced by Major General Hodes. Such a change is a major event in the military and was the occasion for a parade featuring the 7th Army band, elite troops in sparkling regalia passing in review, some speeches and much saluting and marching about. Not that I mean to belittle the ceremony, for the whole ritual made me feel very proud to be a part of this fine Army corps and to have served under such a gallant figure as General Gavin.

Our new commanding general supplied an unwelcome change and an unexpected but significant increase in the number and frequency of general courts-martial in the VIIth Corps. Major General Henry I. Hodes next previous assignment had been to act as one of the chief negotiators for the United Nations Forces at the armistice talks with the Chinese and North Koreans which, after two years of bargaining, had finally resulted in a cease fire, ending the Korean War. Before that he served as deputy commander of the Eighth Army in Korea. His style proved vastly different from that of General Gavin.

I never met General Hodes. For that matter, although we worked in the same building, I don't recall ever seeing him. Perhaps that was because I traveled so much, and I must assume, since corps units were so dispersed, so did he.

In a nutshell, General Gavin followed the recommendations of his staff judge advocate. General Hodes did not.

Charges against a soldier in the American army usually originated with the commanding officer of the soldier's unit. Once the investigation of charges was complete, the file was sent forward, ultimately reaching our office. We would assign counsel and set the matter for trial, unless we determined that there was some reason not to do so. Sometimes the assigned prosecutor would, after reviewing the file and talking to the witnesses, decide that it was unlikely the case could be proved. The charges might be dropped if there was a valid legal defense or, perhaps, if the case was more deserving of resolution at a lower level, by a special or summary court-martial. In any of those events, the matter would be taken up with the staff judge advocate, Colonel Guimond at first, later Colonel O'Connor, and if the SJA agreed with the recommendation (I cannot recall an instance when he did not agree) he would take the case and the recommendation to General Gavin or General Hodes for further action. General Gavin always followed the advice of his chief legal officer. General Hodes followed the recommendation of the commanding officer who had originated and pressed the charge, notwithstanding a contrary opinion from his legal staff.

I thought the difference in style surprising. One might think that the highly decorated and legendary combat general who had risen from the ranks and jumped with his paratroopers on D-Day (Gavin) would side with his field commanders when their opinions on military justice differed from those of his legal staff. On the contrary, he supported the recommendations of his lawyers. General Hodes, who seemed to us more an administrative than combat type, rejected such advice. If Hodes' commanders wanted a general court-martial trial for an offender, they attained that objective over the objections of Hodes' legal staff. The result was that after Hodes arrived our workload increased by about fifty per cent. In the fifteen months I had been at VII Corps, we prosecuted only one officer. After Hodes arrived we tried three in one month. The acquittal rate also increased. In my opinion, many cases were tried that should not have been.

This difference in command technique presents an interesting philosophical question: is Hodes' style or Gavin's more likely to produce the qualities a military commander would want in his men? Those qualities would include high morale, motivation, preparedness, efficiency, discipline and skill. In deciding whether to require a member of your command to stand trial before the highest military court, a court that has the power to impose the death penalty, do you follow the advice of you field commanders or your legal staff?

I know what I would do. But of course, I have a dog in the fight.

*   *   *

Dear Mother and Dad,   *12 June 1954*

This is being written while I take a short recess from my duties as officer of the day, an assignment I receive about once every six weeks. There is a different OD every day. The job is rotated among the company grade officers stationed at or near the Kaserne. The OD's primary responsibility has to do with maintaining the security of the Kaserne. As OD I have about 150-armed troops under my command some of whom are posted at various places around the Kaserne: such as the ammunition dump, the gas dump, motor vehicle pool, etc., guarding these valuable supplies. The OD must post the guards, relieve and replace them at the appropriate time and check to be sure they are awake and alert at random intervals throughout a 24 hour period. I wear a steel helmet, carry a pistol and know the password. The job is necessary but not very demanding. The duty begins with a military formation at which the officer of the day being relieved turns the command over to the new one. There is a ritual and protocol, which must be followed. I learned all this in advance from others more familiar with the procedure and after having held the job a couple of times, I am comfortable with it. Inspecting the guard can take on dangerous aspects should the OD attempt to slip up on an alert guard – or for that matter, a sleepy one – since both OD and the guard are armed with live ammunition.

This time I am OD over a weekend, which I really don't mind so much since that means I won't have the weekend assignment again soon. I didn't have any plans this weekend anyhow, and this duty gives me a chance to look over and do the paper work for eight new cases I was handed yesterday. I can't remember when we have had so much work. Our trial schedule is set for the next three weeks.

My standing at VIIth Corps Headquarters, and especially with the 321st Signal Battalion has lately attained a new enhanced stature. This is as a result of a trial last week in which I defended two master sergeants from the 321st charged with rape, adultery and sodomy. The proceedings attracted an overflowing of spectators and much local interest. Although both accused were convicted of adultery they were found not guilty of the more serious charges and were only fined, with no loss of rank. Not a bad result when you consider they could have been given the death penalty.

I have received much praise for my efforts. One of the nicest compliments came from a Kaserne guard who mentioned the trial not knowing I was involved, and said, "A couple of my buddies saw the trial and told me the defense counsel did a brilliant job."

However, I don't always win. Yesterday my client, charged with knifing an unarmed fellow soldier while in an unauthorized uniform and in possession of a false pass, was sentenced to prison for three years.

We read that communist forces under Ho Chi Minh have defeated the French colonial forces at Dien Bien Phu. The veterans of World War II with whom I am in contact don't have an abundance of respect for French military competence. The prevailing opinion among them seems to be that if have to fight the Russians we shall be much better off with the Germans on our side, rather than the French.

*   *   *

During the third week in June, 1954, I prosecuted two officers, both first lieutenants, one for larceny of funds turned in when the scrip was converted, the other for striking an enlisted man. I don't recall the result of the second case, but wrote home concerning the one tried for larceny by embezzlement.

I was slightly acquainted with the officer charged. He had been in the service since 1941, had fought in World War II, worked his way up through the grades of non-commissioned officer and finally received a battlefield commission in Korea. He was despondent over the fact that he had been passed over for promotion and because he was unable to have his family (wife, son 15, daughter 9) join him in Germany. He had stolen $1,000. Upon his conviction he was stripped of his commission, dismissed from the Army, forfeited all pay and allowances and sentenced to two years confinement at hard labor.

The trial and punishment disturbed me greatly. Colonel Oeding, who was sort of a father figure to me, and I discussed my distress at having to prosecute this fellow lieutenant and in general about dealing with the psychological pressure associated with being a trial lawyer. He didn't offer much by way of a solution. He had been a court room lawyer all his life and was skilled and compassionate.

"When will I get over being so subjectively involved in these trials?" I asked.

"You won't," he replied. "That's what makes you a good trial lawyer. You care about what you are doing. Of course, that leads to a great deal of stress and you are going to have to learn to deal with that."

I pursued the inquiry. "How do you manage to deal with the tensions associated with trial work?"

He paused.

"Well, that's a good question. There are several answers, some better than others, but none very satisfactory. You can learn to compartmentalize. Leave the trial at the courthouse. Don't take it home with you. That's hard to do but it sometimes it can be done. Some trial lawyers try to escape, by physical exercise. They play tennis, golf or some other sport. Some seek diversion through entertainment or travel or becoming engrossed in a hobby, art or creative writing or maybe flying an airplane. Lots turn to alcohol, and that's o. k. as long as you are able to use it in moderation, but unfortunately, many can't. There are many alcoholic trial lawyers. Others just surrender to the law as a 'jealous mistress' and work all the time."

243

He was thoughtful, paused briefly and continued. "It's something you will have to work on all your life in order to find your own answer. About the best I can suggest is that you not be a lawyer all the time. Take on other interests and become absorbed in other activities. Also, being involved and curious about everything around you will make you a better lawyer."

*   *   *

Things got worse. We had a wall chart in our office where we listed all the cases referred for trial but not yet tried. There were seventeen horizontal lines upon which we entered the style (name) of each case. Before, it had never been more than two-thirds full. After General Hodes arrived we had to construct a new chart – twenty-five lines – and counting. Also, before Hodes, many times the defense was able to negotiate a guilty plea for an agreed sentence, in the vernacular, the accused could "cop a plea." No more. The word came down: no negotiated pleas. All cases would go to trial. For the first time we were unable to keep up with the trial referrals; we fell behind.

About this time, I was advised that Captain Fenig and I had been selected to prosecute a first-degree murder case to be tried in Straubing in July or August and that the government would seek the death penalty.

*   *   *

THE TIMES: In July 1954, in Memphis, Tennessee, Sun Records Owner Sam Phillips thought he heard something new in the plaintive and emotional voice of Elvis Presley, a white vocalist who graduated from Humes High School in 1953 and could sing the blues. Phillips teamed Elvis with guitarist Scotty Moore and bassist Bill Black. The trio produced and recorded "That's All Right" and "Blue Moon of Kentucky"—blues and country songs, respectively—in a solid up-beat style that served as the construct for rock 'n' roll.

Elvis was later drafted into the Army and served a two-year tour of duty as an enlisted man stationed in Friedberg, Germany.

*　　　*　　　*

In July 1954 the Danube River in Germany and Austria flooded, prompting a massive American rescue and relief effort. The need for medical relief was insignificant, although the Army furnished Linz, Austria, with emergency stocks of typhoid vaccine. The primary American contribution was flood control by the army engineers and reconnaissance flights by army helicopter units and, when necessary, rescue. Such recovery efforts proved popular with the victims. On one mission a pilot plucked several people from an isolated housetop and noticed that one of them looked familiar.

"Didn't I bring you out a few hours ago?" inquired, the curious aviator.

"Yes," answered the man, "I enjoy riding in a helicopter and so I went back by rowboat."

*　　　*　　　*

COMING IN ON A WING AND A PRAYER

Dear Mother and Dad, 19 July 1954

This is being written from the court room in Straubing where we are waiting for an "alert" to end so that we can get on with a trial. We have been here since last Monday. The area where the 6th Regimental Combat Team usually deploys when on alert, is flooded, so all the vehicles are here in the Kaserne. The noise is deafening: tanks, jeeps, half-tracks, armored personnel carriers and trucks, moving in and out of position. If any American Army unit needs to be ready at all times it is this one. A Russian jet could take off from communist territory and be here in four minutes.

Last week Captain Sadler, a helicopter pilot, invited me to accompany him on a flight over the flooded Danube. I wanted to see the flood area and he wanted me to help him deliver some bundles of burlap bags to be filled with sand and used by the engineers for flood control. The flood wasn't as bad as I expected – maybe because I live in Memphis where we are somewhat accustomed to such phenomena. We landed several times and delivered the bags to U. S. Army engineers who were doing a great job of flood control. They are somewhat disappointed in the effort being made by the Germans who live here and who are supposed to be helping to contain the flood. The Germans seem inclined to sit back and let the Army do all the work. Some of these soldiers have *worked fifteen hours a day for a week and are not very happy about the local help – or rather, lack of help.*

*   *   *

Although there was no mention of it in the above letter – nor would there be in any subsequent letter -- our trip from Stuttgart to Staubing the previous week, had been eventful.

We had left Echterdingen Airfield on the morning of July 12. The weather was ideal; a sunny day. What occurred en route is described in the following report I wrote at the request of the trial team, Law officer Fenig, Defense Counsel Hamm and Court Reporter Hall, on their and my own behalf. The report, describing the events of the flight and in praise of the skill of pilot Captain Hix, was sent to the chief of staff of VII Corps and later placed in the Hix's personnel (201) file.

Date: 22 July 1954

To: Chief of Staff

Through: Staff Judge Advocate

From: Captain Edward Fenig, 1/Lt John J. Thomason, 1/Lt O. K. Hamm and DA Civilian Jerry B. Hall

Subject: Captain William J. Hix

> *1.   The undersigned persons, Captain Edward Fenig, 1/Lt John J Thomason, 1/Lt O. K. Hamm and DA Civilian Jerry B. Hall, all of the JA Section, Headquarters VIIth Corps, were passengers in a twin engine L-23 aircraft on Monday, 12 July 1954. This plane was piloted by Captain William J. Hix, Headquarters Company, VII Corps.*

2. The above parties departed Echterdingen Airfield at approximately 0920 destined for Mansfield Kaserne, Straubing, Germany, where the passengers were to participate in general courts-martial activities during the following week. After having been airborne for approximately thirteen minutes the aircraft was suddenly and without warning subjected to a severe jolt followed by vibrations of a most serious nature. At the instant of the initial shock the right wing pitched downward at a disquieting angle and the starboard engine and the entire aircraft began to shake violently. Almost immediately Captain Hix halted the crippled engine and was able to right the craft, quiet the engine disturbances and set a return course for Echterdingen. The return trip was completed on one engine, the starboard propeller having broken and the broken portion of the propeller having passed through and damaged the fuselage of the aircraft.

3. The prospect of landing under such conditions was viewed by the passengers with apprehension. To our great relief, however, Captain Hix managed to return the aircraft to the airfield without further difficulty. The landing itself would have been considered quite superior under the most ideal circumstances.

4. Subsequent to this incident the undersigned persons have learned that the starboard engine of the aircraft was nearly severed from the wing. Apparently, we were in far greater personal danger than we had suspected; that such imminent danger was not appreciated at the time may be explained only by Captain Hix's quiet demeanor and masterful piloting of the aircraft. We should like to record our profound appreciation of Captain Hix's proficiency as a pilot and his performance during the incident described.

*   *   *

The incident report was signed by the four of us and sent up the chain of command.

Notwithstanding the sterile military language of the report, the broken propeller incident was quite unnerving. The noise when the propeller broke and about one third of the blade went through the airplane sounded like an explosion. The pilot acted quickly, shut down the disabled engine, brought the plane back to level flight, radioed the tower and completed a one hundred eighty-degree turn heading back to the airport. When the airfield came into view we saw ambulances, fire trucks and staff cars lined up on both sides of the runway. That is when I really got worried. None of us had parachutes on although there were two in the plane. Making a quick assessment, I determined that I ranked third in seniority, behind the two Captains -- no parachute for me. The matter of seniority was of no consequence, however. We were flying too low for anyone to have had time to strap on a parachute, bail out and escape from the disabled aircraft before a possible crash.

Captain Hix made a masterful landing on one engine – smooth as silk. When we finally got on the ground and warily inspected the damage, we observed that all the rivets and mechanical fasteners holding the starboard engine in its cowling on the wing had been sheared. The only engine support still holding the heavy motor in place was the flexible fuel and oil lines leading to each of the cylinders. Had those failed and the engine fallen away, the airplane would surely have become unstable, lost its ability to fly, and without doubt we would have crashed. It was indeed a close call; a near fatal accident of which my parents never learned.

From the airport we went back into downtown Stuttgart and caught the next train for Straubing and arrived there safely but much later than originally anticipated.

*   *   *

THE TIMES: August 1954. The French proposed the creation of a "European Army," which would include German soldiers. A treaty was prepared establishing such a European combat force, including twelve German divisions. Other member nations were to contribute their forces but would retain national military identity. West Germany, by contrast, would not. Germany would have no national force, no ministry of defense, or general staff.

Although a French idea, in August 1954 the French National Assembly, afraid of re-awakening German militarism, rejected the treaty and killed the plan. Fortunately, the feared Soviet invasion did not occur and after Stalin's death in March 1953, new Soviet leadership seemed more interested in peaceful co-existence and appeared ready to negotiate with the West.

*   *   *

By the end of July 1954, a bowling alley and tennis courts had been constructed at Kelley Barracks. In the summer the sun didn't

250

set until almost nine p.m., so, frequently we could get in three sets of tennis after work. Opportunities for recreational exercise elsewhere, however, were rare, except that golf was available at Mansfield Kaserne in Straubing. In contrast, Germans enjoyed many forms of sports and often formed clubs where they banded together to participate in a favored recreational activity. In later years, Americans were welcomed into many of the German sports clubs, however, in the early fifties there was not much cross participation. Occasionally, a German boxing club would come to Kelley Barracks for competitive fights in most weight divisions, but since in those days the Germans didn't play baseball or football and we didn't play soccer, there was little other sports competition between us. The American occupation of Germany ended in May, 1955, almost exactly ten years after the conclusion of World War II. From then on American soldiers were in Germany not as occupation troops but by agreement between the American and German governments. Sports opportunities for Americans improved when the occupation ended and joint German-American sports activity became common. However, there were other opportunities for recreation.

Movie theaters featuring fairly current cinema offerings were available at all the military installations. One evening at Mansfield Kaserne after viewing a film, I was walking back to the transient officers quarters when a captain with whom I was slightly acquainted fell into step beside me.

"Interested in some night flying?" he inquired.

It was a clear night; there was no moon but the stars were out and shinning brightly. The captain was an army flyer. Even after the U. S. Army Air Corps became the Air Force in 1947, some aviators

251

remained in the army. They flew various small, propeller driven aircraft including the twin engine six passenger Beechcraft L-23, single engine two passenger Cessna L-19 "Birddog" reconnaissance planes and helicopters.

The L-19 resembled the well-known fabric covered, always yellow Piper Cub. However, it was all aluminum, a high winged observation plane, with lots of windows and short take-off and landing requirements. Built by Cessna and painted olive drab, the Birddog was very maneuverable, slow and easy to fly.

"What do you have in mind?" I asked.

"I've got an L-19 out on the strip," the captain said, "and I need to get in some night flying time before the end of the month. I thought you might want to go along for an hour or so. It's a beautiful night for flying."

"It sure is," I agreed. "Let's go."

It wasn't far to the airstrip where the plane was parked. As we strolled over to the hangar we talked about the movie I assumed we both had seen that night. In fact, the captain had seen the movie on the previous night. This evening, while I had been at the movie the captain had been at the officer's club bar. I didn't realize that until later.

I hopped in the front seat after the captain was settled in the rear, and we took off. It was pretty late and not many lights were visible. After we climbed to about 1,500 feet and flew the short distance to the town of Straubing, the captain shouted to me, over the engine noise,

"Let's have some fun. We'll make these Krauts think World War III has started."

With that, he turned off the ignition, pushed the stick forward into a shallow dive with the airspeed turning the propeller and, after about ten seconds turned the ignition switch back on, which caused the engine to backfire. Indeed, the sound of the tremendous backfire explosion sounded as loud as a huge cannon and lights began to appear in the town.

The captain thought his prank and the reaction of the townspeople was very funny, so he repeated the trick several times. By now there were lights on all over Straubing, and I'm sure if the German air force had still existed its interceptor squadrons would have scrambled.

I didn't think his joke was very funny but I knew of nothing that I could do to bring a stop to the captain's antics. After a while he wearied of the game and turned back toward the Kaserne.

"Do you know how to fly?" he shouted to me.

"I've taken the controls a few times," I shouted back, "but I've never had any lessons."

"Go ahead." I heard the captain say. "You've got it!"

I had only rarely flown a plane and never before at night and had difficulty seeing where the earth met the sky. I found myself "chasing" the indicator on the artificial horizon instrument in the plane so that we were experiencing a slight roller coaster ride.

I turned back to the captain, "You'd better take it back. I'm not comfortable with this."

"You're doing fine," he replied. "Look at the horizon. Don't chase the needle."

But I couldn't see the horizon and my performance didn't improve. At length, upon my repeated insistence the captain took back the controls.

"I think I'll do some touch-and-go landings." I heard him shout. "I need the night practice."

We flew toward the airstrip until we had it in sight; then he started down.

Our first landing was not a good one. We hit the runway on one wheel and a wing tip. The pilot immediately poured on the power and we were climbing again. I was beginning to get suspicious.

"Did you go to the movie tonight?" I shouted.

"No, I went last night," he yelled in reply.

"Where had you been when we met on the walk?"

"The 'O' club," he said.

I didn't pursue the point but I was sure he had been at the bar. About that time we made another landing, a little – but not much - better than the first one. How was I going to get out of this? I pondered. I was afraid that I might make him angry if I accused him of being drunk, and besides that, he was a captain and I was a lieutenant. I didn't know what to do, but I was positive I needed to get out of that airplane.

"I've got to go to the toilet," I shouted.

"You should have thought of that before we took off."

"I know it, but I didn't. I really need to go, bad."

We circled back to the strip and landed. The captain taxied to a stop in front of the hangar. I jumped out of the plane. The captain taxied away and took off again. I think he was tiring of my company and I know I was tiring of his.

*   *   *

<u>UNITED STATES</u>

<u>V.</u>

<u>SAMUEL A. CARVER</u>

On the afternoon of May 22, 1954, Sergeant Samuel A. Carver left Mansfield Kaserne where he was stationed and went to the nearby town of Straubing. He had a pass and was supposed to be back at the Kaserne no later than 1:00 a.m. He actually returned at about 4:30 a.m. As he entered the main gate, he showed his pass to the gate guard, Corporal Pannett, who took it from him and refused to return it. Pannett had orders to take and hold the passes of any soldiers coming in after 1:00 a.m.

Carver protested Pannett's action. Since he was only following orders, Pannett suggested that Carver see the officer of the day at the nearby guardhouse, a small building close to the gate where ten or so off duty guards slept and the OD had his desk. Carver walked across the street to the guardhouse but the OD, after listening to Carver's complaint, refused to intervene on his behalf and sent him on his way. Carver returned to the main gate, asked Corporal Pannett to identify himself and upon receiving his name threatened to kill Pannett. Pannett thought the threat to be only the idle chatter of a drunk and dismissed it, but Carver warned the corporal a second time and then stomped angrily away toward his company area.

An hour later, Carver appeared in his company orderly room, surreptitiously obtained the keys to the arms room and removed two carbines. Moving a selection lever on these weapons allowed them to be fired one round at a time, or on full automatic. In the latter mode the rifle continues to fire as long as the trigger is held back.

Carver then went to the ammunition dump, surprised and held up the guard on duty there, threatened him and tied him hand and foot with wire he ripped from the telephone. He next filled his pockets and a pack with more than 500 rounds of carbine ammunition, located the keys to a truck parked close by, detached a trailer from the truck and headed back in the truck to the main gate.

Meanwhile, the 6:00 a.m. guard relief had been posted and an ill-fated Corporal Shelton had replaced Corporal Pannett at the Kaserne entrance. Corporals Shelton and Pannett were of similar height and build and were dressed alike. Corporal Shelton and a German civilian policeman were inside the gatehouse, a small structure in the middle of the Kaserne access road, the entrance to one side of the gatehouse, the exit to the other. Carver drove the truck to the exit side of the gate and stopped, so that the gatehouse was on the driver's side of the truck. As Corporal Shelton stepped from the gatehouse to check the truck driver's identification papers, Carver pushed the two carbines through the open truck window and opened automatic fire, point blank.

Corporal Shelton went down. Carver stepped from the truck and fired more shots into his prostrate body. A total of about 25 entrance and exit bullet wounds were later found on Shelton's corpse. It was estimated that he had been shot thirteen times. Carver then turned his attention to the unarmed German civilian guard.

The German ran outside the gatehouse, keeping it between himself and his assailant, as Carver fired both carbines from the hip. Luckily, none of the shots found its mark.

Lieutenant Goellner, the officer of the day, aroused by the noise of the first burst of gunshots, ran from the guardhouse to investigate. He quickly appraised the situation and, being unarmed, retreated back into the building. Carver shouted at him and sent a burst of gunfire through the guardhouse door behind him. The door splintered as Goellner closed it but no one was hurt.

Lieutenant Goellner armed himself and, from inside the guardhouse, attempted to engage Carver in a gunfight. Carver, however, took cover beside the guardhouse outside wall, where he was out of Goellner's line of fire, and reloaded the clips to both his carbines. Other soldiers inside the guardhouse attempted to get out, but each time the door moved, Carver fired several rounds through it, effectively containing the relief guards within. Meanwhile Lieutenant Goellner, armed with a carbine and five rounds of ammunition, slipped out a rear window so he could approach Carver from the side.

Goellner fired and called on Carver to surrender. Carver's reply was another burst of gunfire. Goellner fired again as Carver dashed back from the gate, taking cover behind a parked truck about thirty yards away. Looking under the truck Lieutenant Goellner saw Carver's legs and fired his third shot in an effort to ricochet the bullet from the pavement beneath the truck up into Carver's body. He was successful, wounding Carver in the knee, but the fugitive limped away from the truck and took shelter behind a tree further up the street as Goellner fired his fourth round.

Carver reloaded the clips for both carbines and settled in behind the tree for a duel to the death with Lieutenant Goellner. The officer knew he had but one shot left and so maneuvered to a position where he had a clear field of fire. While Carver directed his concentration toward his front, where he had last seen the officer of the day, Goellner achieved the situation he sought, stood with his carbine raised to his shoulder in firing position -- Carver firmly in his sights -- and told the renegade sergeant to surrender or be shot.

Carver, realizing that his position was untenable, threw down his weapons and gave up. He had been wounded in the knee and the chest during the exchange. Lieutenant Goellner was two for four, with one shot remaining.

*   *   *

Carver was charged with premeditated murder, robbery and assault with intent to commit murder in violation of Articles 118, 122 and 134 of the Uniform Code of Military Justice. Lieutenant Colonel Hodges was named law officer. Recently promoted Major Fenig and I were appointed trial counsel (prosecutors); Major Ailor, borrowed from the SJA office of the 43rd Division in Augsburg, and Lieutenant Addis were appointed to the defense. The trial was set for July 28, 1954 at Straubing, but was continued at the request of the defense so that Carver could be subjected to a psychiatric evaluation.

The trial began on Wednesday, 25 August 1954, at Mansfield Kaserne. The eleven-member court consisted of three full colonels, four lieutenant colonels and four majors. The prosecution sought the death penalty. For that sentence to be imposed, the law required all members of the court to concur. From the evidence it was clear there was no factual question to be decided; only the question of an appropriate punishment was in dispute.

Major Ailor was unknown to us but appeared to be an effective trial lawyer. We knew Dave Addis was experienced, capable and smart. We expected Addis to take the lead for the defense, and we were correct. Major Fenig and I divided up the prosecution responsibilities equally, except that Fenig undertook the most difficult task – cross-examination of the defense psychiatric expert. As prosecutors, we believed the facts of this premeditated and brutal murder called for the capital punishment of the accused; therefore, our task was to obtain a unanimous verdict imposing the death penalty. The task confronting the defense was to convince one member of the court that the accused should not be put to death. The goal of Carver's defense, simply put, was to prevent his execution.

The usual sequence of events in a criminal trail, military or civilian, is for the prosecution to present its case following which the defense offers its proof. Thus, we were prepared to call the witnesses for the prosecution when the Carver court convened. To our surprise, however, when we asked the defense attorneys at the beginning of the trial how did Carver plead, guilty or not guilty, Lieutenant Addis stood and said,

"The defense moves for a finding of not guilty as to all charges and specifications by reason of the fact that the accused, Samuel A. Carver, was legally insane at the time these events occurred."

"Further," he continued, "before the defense enters a plea of guilty or not guilty, we request permission to call witnesses and adduce other evidence in support of our motion."

Of course, permission was granted and so, the defense began to establish the facts of the case by summoning the witnesses the prosecution had intended to call and a few we had not.

Some of the evidence offered by the defense in support of the insanity motion did paint a strange picture of Carver. It was shown that when he returned to the Kaserne early that morning he carried a live bird in his hand, which he petted occasionally with one finger. It was also established that he had concealed a kitchen knife under his shirt and that when he had appeared in his company orderly room and awakened the soldier stationed there, he stood silently for a time looking down at the soldier, holding the bird in one hand and the knife in the other. Of course, Carver, a sergeant in the company, was well known to the personnel of the orderly room. They had no reason to be suspicious of him. Carver knew the location of the keys to the arms room and had no difficulty in acquiring them, unlocking the arms room door and removing two carbines. A dead bird was later found in the doorway to the arms room, after Carver had stolen the two weapons.

Defense witnesses testified that Carver had been drinking; that he had a vicious temper when under the influence of alcohol and that in the past, when intoxicated, he had become violent. In addition to the lay witnesses who testified about Carver's unusual behavior, sometimes even when sober, the defense called an expert witness, Captain August, a physician and psychiatrist who testified at length as to the accused's sanity at the time of the offenses.

Based on Carver's history, the facts of the occurrence and his personal interviews with the accused, Captain August voiced his opinion that Carver was suffering from a form of insanity known as schizophrenia.   He testified that at the time these offenses were committed, Carver was unable to distinguish right from wrong and was, therefore, not responsible for his actions.

The defense expert psychiatric witness was then vigorously, and I thought, effectively cross-examined by Major Fenig. It seemed to me that Captain August had overblown his credentials, exaggerated his experience and inflated his expertise.   Fenig tore into him with sarcasm and scorn in an effort to belittle his expert opinion.

Beginning his cross-examination, seemingly with unsophisticated curiosity, Major Fenig queried,

"Captain August, I believe you stated on direct examination that you are chief of the psychiatric department at the Augsburg Military Hospital, is that correct?"

"Yes, that is true," said Captain August assuredly. "I am chief of the department."

"And how many others are in the psychiatric department of the Augsburg Military Hospital?" Major Fenig inquired.

Captain August registered confusion.

"What do you mean?"

Without hesitation, Major Fenig explained what he meant. "How many other people are assigned to and work with you in the department of psychiatry of the Augsburg Military Hospital?"

Captain August hesitated, then answered with slightly less assurance.

"Well, actually, I'm the only one in the department," said the psychiatrist, apprehensively.

"So, you're the chief and all the Indians as well. You're the whole tribe. Is that correct?"

August didn't answer.

Fenig went on, relentlessly. Utilizing medical and psychiatric textbooks and articles from authoritative journals furnished to him by the expert psychiatrists for the prosecution, Major Fenig disputed Captain August's opinions, questioned his methods and contradicted his conclusions. He derided the assertion that the viciousness of the murder was evidence of insanity and that the presumably murdered bird was significant in making a determination of Carver's guilt or the appropriateness of his punishment.

Captain August must have thought the cross-examination lasted for a long, long time. He seemed uncomfortable. His suave assurance melted in the face of questions framed by an experienced trial lawyer who had done his homework. His opinions, so well expressed on direct examination, were less convincing when closely examined or disputed. Although Fenig was effective in puncturing the expert's theories and discrediting his opinions, Captain August was unswerving in his ultimate conclusion, that Carver was legally insane.

One member of the court, Major Kelley, was obviously offended by Fenig's vigorous cross-examination. He seized upon the right of a court-martial member to ask questions as a means to discredit Major Fenig's attack and rebuild the credibility and prestige of Captain August, whose testimony Kelley apparently believed. From Major Kelley's questions and comments it was obvious that he thought August had been unfairly belittled. As a stratagem, he claimed to be interested in the principles of psychiatry and sought to have the defense expert verify his beliefs, which we perceived to be favorable to Carver.

*　　　*　　　*

Dear Mother and Dad,　　　　　　　　　*26 August 1954*

I am writing this letter under rather peculiar circumstances. It is now 11 p.m. on the second day of the trial of U. S. v. Carver. The charge is premeditated murder.

Court was adjourned at 3 p.m. this afternoon when the prosecution requested and was granted a continuance until tomorrow so that we could fly in another psychiatrist; he will be the fourth such expert witness to testify.

Actually, the accused has not yet pleaded to the charges. We are still hearing evidence on a motion made by the defense to dismiss all the charges and specifications by reason of the fact that the accused, at the time of the offense, was unable to distinguish right from wrong or to adhere to the right. However, all the evidence on the merits of the case has been introduced in support of the defense motion and once there is a ruling on the motion the trial will just about be over.

We were taken by surprise by the defense tactic. In presenting evidence in support of the motion the defense called almost every one of the witnesses we had intended to call and examined them as if they were defense witnesses. That tactic made our task somewhat easier since we were thus allowed to cross-examine our own witnesses by asking leading questions. We were also able to introduce some evidence not otherwise likely to be admitted as part of the prosecution proof and, since the defense could not ask leading questions of its own witnesses, some testimony we felt might be unfavorable to the prosecution side of the case was not introduced.

The only obstacle for the prosecution in this case arises from the fact that the defense is able to produce an expert witness, a psychiatrist, whose opinion is that the accused was not responsible for his acts on the day he shot and killed the gate guard at this Kaserne. We have presented two examining psychiatrists who disagree with that opinion. A third will testify tomorrow morning. But now we have another problem.

One member of the court, a major, has from the outset, by his comments and questions lead us to believe that he is prejudiced in favor of the accused. His bias became particularly clear after Major Fenig's cross-examination of the defense expert. It is evident that he resented a perfectly legitimate, although spirited, inquiry into the qualifications and opinions of the defense psychiatrist. I think he has accepted the theory of the defense expert and is not listening to the contrary testimony of our better-qualified witnesses. Our remedy is to challenge him for cause. If we do that the court will vote on whether to sustain our challenge. The challenged member will not be allowed to vote – that leaves ten. We need a majority, six votes, to sustain the challenge. We expect to make the challenge tomorrow morning. If we lose the challenge I expect that Carver will escape the death penalty because the challenged major will defeat the unanimity required to impose that sentence; if we win the challenge I think the decision of the court will be unanimous and Carver will be sentenced to death.

*   *   *

Next morning, the third and final prosecution expert witness, an imminently qualified and experienced practicing psychiatrist testified in rebuttal to Captain August. All three of the prosecution experts opined that based upon their knowledge and experience as psychiatrists and their examinations and interviews with Carver, he was sane at the time the offenses were committed; that he knew right from wrong and, if he had wanted to do so, could have adhered to the right.

Then a series of unusual procedural events took place.

The defense motion for a dismissal of all the charges on the ground that the accused was insane was withdrawn. Apparently the defense had made the motion so that the defense lawyers would be in control of the order of proof and the sequence of witnesses. Then defense counsel, on behalf of Carver, entered a plea of "Not guilty by reason of insanity." The effect of the plea was to remove the determination of Carver's sanity from the law officer, who, in ruling on the motion, would have decided the question as one of law. It was now the responsibility of the court to make a factual decision as to Craver's sanity based on the proof and the conflicting expert testimony concerning his mental capacity.

The prosecution announced that all the evidence had been adduced and that it would call no additional witnesses. Then, the prosecution rested.

The defense announced it had no other witnesses to call. The defense rested.

At that point the prosecution, taking a most unusual step, challenged Major Kelley, the court member, for cause, and requested permission to question him under oath.

Permission was granted by the law officer, and Major Kelley took the witnesses stand.

The court member's testimony as to his own mental attitude appeared, as suspected, to favor the accused and support the expert opinions of Captain August. It was obvious, however, that Major Kelley wished to remain on the court and participate in the deliberations, so he vacillated in his responses in what we thought was a transparent effort to show that he was even handed. He insisted that he was not prejudiced in favor of either side. Then the challenged court member, Kelley, made a critical error.

In summing up his position, Major Kelley stated that if he were called upon to decide a close question he "might be inclined to bend over backwards in favor of the prosecution."

The defense, even in the face of that comment, stated it had no objection to Major Kelley's continued participation. The prosecution, however, seized upon Kelly's remark arguing that such a predisposition did violence to the principles of the presumption of innocence and the necessity of the prosecution proving its case beyond a reasonable doubt. Kelley had said, in effect, that deliberations should be undertaken with the scales of justice weighted in favor of the government. Although Kelley's other statements, questions and remarks indicated a prejudice in favor of the accused, his assertion that he "might bend over backwards in favor of the prosecution" put him in an untenable position. At the beginning of a court martial trial, court members take an oath that they will "faithfully and impartially try (the case), according to the evidence, (their) conscience and the laws and regulations provided for trial by courts-martial." They are not allowed to "bend over backwards" for either side.

When the prosecution's challenge of Major Kelley, to remove him from the trial panel for cause, was voted on by the other members of the court, the challenge was sustained. A disgruntled Major Kelley departed. And then there were ten.

All the proof on the charges having been heard, it was time for closing arguments by the lawyers and instructions pertaining to the applicable law from the law officer. First came the instructions, then the summations. Since the prosecution was required to carry the burden of proof, we had the right to argue first; then the defense had an opportunity to respond and finally the prosecution could reply to the defense, but the total time allowed to each side for summation was equal. I opened for the government.

In a letter home, dated 2 October 1954, I wrote:

Unknown to me, Major Fenig had several copies of my closing argument in the Carver case prepared by the court reporter. That is quite a compliment. He did not go to the same trouble with respect to his own remarks. He said he wanted the transcript for his own use but I suspect he did it because he knew I had worked so hard in preparing it and thought I would like to have a copy. Anyway, I am happy to have the record and am enclosing a duplicate for your critique.

*   *   *

TC: (1ˢᵗ Lt Thomason): Gentlemen. By reason of the withdrawal by the defense of the motion to dismiss, all the evidence is at long last before the court. You have only to hear the summation of counsel and the instructions of the law officer before retiring to determine the issues that have been brought before you. The time for decision is close at hand.

On behalf of Major Fenig, and on my own behalf, I would like to express my appreciation to the court, both individually and collectively. You have obviously weighed every word of each witness. We thank your for your attention to the witnesses and your patience with counsel.

No court proceeding could be more important than this one. You decide today whether Samuel Carver shall live or shall suffer the law's most severe penalty. And so, we submit this inquiry to you in the name of our cause, in the name of justice and in the name of Corporal Frank Shelton, who died a little more than three months ago today.

*   *   *

We congratulate the defense team, Major Ailor and Lieutenant Addis. They have ably managed the task assigned to them. They have shattered all the laws of physics – they have created something where there was nothing. Through them Samuel Carver has been given shelter in the very law he has defied. Psychiatry is their smoke screen.

It would appear from the questions asked by the defense and from the manner in which they presented the defense case, that the facts here are not contested. It is the meaning of those facts about which we differ. It would appear that the defense is eager for you to forget the circumstances of this brutal killing. The defense cannot fight us on the issues, so by concentrating on Carver's state of mind rather than the brutality of his act they have engaged the prosecution in a sort of rear guard action, a sniper's indirect tactic. But, shocking and repulsive as they may be, the facts must be placed before you.

Captain August, a psychiatrist from Augsburg, tells us that we should not punish Carver for his appalling deed. He would have us believe that, by gazing into the past, he is able to determine the mental condition of the accused on the day in question. Indeed, he was able to ascertain the mental condition of the accused's grandfather, though he has never seen the grandfather.

He says his deductions are not based on the events that occurred on May 23rd last, but upon events that took place years ago. No matter what Carver might have done on that fateful day, Captain August says he cannot be held responsible for his acts because of his background. So says Captain August.

Let us follow the reasoning of Captain August to its reasonable conclusion. If a person has a background like Carver's – and there must be millions with backgrounds much worse – such a person may commit any crime – no matter how brutal, and may commit such crime at any time – no matter how far removed in time from the particular formation of this background, and do so with impunity. If, like Carver, this accused once insulted his first sergeant, once stabbed another with a fountain pen, has one distant relative who is demented and two others who are imprisoned, and last of all, should this accused have Captain August available as a witness in his defense, then you are to believe that this person is to be granted some sort of immunity and may not be punished for his misdeeds. In other words, we are asked to judge Carver by the tale he has told his psychiatrist and to overlook what the evidence shows us he did.

But let us review the facts. These facts show us that Carver was sane, that he was and is responsible, and – most important – that he planned to murder, and murdered according to his plan

*   *   *

At this point in the summation, the testimony of eleven witnesses was reviewed and analyzed. It was the contention of the prosecution that this testimony, and the evidence in its entirety supported a factual finding of sanity, stratagem, planning, malice and premeditation.

Then a series of rhetorical questions were posed for defense counsel to answer, if they chose to do so. And finally,

*   *   *

Gentlemen, a brutal killing such as has been described in these proceedings, tempts counsel to speak in flowery terms on an emotional plane. I have tried to avoid that. We do not appeal to your emotions. We appeal to your common sense and sound judgment. We do not ask that you hate Samuel Carver; we ask only that you hate his deed and punish him for his crime. Mercy to him is but cruelty to others.

This court has a burdensome task before it. Your duty this day is not to be envied. But, gentlemen, in a sense, you are not passing judgment. You are reviewing a judgment already passed.

The verdict in this case was reached on Sunday, the 23rd of May 1954. Thirteen steel-jacketed .30 caliber votes were cast then and there, and the judge who cast then was the accused himself.

*   *   *

Carver was found guilty of all the charges and specifications. The final phase of the proceeding was for the court to hear matters in aggravation, mitigation and extenuation relevant to the sentence. The defense reminded the court of Captain August's testimony and urged the members to take Carver's deprived background and questionable mental condition into account in considering what his punishment should be.

The court adjourned to begin its deliberations. The law officer, the lawyers, the accused and his guards remained in the courtroom. Major Fenig paced, stopping from time to time to look out the window. Lt. Addis sat with his elbows on the defense counsel table, his chin resting on tented fingertips, staring vacantly into space. Major Ailor and Lt. Col. Hodges engaged in conversation. I unsuccessfully attempted to write a letter and nervously smoked several cigarettes. Carver, closely guarded but calm and detached, scanned a newspaper.

After about an hour there was a knock on the door of the deliberations room, the court members filed back in, took their seats and the court came to order. The faces of the court members gave no hint of the verdict. They were uniformly without expression.

The president of the court aligned some papers by holding the edges with both hands, and tapping the bottom of the lot against his desktop. Then he laid the documents on his desk, smoothed them, looked up and addressed the accused.

"Private Carver," said the senior colonel, president of the court. "You will please stand and face the members of the court."

Carver did so without speaking. He had been a sergeant and I could see the stitch marks on his sleeve where his chevrons had been.

The sentence was about to be delivered. I knew the key would be in the number of members of the court concurring in the sentence. The death penalty required a unanimous vote, *all members concurring.* Surely, Carver knew that too.

When Carver stood he had pushed back his chair which made a scraping noise on the wooden floor. Now there was not a sound.

"Private Carver," said the Colonel, "it is my duty as president of this court to inform you that the court, in closed session and upon secret written ballot, *all of the members present at the time the vote was taken, concurring…*"

272

Because the president of the court had said *all ... the members ... concurring* I thought I knew what was coming next. Even so, I wasn't prepared. It was a shock.

"...upon your conviction of premeditated murder, assault with the intent to commit murder and robbery, sentences you to be put to death."

Carver saluted. Somebody with the guards said, "Remove the prisoner," and they took him away.

*   *   *

Even today, almost fifty years later, in my mind, I can recreate that moment when Carver was sentenced to death. I can see him standing stiffly at attention, meeting the sentencing colonel's gaze. I can see Major Ailor and Lieutenant Addis staring down at the yellow legal pads on their desks, and Major Fenig, his eyes narrowed with intense concentration, as he scanned the faces of the court members. I can see Carver salute the court when the guards approached to remove him, smartly execute an about face, and, after being handcuffed, stride from the courtroom, with never a glance in my direction.

Someone once asked me, "Who decides whether the prosecution will ask for the death penalty, and how did you feel when the court granted your request and imposed it?"

As to the first part of the question, I am not certain. I know at some early point in the preparation of the prosecution case, Major Fenig told me, "We are going to ask for the death penalty," but frankly, I didn't think much about it. I knew military law provided for such a penalty in cases of premeditated murder, mutiny and rape, and I thought the circumstances of the Carver case clearly indicated the former. In time of war the list of capital offenses is expanded to include aiding the enemy, desertion, misbehavior before the enemy, attempting to compel a superior to surrender, willfully disobeying a superior officer, etc., and upon conviction of spying in time of war, the death penalty is mandatory.

I knew also that in a case where the death penalty was applicable, trial counsel could properly ask, "Does any member of the court have any conscientious scruples against imposing the death penalty in a proper case?" A prospective court member who answered affirmatively was subject to challenge for cause. We asked that question in the Carver case. Trial lawyers who try criminal cases know that posing such a question to a court or jury indicates that the prosecution seeks a sentence of death.

Military law provided that the death penalty may not be adjudged if the convening authority, here the commanding general of VII Corps, had directed that the case be treated as not capital. No such direction was made in the Carver case.

To put the final nail in the coffin, so to speak, a prosecutor asks for or "demands" the death penalty by asking the appropriate qualifying question when interrogating prospective members of the court or jury, to be certain no one is scrupulously opposed to it; then, in closing argument, by specifically asking for, or demanding that such sentence be imposed.

As to the second part of the question, how I felt when the sentence I had requested was handed down, I was stunned.

I favor capital punishment in proper cases, but not strongly. Surely, the rape and murder of a defenseless child, upon a certain conviction, warrants the death penalty, as does the mass murder of unsuspecting innocents for political purposes.

If I had been a member of the Carver court, in 1954, I would have voted for the maximum penalty, death. On the same court today, with fifty years of law practice behind me, I'm not so sure.

However, I can say with certainty, my participation in that trial, under the profoundly solemn procedures of the American system of military justice, only a few miles from communist territory, where the death penalty is routinely effected without fanfare or due process was an unforgettable and gratifying, although sobering, experience.

*   *   *

THE TIMES: September 1954. When the Chinese Nationalists led by Chiang Kai-shek retreated from mainland China in 1949, leaving it to the communist People's Republic, and established themselves in what was then called Formosa (now Taiwan), the United States adopted a policy not to interfere. However, when the Korean War began, President Truman designated the Formosa Straits, between Formosa and China, as neutral territory and sent in the U. S. Navy to keep peace - primarily by blockading Formosa and preventing the Nationalist forces from attacking the mainland.

When the Korean War ended, President Eisenhower lifted the blockade. During the summer of 1954, about 75,000 Chinese Nationalist troops were transferred from Formosa to the islands of Quemoy and Matsu, both less than 10 miles from the mainland. In response to that troop movement, the communists on the mainland began an artillery barrage against the Nationalist forces on Quemoy during September 1954. U. S. politicians and diplomats supported the Nationalists while searching for some means to end the conflict. The use of atomic weaponry in support of Nationalist China was suggested and that prospect was openly discussed. President Eisenhower's rhetoric and treatment of the Chinese Communists was harsh and diplomatic relations rapidly deteriorated.

TWO WEEKS LEAVE: THE LOW COUNTRIES, ENGLAND, AND FRANCE

The town of Freudenstadt sits on the edge of the Black Forest, two-thirds of the way from Stuttgart to the French city of Strasbourg. It is west of Stuttgart, at the east end of the "Black Forest Highway" which begins in Freudenstadt and runs through a succession of charming little villages in delightful natural settings to Baden-Baden. Founded in 1601 by the Duke of Württemberg and nourished by its silver mines, Freudenstadt became a significant attraction for visitors to the area, probably because it boasts more days of sunshine each year than any other German resort. The town displays a large central square surrounded by Renaissance arches, cafes and shops.

One spring day Bill Bonwell and I drove to Baden Baden and, because the weather was so beautiful we luckily decided to take the long way back to Stuttgart, through Freudenstadt. As we approached an outdoor café near the town center we observed two young ladies having a cup of tea at a table for four.

We circled the block, parked the Morris and inquired about the possibility of our occupying the empty chairs. Upon being welcomed we introduced ourselves and soon learned that we were in the company of two English employees of the British legation in Strasbourg. It was Sunday. They had come over by bus on their holiday to see the Schwarzwald and were required to be back at their desks on Monday morning.

After an hour or so of easy conversation it occurred to us, since these Britishers had never been to Germany before, and the weather was ideal for a drive -- the top was down on my convertible – that we should take them on a short scenic tour, terminating with supper in Stuttgart from which there was frequent train service to Strasbourg. They could depart Stuttgart around ten, and after a two-hour train ride, easily get to their lodgings for almost a full nights sleep and be in the foreign office on time on Monday. They agreed to the plan and off we went.

One of the young ladies, Daphene Low, lived near London and after we had all gotten to know each other and when she learned that Bill and I were planning to visit England in September, invited us to stop by her home in Surrey and meet her family. She had handed me the envelope of a letter from her father so that I could copy her home address. I noticed that her father's name was preceded by the title "sir" which I surmised must mean that he was a knight. I thought a visit to the Low's residence might well be interesting.

Two months later Bill and I departed Germany for the Low Countries, England and France. After driving through Belgium and Holland, putting the car on a ferry and crossing the English Channel we finally arrived in Surrey on the designated day but about two hours later than we had expected. The Low's address was strange to us; no house number, just the name of the house, the name of the street and the name of the county and town: High Gardens,

Hollybank Road, Hook Heath, Woking, Surrey. I don't know how anyone could find such a location unless there happened to be someone available from whom directions might be obtained. After having the way pointed out to us, we finally arrived, tardy and apologetic.

Nonetheless, the Low family, including Daphene, Sir Richard, Lady Caroline, and Daphene's two brothers, had waited, offered us a drink (Scotch Whisky -- without ice) and entertained us for an hour or so in the dark paneled great room of their baronial home. Bill's date, Petrinella, was also there waiting for us. Soon the four of us went out for supper in the nearby town of Woking.

The Low's had booked rooms for us at a nearby hotel. When we returned, late, and after taking our dates home we were introduced to the custom of having to ring the front bell of the hotel in order to wake the doorman, or desk clerk, or whatever he was, to let us in. He was very grouchy about it and made it quite clear that he disapproved of anybody staying out as late as we had, especially Americans escorting English girls. He muttered something, reminding me that in World War II a common English complaint about American servicemen was that "they are overpaid, over sexed and over here."

The next day provided a perfect, sunny opportunity to see the sights of London. Daphene and Petrinella ushered us to many points of interest, some of which they had not previously seen themselves. Near the end of the day we stopped in a café for a glass of wine and with boldness, I decided to tell a joke that necessarily employed the use of what I thought to be my rather clever English accent. When I had delivered the punch line of the story, the laughter of our companions exceeded the level of enthusiasm warranted by the joke, which I thought probably due to the skill of its delivery.

"I'm curious," I probed. "From what region would you expect my English accent to have come?"

"From the region of Tennessee," said Daphene.

*   *   *

Several years later I received a small package mailed from England. In a specially crafted white, formal bond paper box, I found a one-half inch by one-half inch piece of Daphene's wedding cake with a card expressing her engraved regrets that we had been unable to attend the ceremony. I had never before seen anything quite like that.

Daphene's husband, Nigel Haslam, was in the Foreign Service. After the wedding they were off to South Africa and then, as the years passed we received Christmas cards from time to time posted by them out of various exotic places, worldwide.

Many years later they were back in England in the family home near Woking. Once, when our two daughters, Palmer and Suzy, completing a summer as waitresses in the Hard Rock Café in London, needed some assistance getting home, Daphene and Nigel took them in for a night before their flight and got them safely on the plane to America.

*   *   *

After a remarkably rough English Channel crossing – one of those resulting in all the bar glasses being broken, the lounge furniture being thrown all around and most of the passengers being rendered sick-unto-death -- we retrieved the Morris at Boulogne and drove to Paris. Our plans were to visit Joannie and Billy Cowan in their village near Chaumont on our way back to the Stuttgart area.

The Cowans, like other American Air Force officers accompanied by their wives and stationed in France, lived "on the economy." The Cowans' home was a farmhouse in a small hamlet near Billy's base. Of the inhabitants in the village, they were the only Americans, but Joannie spoke French and, as newlyweds, I suspect, they enjoyed the seclusion. There were no living quarters for married couples on the base. The other fighter pilots, mechanics, backup and supply personnel and almost all the enlisted men who were not married or who did not have their wives with them lived on the base in barracks or temporary bachelor officers' quarters.

The situation was different in Germany. Since we were the conquerors, if we needed off-base housing for military personnel, we requisitioned it. As a result, many of the U. S. military people, especially the high-ranking officers, lived in German civilian houses; often the finest homes in the area. Several times I attended social functions in these beautifully furnished residences. Americans in vanquished Germany frequently dwelled in comfort and sometimes in splendor.

In France, however, a country in which we were guests rather than victors, we could not requisition housing. So, if you were an American stationed in France and wanted to live in the French countryside rather than occupy temporary quarters at the American military installation, you took what you could get.

The final mile or so to the Cowan's farmhouse was unpaved. They had sent us a map without which we would not have found the place. We drove into their enclosure, among the cows, goats and chickens, and were greeted by a smiling, blooming, beautiful Joannie, vivacious and looking very French in a simple but pretty print dress. She was hearty, pink-cheeked and happy. Married life, it seemed, even in these simple circumstances, was quite agreeable.

We unloaded our gear and were shown to our room, but were disappointed to learn that Billy was not there. He was with his squadron in Tunisia practicing gunnery. Nonetheless, Joannie had prepared a banquet for us. Before supper she politely inquired if Bill and I would like to bathe.

"That would be nice." I rejoined. "We can knock off the road dust."

"Actually, we don't have a bathroom," said Joannie.

Did I detect a note of pride?

"We ordered a canvas tub from Sears and we use that. It's really not so bad. We fill it with hot water from the stove and cold water from the pump and drain it with a hose into the garden. Here, I'll show it to you. It's on the back porch."

We were taken to the porch where we observed a device that resembled an army cot – a wooden frame with a cloth sack suspended inside. It didn't look particularly comfortable or, for that matter, very safe.

Joannie appeared genuinely crestfallen when we declined her invitation to utilize the portable bathtub. We didn't admit it, but American JAG officers stationed in Germany were unaccustomed to such sparse personal accommodations.

Later Joannie told me that her gossipy French neighbors had taken a dim view of our visit. Not only were they shocked that she would entertain two strange men while her husband was absent, but they had seen the word "Germany" on the license plate of the Morris and had jumped to the conclusion that we were enemy agents or fugitive members of the Gestapo. In fact the plate read "US Forces in Germany," but nobody in the village read or spoke English.

*   *   *

Dear Mother and Dad,   *18 October 1954*

Jerry Hall, one of the civilian court reporters, and I have decided to take our Christmas leave together. We shall take a week off for skiing, rest and relaxation in Switzerland, Austria or Germany. There are plenty of excellent ski resorts available. It's just a matter of picking out one. I have decided to go to one place and remain there for the week because in the thirty days leave I have taken since I have been here I have driven my Morris more than 4,400 miles. I have felt that I have needed a rest more when I returned from leave than I did when I began. So, for me the Christmas holidays this year will be tranquil and serene.

The Fenigs, Major Ed, his wife Maggie, the children, Kathie, Mary and little Eddie leave Wednesday to return to the States; Camp Carson, Colorado. They have all been wonderful to me during my duty assignment here. The Fenigs are an unusual couple: he a practicing Jew, she a devout Roman Catholic. I have enjoyed many suppers at their home and have learned more law, and especially trial tactics, from Eddie Fenig than I could have in ten years of civilian practice. He is a natural teacher and has spent many hours showing and explaining to me how a lawsuit should be prepared and tried. He has taught me how to manage many tasks simultaneously and given me confidence in the courtroom. All of us here in the JA section hate to see them leave.

*   *   *

Although I have requested that I be sent back through the Mediterranean, I think my request is not likely to be granted. Single officers are needed on troop ships. Married officers traveling with their families are the ones who get to depart from Genoa or Leghorn on passenger vessels or from Frankfurt by air. I guess that is as it should be.

*   *   *

THE TIMES: In November 1954, in response to a U. S. Central Intelligence Agency request, the American airframe manufacturer, Lockheed, presented a proposal for the production of what was later to be designated as the U-2, a high altitude reconnaissance aircraft capable of flying long distances and photographing military sites in the Soviet Union using high resolution cameras. The CIA with President Dwight Eisenhower's approval accepted Lockeed's proposal. Operating under a very demanding schedule, the "Skunk Works," a specialized design/production facility at Lockheed produced the new U-2 just eight months later, its maiden flight took place on August 6, 1955. In appearance and performance like a sailplane, on its first flight the lightly loaded U-2 refused to land until the test pilot's fifth attempt.

By the summer of 1955 the first U-2, became operational. On July 4, 1956, a U-2 completed the first overflight of the Soviet Union. Sophisticated electronic and camera equipment was housed in the nose and in a large fuselage bay. Huge fuel tanks enabled the aircraft to fly for six hours a distance of almost 3,000 miles at altitudes in excess of 60,000 feet. After that, operational U-2s flew routinely from bases in Pakistan and Turkey to Norway, overflying vast stretches of the Soviet Union. These flights gathered much important data and particularly revealed that the suspected missile superiority in favor of the Soviet's was unfounded.

For four years the CIA operated these flights until May 1, 1960, when Francis Gary Powers was shot down by a missile over Soviet territory, igniting a diplomatic incident embarrassing for the United States and President Eisenhower and bringing an end to the U-2 flights over the Soviet Union.

THE CHAIN OF CUSTODY

One November day in 1954, Colonel O'Connor, who had replaced Colonel Guimond as staff judge advocate at VII Corps, called me into his office, closed the door, and said,

"You have 'top-secret' security clearance, do you not?"

"Yes, sir," I responded.

Colonel O'Connor continued. "Sit down," he said. "We need for you to handle a very serious situation that has come up in Straubing. You may want to take some notes."

I sat. He handed me a yellow pad.

"Since Mansfield Kaserne is so close to the Czech border, we have some intelligence operatives who use it as a base for going in and out of the Soviet zones of Eastern Europe. One of our people has been in contact with a Czech scientist, a nuclear physicist, for several months and has been trying to arrange for him to defect to the West. The deal was finally put together last week, and three nights ago the scientist, his wife and seven year old daughter were smuggled across the border and taken to Mansfield Kaserne where they were lodged in a house on the base. We thought they would be plenty safe there since they were surrounded by the entire 6th Armored Cavalry. They were to spend one night in the Kaserne, then flown to Frankfurt, and from Frankfurt to the States."

Colonel O'Connor sighed. "A major problem has developed," he said, "and this is where you come in."

I waited for him to proceed.

"On the one night this Czech family was under our protection, a soldier – he must have been drunk -- slipped into the house where they were staying, found the little girl's room, and tried to sexually molest her. She screamed and he escaped through a window. I don't think she was really hurt – just frightened."

"We've got the guy who did it. He dropped his cap in the little girl's room and his cap had his service number written inside. He has no alibi and was not in his barracks when the incident occurred."

"The commanding general wants this soldier court-martialed and the intelligence people want this family out of here, like *right now!* It would be a lot simpler just to throw the accused in the slammer and forget him, but we can't do that. If he is to be punished he has got to be tried and if he's going to be tried we have to keep the Czech family here until they testify. The accused has a right to be confronted by the witnesses who testify against him."

Colonel O'Connor concluded his introductory remarks. "So, here's what I want you to do."

I was fascinated. I sat, pencil poised. I hadn't needed to take notes.

"Get to Straubing as fast as you can. I'll arrange for you to have an airplane. I don't know yet who the others on the trial team will be. It won't be difficult to find a Law officer with top-secret clearance, but a court reporter and defense counsel with high enough security may be a problem. We can get interim clearance for them if we have to."

It was obvious Colonel O'Connor had cleared the decks for action. His concentration was focused and things were moving fast.

"O. K., here's the file. When you get to Straubing, get the trial set up as expeditiously as possible. The regimental commander up there is waiting for you. You will get full cooperation."

The file was sealed and stamped "TOP SECRET" in big red letters.

"I'll handle all the rest of the legal paper work from here. Maybe I should send Lieutenant Hamm up with you, as defense counsel, so there won't be any delay on that end. I'll just have to work out the security problem."

I wasn't sure, as Colonel O'Connor considered the defense assignment and security, whether he was talking to me or to himself.

"Very well, Colonel," I said. "I'm on my way. Anything else?"

"Yes. There is one more thing. This whole trial will have to be secure. You will have to arrange for the necessary military police and keep the courtroom locked. The identity of these Czech people, and the fact that they are here, must not be revealed."

*   *   *

The prosecution of this case would be pretty straightforward. The child was old enough to testify. I had a copy of a translated statement she had given describing what had happened. It was clear and convincing. The only problem was identification of the assailant. The room had been dark so the victim had not seen the soldier's face. The military cap found at the scene would be the only means of verifying identity.

After the intruder had fled, the child had found the military cap by her bed. She had given it to her father, who, in turn, had turned it over to Pfc. Keeney, a guard stationed nearby who was first at the scene after the father had sounded an alarm. When the military police arrived, Keeney handed the cap over to MP Sergeant Vescovo who delivered it to CID agent Conley who turned it over to Warrant Officer Hendrix of the Criminal Investigation Division. WO Hendrix had shown the cap to the accused whom, after checking the lining and seeing his service number acknowledged that the cap was his.

Hendrix kept the cap in his office safe until I arrived, and then gave it to me. The accused could not explain how his cap came to be in the room where the assault had occurred. He said that he had had too much to drink and could not remember where he had been or what had taken place after he left the enlisted men's club. Neither could he account for when, where or how he had lost his cap.

In order for me to prove that the cap shown to and identified by the accused was the same cap that was found in the little girl's room,

I knew it would be necessary for me to establish a chain of custody. In order to do that, I would call each witness who had possessed the cap after it had been found, who would testify when, where and from whom he received the cap, and when, where and to whom he gave possession of it to someone else. I intended to show the cap to each witnesses and ask if the witness could identify it. I knew the guard, the military policeman and the CID agents could do so for they had all noted the service number and WO Hendrix had affixed a tag which he signed and labeled as an exhibit. The child and the father would be able to testify that the cap shown them in the courtroom was the same "type and kind" of cap they had seen in the child's room and passed on to the military authorities who established the chain of custody, which began with the little girl and ended with me. I would not need to take the witness stand because Hendrix could say, when handed the cap in court, that he recognized his signature on the label and that this was the cap he received from agent Conley, signed, labeled and delivered to me, the prosecuting attorney.

Establishing the chain of custody was a complicated process. By calling the child; the father; Keeney, the guard; Vescovo, the MP; and the CID agents, Conley and Hendrix, I thought I would be able to establish that the cap found at the crime scene belonged to the accused. That, I believed, plus the little girl's testimony, would be all that was necessary to get a conviction.

I interviewed Gretchen, the small victim the day after I arrived in Straubing, the day before the trial. Since I had her detailed, transcribed statement I didn't think it was necessary for me to review the facts with her. Instead, I just wanted her to be comfortable with me so that when I questioned her in court she would not be frightened. We talked, in the presence of her parents and an interpreter. I made sure that her mother and father were brought into the conversation and that it was pleasant. I wanted her to think of me as a friend of the family. The discussion was mostly about the impending trip to America and what things would be like when they got there. We talked about my childhood and what might be different for her in her new home, although I had to speak in generalities since none of us knew exactly where in the U. S. the family was to be located. The child was very bright and, after about forty-five minutes I was convinced she would be a convincing witness.

After my interview with the Czech family, I spent most of my trial preparation time making certain the chain of custody witnesses would be ready, that I understood what they knew and how they would answer my questions. Also, time was required to arrange for a secure trial location and the presence of sufficient military police.

My first witness was the father who told about being awakened by his daughter's scream, what he found upon entering her room and that she had given him a military cap which he gave to a guard, Keeney, the first person to arrive after he gave the distress-signal. I showed him the cap. He said it looked like the cap he received from his daughter and gave to the guard, but he couldn't be sure. I had asked him his name but avoided questions about his permanent residence, occupation or why his family was spending the night at Mansfield Kaserne, as did the defense. We had agreed that details concerning the identity of the family were not relevant to any issue in the trial.

The next witnesses, Warrant Officer Hendrix, was shown the cap, testified that he received it from agent Conley, labeled and signed it, and showed it to the accused who admitted that the cap was his.

Then, I called seven-year old Gretchen. I first asked her about her belief in a supreme being and whether she knew the difference between right and wrong. Her answers established that she understood the nature of truth and that persons who told falsehoods would be punished. Once qualified, she took the oath, swearing in the presence of God to tell the truth, the whole truth and nothing but the truth.

Then, very gingerly, my questions turned to the soldier's intrusion and the particulars of his indecent assault. In question and answer form, she repeated the facts described in her written statement. When that unpleasant task was completed I had checked off all the necessary elements of proof, except for the identification of the cap.

"Now Gretchen," I said, "I'm almost finished. I have just a few more questions."

Gretchen was silent.

"After the soldier – the soldier who had gotten into your bed with you – had left, did you find anything in your room that was not there when you went to bed?"

"Yes." She said.

"What was it?"

"A cap."

"What kind of cap?"

"A military cap."

"Do you remember what it looked like?"

"Yes."

"What did it look like?"

"It was a soft cap, sort of tan colored, with yellow edging."

That last answer surprised me. There was nothing in the statement about yellow edging, but yellow was the color designation for the U. S. Cavalry, and the 6th Armored, now a tank unit, many years before had been a horse cavalry unit and its soldiers, of whom the accused was one, wore yellow piping on their caps.

"Where did you find the cap?"

"On the floor, beside my bed."

"What did you do with the cap?"

"I gave it to my father."

I had what I needed to begin the chain of custody, but I sensed there was something more.

"If you saw that cap again, do you think you would recognize it?"

"Yes," said Gretchen.

No ifs, ands or buts; no "maybe." She expressed no doubt. She was emphatic. Again, I was surprised. There was no mention in the statement of a positive identification of the cap.

"How would you recognize it?"

I had no idea what she would say; but I had established the first link in my chain of custody. What did I have to lose?

"I would recognize it because it had a number written on the inside."

Perhaps I paused for a mini-second, but there was no doubt; I had to continue.

"Do you remember the number?"

"Yes."

"What was the number?"

"It was RA 355 883 414."

I couldn't believe it! She had remembered the service number. I reached over to the exhibit table and picked up the cap.

"Look at this cap, Gretchen." I said, handing it to her. "Have you seen this cap before?"

She looked at the outside – and then the inside.

"Yes." She said.

"When and where have you seen it before?"

"This is the cap I found on the floor beside my bed after the soldier ran away. See, it has yellow edging and the number inside is the same, RA 355 883 414."

Of course, it was the cap the accused had identified as his.

The rest of the chain of custody witnesses, Keeney, Vescovo and Conley, were sent home and, the prosecution rested.

ORDERS HOME

HEADQUARTERS VII CORPS
APO 107   NEW YORK, N. Y.
Letter Order 11-157   30 November 1954
SUBJECT: Redeployment Orders – Separation
TO: 1ST LT JOHN J THOMASON, 01878077, JAGC, Cat III,
Cat expires 28 Feb 55, PMOS 8103, Cau, DOR 21 Aug 52
Rotation date 31 Jan 55.

You are released from assignment at Headquarters VII Corps ... and assigned to the   7802nd Embarkee-Debarkee Transit Detachment, Bremerhaven Port of Embarkation, Bremerhaven, Germany, for further assignment to the 2048th Army Service Unit,

Fort Knox, Kentucky...You will proceed from Moehringen, Germany to Bremerhaven Port of Embarkation...and report to the Commanding Officer there on the date specified in firm port call to be issued by Headquarters 7th Army, for processing and movement by U. S. Government transportation... Travel will not commence until a firm port call is received...Effective date change of station accountability is 31 Jan 1955 and is subject to adjustment upon receipt of firm port call....

BY COMMAND OF LIEUTENANT GENERAL HODES.

* * *

Actually, the orders were written in army abbreviations. I have translated them here for the convenience of the reader. The orders also contained much more detailed information than is reproduced here, e.g. that pet space was not required and which financial account was to be charged for various kinds of travel. By this time in my military career I could read orders, abbreviated or not, without stumbling or hesitation, so long as they were in English.

The receipt of these orders also meant that I would have to drive my Morris from Stuttgart to Bremerhaven, a distance of about 735 miles, sometime in January so that it could be shipped to New York and be ready for me to pick up when I arrived there. Although they seemed certain, the orders did not mean that I would definitely ship out of Bremerhaven. They contained contingency language that could be altered by supplemental orders and which would allow me to get to New York by a ship out of Genoa or Leghorn, through the

Med, or a plane from Frankfurt. I was keeping my fingers crossed hoping for a more scenic or shorter trip.

*   *   *

THE TIMES: In December 1954, The North Atlantic Treaty Organization agreed to integrate tactical nuclear weapons into its defensive strategy. Beginning then, tactical nuclear weapons from the U. S. began to arrive in Germany. The Army had developed tactical nuclear weapons to counter similar Soviet creations. It had an 85-Ton mobile cannon capable of hurling an eleven inch (280 mm) conventional shell or atomic missile twenty miles into enemy territory.

The cannon, with a forty foot barrel, was mounted on twin cabs, the rear driver connected by telephone to the front. The nuclear artillery projectile could produce a yield 2/3 the size of the bomb Hiroshima, Japan, had experienced in World War II. Such a weapon could vaporize an entire hill along with the garrison occupying it. The U. S. also developed ground launched, short-range nuclear missiles. By the end of 1960 there were 2,500 U. S. tactical nuclear weapons deployed in Western Europe.

In addition, the Air Force had a plan in place whereby, in the event of war, "small" nuclear bombs would be dropped on predetermined targets by jet fighter-bombers. When ordered to attack the jets were to fly in at low altitude, avoiding radar detection, and when over the selected target (a city or military installation) pull up with maximum thrust to effect a vertical ascent, flying straight up. At a predetermined altitude the nuclear bomb would be released, the plane would turn and depart at top speed. In theory, the bomb would continue straight up until the pull of gravity overcame its movement inertia, then the bomb would turn and fall back to earth exploding at a fixed altitude over the target city, or on impact. By the time of the explosion it was thought that the plane and pilot that had brought in the bomb would probably be out of range.

*   *   *

Dear Folks,   *5 December 1954*

I'm officer of the day again tonight, so, I have time to write. I shall probably be assigned this job one more time this week because many of the Kelley Barracks troops are out in the field. There are but few of us of company grade officers around to undertake such duties.

I have been sitting here talking with the corporal of the guard. I am amazed that he knows so much about me and what goes on in the JA section. His regular job is such that he has access to trial records and exhibits before they are sent to Washington. He finds the transcripts to be quite interesting and is thinking about going to law school. He asked me about several cases, why I did this instead of that, and the significance and meaning of some points of law. He knows what cases I have won and which ones I have lost and that I have defended two officers, both of whom were acquitted. He is a very bright fellow and I have enjoyed our conversation.

I am also surprised that I am known by name by so many soldiers here. As often as not, when I am saluted on the

John J. Thomason

street I am also greeted by name, "Good morning, Lieutenant Thomason." On the other hand, maybe it's not so peculiar. This is a relatively small place, only about 1,200 soldiers stationed here – a small town, so to speak – and I suppose what goes on in the JA section, who gets tried, for what, and the result of the trial, is what is interesting in this little community. In addition, I have been here almost two years now. I am one of the "Old Timers," at Kelley, and a "Short Timer," in the army, meaning I will get out soon.

*   *   *

A NOT SO MERRY CHRISTMAS

Dear Mother and Dad,   17 December 1954

Today is "Bad News" day. This morning I found out that all my plans to get home by some easy or pleasurable means have gone asunder. I shall not take that delightful cruise over the blue ripples of the placid Mediterranean; nor shall I wing my way in a few short hours over the clouds and swells of the heaving Atlantic.

No! Instead, I am scheduled to board a train in Stuttgart on the 23rd of January, a Sunday, and begin the long trek to the Northern Hinterlands, to the very city whence I came: Bremerhaven! And that is not the worst of it. Once I arrive at the port of debarkation I shall step aboard a troop ship, not just any troop ship, but a special troop ship – the very same troop ship I came over on, the _Haan_!

296

*   *   *

Jerry Hall and I shall depart on Sunday, the 19th of December for my final leave, eight days of skiing in a little town in the German Alps, Oberstdorf. We have booked rooms at the Höfatsblick, a resort hotel on top of the Nebelhorn, a high mountain near there. We shall be in an area called the Allgäuer Alpen, in English, the Algau Alps, about five miles from the Austrian border. I'm sure we shall have a noteworthy vacation and an unforgettable Christmas.

*   *   *

Jerry and I arrived in Oberstdorf, by way of Ulm and Kempen, on a beautiful, sunny Monday afternoon. We were about sixty miles west of Innsbruck, Austria, surrounded by the highest mountains in Germany. All round us the towering Alps were covered by a deep mantle of bright snow. After outfitting ourselves with all the necessary rental ski equipment we rushed over to the Nebelhornbahn, the two stage cable car which would take us to our hotel, on top of the 7,000 foot mountain, Nebelhorn, only to find it closed for repairs. There was no other way up, except to undertake a ten hour climb, an impractical solution since we had brought considerable luggage. So, we spent a pleasant evening in the town.

The next morning the cable car was in operation, but the sky was overcast, and as we ascended the weather deteriorated. By the time we reached the summit the fog was so dense we couldn't see anything, and afterwards the wind began to blow furiously, probably fifty to sixty miles an hour. Following our ascension, the cable car was shut down because of the frightful storm; we were the only guests at the hotel. For the next three days we were isolated. Although our skis were waxed and ready, we couldn't leave the hotel – couldn't even open a window. Whether it was snowing or the snow was just blowing we were unable to say. It was probably a combination of both. Whatever the case, there was nothing for us to do but read, play gin rummy and eat. We got plenty of service from the staff, who seemed to be enjoying themselves judging from the sounds of a remote party somewhere, but we weren't invited.

Finally, on Christmas Eve the weather improved sufficiently for us to descend, which we did, taking up residence in an inn at the bottom cable car station, The Nebelhornbahn Hotel. It was a great relief to be able to move about again although the elements remained unsettled and blusterous.

That evening at supper, a young man who introduced himself as Carl Maul, the Stuttgart manager of a German shipping firm, joined us. In Europe, I have found, It is not unusual for a stranger to ask to be seated at a dinner table where there is an empty chair, a custom I applaud. Carl, a bright and friendly vacationer who spoke excellent English, was a welcome addition to our table.

The three of us got on quite well and agreed to meet the next morning so that we might ski together, assuming the weather improved. It was lucky for both Jerry and me that we met.

Although only a few years older than we were, Carl had been an enlisted man in the German army during the final year or so of World War II. He told us some interesting war stories. Carl was assigned to an infantry unit on the Eastern Front, fighting the Russians. As the war was coming to an end his battalion was in retreat, somewhere in southern Germany. He and his comrades knew that the American army was not far to the west. They also knew that they would be captured in a matter of days and preferred to be prisoners of the Americans.

As the Germans fell back they encountered advance units of the American Third Army under the command of General George Patton. They surrendered to the highest-ranking American officer they could find, a major. The main body of the American troops was still several miles to the west. According to Carl, the American major ordered the Germans to keep their weapons and to take a position on the western bank of a river, to defend the position against the Russians and prevent them from crossing, which they did. So, Carl told us, this unit of the German Army held off the Russian advance for three days under the command of an American officer, until the American Army arrived and relieved the German defenders. The German soldiers were then disarmed and sent to the rear to be processed.

Processing consisted of being put in a loosely guarded pen, fed and interrogated to determine what part of Germany each soldier called home. Unless there was reason to believe the prisoner deserved special treatment, or was a war criminal or a member of some particularly blameworthy part of the Nazi organization, after a week or so they were allowed to start walking home. The only complaint Carl had about his treatment was that the American captors did not hesitate to relieve their captives of wristwatches and cameras.

When the Germans realized they were being sent back to their hometowns, it also became clear to them that if they had come from a place in eastern Germany they would be turned over to the Russian authorities. So, when asked their place of origin, it was commonplace to give an address in the western part of Germany, where the occupation troops would be British, French or American, not Russian. Frequently, to avoid being sent east, prisoners selected the address of a building or street in the western part of Germany that had been destroyed in the allied air attacks. Such addresses were easily obtainable from fellow prisoners who were legitimate residents of one of the heavily bombed cities, of which there were many. After giving an address in the western part of Germany, the prisoner would be sent "home" to an area occupied by the Allies.

Jerry and I decided to attend midnight services that evening at a small church nearby, so left Carl about 11:30 p.m. The chapel was packed. We could scarcely get inside the door, much less find a seat. Still, the experience was unforgettable; the music simple but familiar and harmonious. By that time my German was good enough for me to piece together the Christmas story when the minister recited it. After the wearisome experience on top of the mountain waiting for the storm to abate, I was finally beginning to feel the Christmas spirit.

The next morning, Christmas day, the weather improved considerably. We met Carl for breakfast and excitedly set out for the summit of the Nebelhorn where the snow, we were told, was fresh and powdery. However, when we arrived at the summit it was snowing again and the sun was not to be seen.

We waxed and donned our skis and pushed off down the slope. Carl was first, I was second and then came Jerry. The slope was steeper than I had expected and the blowing snow was blinding. Jerry fell, but was quickly up laughing, ready for more. Carl was a better skier than either of us. We regrouped at the bottom of the slope we had descended in a cup-like depression at the top of the mountain, where Carl offered some appreciated advice.

After climbing by "herringbone" back up the slope, we started down again. The slope was very fast and the snow, again, blinding. I fell about half way down, but was soon up again and made it to the bottom where I stood talking with Carl. Jerry started down and Carl saw him fall. I didn't see him, but I heard him call out,

"Bud, help me. Come quick."

I could tell from the tone of his voice that something serious had happened.

It couldn't have taken Carl and me more than a few seconds to cover the forty meters separating us from Jerry. He was in a sitting position holding up his left leg with both hands. His leg, between his knee and ankle, angled queerly outward and upward at about fifteen degrees.

I knelt beside Jerry and, in an effort to comfort him, said, "Maybe it's just a bad sprain."

Ever articulate, Jerry replied, "I think we can dismiss that possibility."

There were thirty or forty Germans on the slope and without a word one was immediately away to get help. Carl, another German skier and I stayed with Jerry. Other than take off his skis and shield him from the blinding snow, there was little we could do. In about fifteen minutes help arrived in the form of a sort of aluminum, boat-like litter accompanied by a take-charge skier who said he was a physician. We managed to get Jerry into the "boat" without moving his foot and then, for me, the real torture began.

301

Six Germans were attempting to move Jerry and the litter as I tried to keep up while carrying our skis and ski poles in my arms. All of us were on foot. With each step I sank in the snow to my knees, sometimes above my knees, almost to my waist. The litter was about fifteen meters in front of me and I could see that the rescuers were encountering extreme difficulty as they reached the steeper parts of the hillside. Jerry, in order not to lose his balance, had to release his grip on his leg and hold onto the sides of the litter, leaving his leg and foot unsupported and causing him great pain.

I followed Jerry, the litter and his rescuers upward, toward the cable car station on the mountaintop. I suspect it would be difficult for a single person to carry four skis and four ski poles under any circumstances, but to do so in waist deep snow, up a thirty-five percent grade, as fast as possible in a blinding snowstorm is well neigh impossible. I had taken off my jacket and given it to cover Jerry, as had several of the others, but sweat soaked my wool shirt despite the biting cold, the chilling wind and swirling snow. From time to time, a ski would slip loose and I would have to reclaim it without losing the others. Then, in the midst of all this travail, my nose began to bleed.

Bright red blood on white snow produces a striking pattern, I briefly thought, but I had no time for musing. I was beginning to lose hope of keeping up with the rescuers and of reaching the cable car station in time to descend with Jerry. I could see the cable car station ahead and above, through the whirl of snow, but reaching it seemed impossible. Then, oddly, some advice Major Fenig had given me when I had seven cases to try in one week popped into my head.

"Just try one at a time," he said. "Don't try to do them all at once."

"So," I said to myself, "I'll just take one step at a time, and I'll get there."

I think that is what all of us did and we all got there, panting, coughing and sweating with tears flowing from our eyes and blood and mucus streaming from my nose.

The cable car departed as soon as we reached the station. There was an ambulance at the bottom and within two hours of his fall Jerry's leg was set and in a cast. To say that I was grateful we had not been alone, and that Carl had been with us, would be to grossly understate.

Jerry was taken to a hospital in Sonthofen, about ten kilometers from Oberstdorf. I stayed with him for the remainder of the day, until about eleven p.m. when the nurses sent me away so Jerry could get some sleep. Alone, I walked toward the small railroad station where I could board a train back to Oberstdorf, and my hotel. Except for me, the roadway through the village was empty. It had stopped snowing but a deep blanket of white covered everything and muffled any sound – until, faintly in the distance – I heard Christmas carols. So much had happened, I had almost forgotten, it was Christmas night.

The train to Oberstdorf wouldn't arrive for an hour, so I walked toward the sound of the singing. The carol, *Stille Nacht! Heilige Nacht!, (Silent Night! Holy Night!)* was being sung by the occupants of a private home. One hundred thirty-six years before, that carol had been written and presented for the first time on Christmas Eve, in the little Austrian village of Oberndorf, close-by this very place.

When I found the source of the music I approached a window. There were eight or so family members, old, middle aged and young,

303

gathered around a Christmas tree, alight with candles such as I had seen at the Barre's in Munich the year before. In the candle glow, I could see their faces, with radiating expressions of joy and love. I stood outside and listened. They could not see me, nor did I want them to. I paused in the deep snow outside their window for a long time, enthralled by the experience. When it seemed I should, I turned and made my way to the railway station, reexamining in my mind the events of that Christmas day.

Two days later Carl Maul, who was traveling by auto and who lived in Stuttgart, arranged the interior of his car so that Jerry and his cast could fit comfortably in the rear seat, and returned us home to Kelley Barracks.

*   *   *

<u>STOCKHOLM, SWEDEN</u>
<u>January, 1955</u>

Reluctant to return to the ski slopes after Jerry Hall broke his leg, nevertheless, upon the urging of newly arrived George Gallup, I decided to spend New Year's Eve in Garmisch, and met Sally. Two weeks later, back at Kelley Barracks, without much hope it would be delivered, I dropped a letter in the mailbox. It was addressed to:

"Miss Sally Palmer, An American Graduate Student studying at a University which teaches Political Science in English, and which, I believe, is located in Stockholm, Sweden."

*   *   *

The third week in January is not the most agreeable time of year to be in Stockholm, and Tuesday, January 18, 1955 was no exception. Daylight began about nine a.m. that day and ended at three in the afternoon, but the sun was not to be seen; it was chilly, bleak, overcast and gray.

In the student cafeteria at the University of Stockholm, not far from the city center, Sally Palmer of Bakersfield, California, and Barbara Hale, of Canton, Ohio, reflected on the sunny days they had relished in southern Germany, where they had skied over the New Year's holidays. Lunch ended, Sally picked up her book sack and headed for an afternoon class. She was in no hurry; class would not begin for half an hour.

"Sally, wait a minute."

It was David Lawton, another American student, from New York City. David owned a Leica camera and had become the unofficial class photographer.

Sally paused. "Hi, David. What's up?"

"There's a letter for you up at the University office," he replied.

That was odd. Sally lived with a Swedish family in a suburban home. She received her mail there. The only mail that came to her University address, were notices from the school.

"Thanks, David," she said. "I'll go see."

She walked up the hill to the University office, past the small park with its concrete benches surrounding a well-known statue by the contemporary Swedish sculptor, Carl Milles. At the office she was given a letter addressed to her in a round about, descriptive style; a letter from the young lieutenant she met while skiing on the Kreutzeck.

Exhilarated and excited by the unexpected arrival of this communication, Sally seized a nearby letter opener, hastily cut the envelope and while the University office personnel inquisitively watched, devoured the writing within.

"Wow!" she exclaimed, ran back to the Milles plaza, sat on a bench, and read the letter again.

Then she jumped to her feet and eagerly ran down the hill to the cafeteria where Barbara was still at the lunch table.

"Barbara, look! I got a letter from that guy I met in Germany!"

*   *   *

On the same day, at the office of the staff judge advocate, Kelley Barracks, Germany, a VII Corps courier sauntered into our trial team office and said,

"Hey, lieutenant, I've got a letter for you."

"Since when are you the mail man?" I questioned.

"I'm not, but I've got a letter for you anyway. I was over at 7th Army picking up some stuff at the post office," he said, "and I noticed this letter on the postmaster's desk with a lot of stamps and writing on the envelope, like it had been forwarded all around the European theater. So, I got curious, and even though I had to read the address upside down, I made out your name. 'Hey, I know that guy,' I said. 'He's over at VIIth Corps.'"

"'Cool,'" said the postmaster. "'We had about given up on finding him. Take this letter on over to him when you go back.'"

"So, here it is," said the courier, and handed me the letter.

It was from Sally Palmer in Stockholm.

Before she received my letter, bearing my return military address, Sally had decided to write me.

The letter given to me by the courier was addressed to *"Lt. John Thomason."* That was correct.

"c/o Adjutant General's Office." That was wrong. I was in the office of the staff judge advocate.

"APO 46." That was wrong. I was at APO 107.

"Stuttgart, Germany." That was wrong. I was at Möhringen, Germany.

So, I got Sally's letter and she got mine.

*　　　*　　　*

HEADING HOME ON THE HAAN

Dear Mother and Dad,　　　　　　　*Saturday, 29 January*
　　　　　　　　　　　　　　　　　　　　　1955

This will be the last time you will hear from me until you get a telephone call from New York.

I write this from the casual officers' billet at Bremerhaven, Port of Embarkation where I arrived this morning at 0700. I have absolutely nothing to do until I join the advance party and go on board the Haan *at about noon tomorrow. Tomorrow night I shall spend aboard, then we shall take on about twenty-five hundred troops and be on our way home. So, I expect to depart from the European continent on 31 January and arrive in the U. S. about 11 February. My car will be waiting for me. I shall drive to Fort Knox, Kentucky, to be separated from the service and then head for Memphis.*

I have shipped one large wooden crate and two foot lockers directly to my home address. I expect them to arrive about two weeks after I do.

This has been a hectic week. There are uncounted responsibilities to be completed in connection with the departure process. All the while, I still had my work to do, added to which has been an almost unending round of good bye parties. Then my departure date was extended four days and the parties started all over again.

Colonel Hodges, Mrs. Hodges, Colonel Oeding, Mrs. Oeding, Dave Addis and John Tinnerello all came down to the Stuttgart train station to see me off. It was a sad parting for I greatly care for all these people. This is the first time in my life I have left a place where I have been for a long time and to which I am not likely to return. I also doubt that I will ever see any of these folks again. That is an unhappy prospect for these people have been my family for the better part of the last two years.

Being part of the American Army in Germany during this dangerous phase of the Cold War has been an unforgettable experience for me.

*   *   *

By the time I reached Bremerhaven ready to sail for home, I had lived in Europe almost exactly two years. I had learned a lot, about the army, about Europe, about how to manage multiple tasks simultaneously and how to try a lawsuit. My last few days at Kelley Barracks had been filled with farewells, departure parties, packing and tending to all the details involved in leaving a place where I had lived for so long. Now, after 168 general courts-martial trials, the stress of being in the middle of the Cold War and scores of new experiences in Europe, it was all finished.

My Morris was on its way to New York and all my belongings were packed and on their way to Memphis.

Because I had come over on the *Haan* I became known as something of an authority on the intricacies of the ship and found myself named as assistant adjutant for the voyage home. The adjutant, a lieutenant colonel, was stricken with an acute appendicitis two days out, so I became acting adjutant, which made me responsible for all the administrative details of the 2,500 troops on board. The ship itself was administered by the ship's company.

I was in charge of seeing to it that everybody who got on the ship, got off; that all assignments for work details were filled; MPC scrip was exchanged for dollars at the appropriate time and a host of other things. But just as I had become seasoned by my two and a half years in the military, so had these soldiers, most of whom had been in the Army long enough to learn the system, and sometimes how to outsmart it. Most were also headed home to civilian life, therefore not particularly interested in establishing an auspicious army record and many were less than eager to work while en route to the States.

My first responsibility, which I thought would be easy but turned out to be daunting, was to call the role – to make certain everybody who had boarded the ship in Bremerhaven was still on board.

I was not concerned with the 300 prisoners. They were under the control of the military police, a completely separate organization. The prisoners were locked in the forward compartment and, I think, never left there for the duration of the voyage. I had watched them as they boarded, taken singly from their prison train which had halted on a siding near the pier, and marched quick-step to the ship's gangway under the surveillance of two fifty caliber machine gun crews; a humiliating experience, I am sure. I wondered, as I watched them board the *Haan*, if there were among them some whom I had prosecuted or defended. Undoubtedly there were. As on the journey over, the other soldiers were in compartments, 150 to 200 men uncomfortably packed into each.

As acting adjutant, I ordered each compartment commander to call the roll and report back to me. They did so. Five hundred twenty-seven men were missing. It didn't take a rocket scientist to figure out what was going on. If you didn't answer the roll call the authorities didn't know where you were and therefore, couldn't assign you to a work detail.

I was resolute. Plan "B" was to require all compartments to be emptied and all soldiers to report on deck at a certain hour on a certain day. We would then take the roll on deck and while the compartments were empty, a search team would explore each compartment looking for whomever might be hiding. That was fairly effective. In some of the compartments we found little houses that had been formed by piling up barrack bags. In these makeshift shelters, there might be four or five soldiers hiding out, playing poker or sleeping, but not answering the roll or being put on work details. We found numerous other hiding places ingeniously fashioned

310

among supplies and in storage areas. When that exercise, Plan B, was complete and the names of those answering the roll was compared to the embarkation list, there were still about two hundred missing.

Determined to find every man, I next established checkpoints at each mess line, so that a soldier had to identify himself before he could get anything to eat. Slowly the number of missing troops began to dwindle. Sudden, unannounced inspections at odd hours produced more previously missing persons as did requiring positive identification of each enlisted man when MPCs were exchanged for dollars. There was no punishment for those we finally caught. There was little we could do except assign the delinquents to work details. The ship's brig had only two cells. I could order a miscreant to be confined to the ship, but that was no punishment because *everybody* was confined to the ship while we were at sea.

The only effective punishment we could impose aboard the ship was confinement in the brig for three days with nothing but bread and water to eat. That sentence was imposed by the troop commander, the highest ranking army officer on board -- a full colonel -- on two soldiers who refused to obey a direct command from a commissioned officer. It was my responsibility to take them the bread each day. The cells were equipped with a supply of cold, fresh water. The brig was near the stern of the ship on the main deck. To get there it was necessary to go outside. About four days out, the sea got very rough. In fact the ship was pitching so much that the screws were coming out of the sea as the ship pitched, the stern arose and the bow went down. When that occurred, the whole ship vibrated as if it were coming apart.

The first day I took each of the brig prisoners two slices of bread, on three occasions. On my very precarious journey to the cells I held fast to the railing, trying to keep the bread and myself dry while the *Haan* pitched and rolled dangerously. There was no one on deck but me. If I had gone overboard, no one would have noticed. After three trips on the first day I reached a decision.

"Listen you guys," I told my prisoners. "If you think it's any fun for me to bring your bread supply out here three times a day, you're wrong. So, I am making a change. From now on I am coming out here once a day and I am bringing each of you six slices of bread. If you want to have a feast and eat all six slices at once, that's O. K. with me. If you want to ration your bread supply to have breakfast, lunch and dinner, that's all right too. But I'm only coming out here once a day, and that's that."

However, I was required to make a supplemental trip.

When the troop commander asked me how our prisoners were doing I told him about my one trip a day plan, and he agreed. I also told him that our prisoners seemed to be having a pretty good time. One had a harmonica which he played while the other sang. The colonel thought about that a moment and then said,

"Go take the harmonica away."

I was a little surprised, but replied, "Yes, sir," and went back out into the storm. When I succeeded in making my way back to the jail, I found the prisoners as I had left them playing the harmonica and singing. I then employed a subterfuge of which, even to this day, I am a bit ashamed.

"That's a pretty good sounding harmonica, Mitchell," I said.

"What kind is it?"

"It's a Hohner, sir, I got it in Germany. It's really a nice one."

"May I see it," I asked.

"Sure, lieutenant," said Mitchell handing me the precious instrument through the bars. "You're welcome to give it a try, if you'd like."

"No," I said. "I won't try to play it. I'll just put it up here on this shelf across from your cell and give it back to you when you get out."

Mitchell was crushed by my betrayal. But, after all, they were supposed to be undergoing punishment, not having a good time.

Three days on bread and water must be just about the right duration to be effective. On the third day my prisoners presented me with a calculation which took into account all the time zones we had passed through as we headed west and which resulted in their being released a few hours earlier than I had calculated they would be. As I unlocked the cells, returned Mitchell's harmonica to him and set them free, they said they would be happy to volunteer for a work detail, if I had any vacancies.

*   *   *

Finally, thirteen days after we had departed Bremerhaven, when the *Haan* arrived at the port of New York, I had located and accounted for all but twelve of the troops who boarded.

Nonetheless, everyone who got on in Bremerhaven got off at New York.

The ship unloaded troops from separate gangways at many locations and I could be in only one place. So, I could not question each of the missing soldiers as they debarked, but I had the names of the men for whom I was still searching and one of them happened

313

to come down the unloading ramp where I was standing with my clip board. I called him out of line and asked,

"Where the hell have you been, Zumas. I've been looking for your ass ever since we left Germany. I've turned this ship upside down looking for you."

"Gosh, lieutenant," Corporal Zumas said with a smile. "That's peculiar. I've been standing right behind you the whole time."

*   *   *

LETTERS CROSSING IN THE MAIL

The descriptively addressed letter Sally received from me and the incorrectly addressed one I received from her, provided each of us with a correct return location. But time was short –a few days after I received her letter I was scheduled to ship out from Bremerhaven and return to America. Knowing that, when Sally received my letter, she promptly replied,

Needless to say, I was very happy to hear from you, Bud.
In answer to your query, I don't know when I've had a better
time.

I scanned her chatty account of the journey back to Sweden and school activities in Stockholm, searching for the response to my invitation to visit Memphis.

Although I've traveled nearly half way around the world to get from California to Stockholm, I've never been south of the Mason-Dixon Line in my own mother country – which leads me to believe that something should be done about that!

What I'm trying to say is that I hope those Southern Belles don't prove to be so charming that you won't have time to say "hello" when a homeward bound student is in the vicinity – which will probably be sometime in June.

More talkative narration concerning student life in Sweden was followed by her salutation, which I studied carefully, seeking some clue to her feelings.

Say "Hi" to George and 'bye for now, Bud. Bon Voyage.

Love,

Sally

I answered at once, and once again our letters crossed. I mentioned that I had written her using a descriptive address – a letter which I did not think she would receive – that I would be leaving Stuttgart in two days and furnishing my home address in Memphis. I was on shaky ground. I would be out of touch for a month and heading west, away from Sally, not north east, toward her. There would be no way I could communicate with her from the ship.

Oh well, what the hell.

You have no idea how much I have thought about you since our parting. It would seem that I have known you for a year and that we are old flames, for you occupy an inordinate amount of my thinking time. Time and again I ask myself these questions, why didn't I go back to the mountain top with you that afternoon I saw you at the ski jump, so that I could have been with you again; why didn't I ask you to stop by Stuttgart?

For some reason, I believe if I had asked, you just might have done it.

Then, leaving myself an escape in case she was cool to my entreaties, I rationalized that I was infatuated with her because she was the first American girl I had dated in two years. The suggestion was made that we continue to correspond because it might turn out to be "successful and interesting." I closed with "Love?"

The next letter Sally received from me was dated March 1955. I was home, out of the Army, again associated in the law practice with E. W. Hale, Jr., with nothing to do. I had no clients and no income. I had plenty of time to write letters and wrote Sally frequently.

. Then, in April, things changed. I applied for and obtained the position of Shelby County Assistant Public Defender. Hugh Stanton, Sr., the Public Defender, had one assistant, me. The job was to be part time and pay $200 a month. My legal activities immediately increased explosively. Memphis then had two divisions of Criminal Court. Mr. Stanton and I represented all indigent defendants in both. My military trial experience perfectly suited me for the job and I thrived in it until, a year and a half later, the demands of a developing personal law practice required me to resign.

Meanwhile, my letters to Sally, although less frequent, were more about Memphis and this Mid-South area. To arouse her interest in my hometown was my objective. Some of my communiqués could have been written by the Chamber of Commerce. Take, for example, this description of the then-in-progress Memphis Cotton Carnival. I include it because the description is a period piece of Memphis in the 50s, because the Memphis carnival was so unlike a European counterpart and so different from such a festival in Memphis today.

Dear Sally,   *Thursday, May 12, 1955*

Things have been crowding in on me of late and I find myself exceptionally busy. In addition to my regular duties over at criminal court, I am involved in the Cotton Carnival, which fills part of each day and almost every night with activities of a more social but equally time consuming nature. I went out on the Mississippi bus tour on Monday, May 2, an all day job of speech making, balloon blowing, smiling, drinking and other promotional activities designed to encourage the citizens of small nearby Mississippi towns to come to Memphis for the Carnival. I am also one of many parade marshals for four large parades, an integral part of the Carnival. Two are over, two remain: the children's parade tomorrow at noon, in which 20,000 children will participate and the Grand Carnival Parade on Saturday night.

The Cotton Carnival is a wonderful party – not all good parties are in Europe. Let me tell you what you are missing. There are about six secret societies, which have parties every night for a week. Further, all the private clubs in town have at least one extra large blast during Carnival week. Add to that four parades, featuring 135 bands from as far away as Oklahoma and Texas, about 65 floats, fashion shows, fire works, street dances and frivolity abounding, all of which makes for some really fun times. The only difficulty is that everybody is expected to keep on working at his or her regular job throughout the festivities. Many, and I am one, at this point need a little sack time.

*　　　*　　　*

I note that you will arrive in Memphis at 11:20 p.m. on Tuesday, June 21. In case you're fearful that you won't recognize me, just look for the happiest person in the reception area.

*　　　*　　　*

Let's talk about us.

You needn't worry about any competition from the girls here. Somehow, I don't compare you with the girls I date here, because you are not here! You are far away, in a romantic dream and in a class by yourself. This has its good and bad aspects. The good side is that when we finally get together, if we are disappointing to each other, there is absolutely no reason why we should worry about it; there will be 2,000 miles between us. The bad side is that if you are really as cute and interesting as I remember you to be – and you are not too repelled by me – we are going to be involved in a real and virtually unsolvable dilemma, and I will be saying, as I am saying now, "Why can't you be from Little Rock, or somewhere closer to Memphis than California?

*　　　*　　　*

THE TIMES: In January 1955 the Soviet Union declared that its state-of-war with Germany was terminated. Four years earlier, in July 1951, the United Kingdom, France and the United States, had done the same. On 7 October 1949 the Soviet Occupation Zone had been declared to be a separate state, named the "German

Democratic Republic," or "GDR." The GDR followed the pattern of the "people's democracies" set up in east central and southeast Europe as Soviet protectorates. In these states elections were based on "Unity" lists of candidates – the voter had no choice of candidates and strict control and direction of government and society was exercised by the Socialist Unity Party. By 1952, the border between the east, controlled by the Soviets, and the west occupied by the United States, Britain and France, was effectively closed. An Iron Curtain had descended and was in place.

As a result of the East-West conflict, Germany had become two states, each claiming to be the model for a single united Germany that was to be created in the future. However, the ever increasing number of refugees fleeing first from the Soviet Occupation Zone, then the German Democratic Republic, and the June uprising of 1953, clearly demonstrated that the East German state did not have the support of the great majority of the people who were forced to live there. The external and internal stability of the Soviet dominated state depended above all else on Soviet authority, which alone guaranteed its existence. This fact essentially remained unchanged until 1989 when the Berlin Wall was destroyed, the Soviet dominated East German State ceased to exist and Germany was reunited.

*   *   *

At noon on Friday, May 6th 1955, ten years of occupation by British, French and American troops officially ended in West Germany. The Federal Republic of Germany, emerged a free and sovereign nation with full authority to govern itself. The Allied troops remaining in Germany did so by consent of and agreement with the German government and not as conquerors of a vanquished nation.

MEMPHIS IN JUNE

The American Airlines flight from New York was a few minutes late. When, finally, the big, four engine DC-4 landed and taxied toward the ramp my feelings of excitement were being replaced by anxiety and apprehension.

Would I recognize her? After all, I had been with her only a few hours, and that was six months ago. I should have asked her to send me a picture, but until just a few weeks past I hadn't been certain she would actually detour through Memphis. Her family, especially her father, had not been too keen on the idea. Her parents had not seen her for a year and thought my suggestion that she spend four days in Memphis on her way from Stockholm to Bakersfield was ill considered. I had written her father, lawyer to lawyer, assuring him that proper arrangements had been made to accommodate his daughter and that appropriate chaperones were in place. At length, after fervent entreaties, written by both Sally and me, the Palmers acceded to the visit, though reluctantly.

The giant, silver airliner came to a stop fifty feet from the chain link fence separating the ramp from the reception zone. As the slowly rotating propellers came to a stop, a rolling stairway was pushed against the fuselage, the rear door was opened from the inside and the passengers destined for Memphis began to emerge.

There was Sally! At least, I think it was Sally. I saw only one unaccompanied female of the appropriate age exit the plane, so, I assumed, it must be Sally.

As she advanced toward the terminal entrance, she scanned the waiting crowd of twenty or so persons, obviously excited, but composed. I approached her and said, "Sally....? Hi, it's me."

She smiled as I took her hand baggage and guided her toward the luggage claim, and then, our lively conversation bubbling, on to the dependable Morris Minor. We were both tentative but ebullient in this new and intriguing friendship, now in circumstances so different from where it began. I squeezed her suitcase into the small trunk of the car and we set out for the city and to get to know each other.

*   *   *

Seventeen months after we met outside the Höllentalklamm Hütte -- in the California, San Joaquin Valley city of Bakersfield, five thousand nine hundred and forty-six miles west of the Kreutzeck, committed to each other after eleven traditional dates in Memphis, Corinth, Mississippi and the West Coast, and the exchange of one hundred fifty-seven letters -- Sally Palmer and I were married.

Included in the wedding party was one George Gallup, who came all the way from New York City to be in our wedding in California – a big deal, in 1956. If you carefully examine the nuptial photographs, you may observe in George a faint resemblance to that matchmaker, Cupid. Admittedly, and contrary to customary portrayals, George possesses no bow or arrows, at least none are in sight -- perhaps he concealed his weapons when he noticed the photographer.

*   *   *

Over the years, Sally has contended that she "picked me up" at the Memphis airport that June evening in 1955 -- that she had never seen me before that night. Since I wasn't certain I recognized her when she stepped off the plane, she maintains I met and fell in love with someone else, some other "Sally," that New Year's Eve on the Kreutzeck in Germany.

*   *   *

But, I think she's teasing.

CONCLUSION

Mikhail Sergeyevich Gorbachev was born on March 2, 1931 in the southern Russian village of Privolnoe. From May 25, 1989 until March 15, 1990 he served as Chairman of the Supreme Soviet and from March 15, 1990 until Christmas day, 1991, President of the USSR. In 1990 he received the Nobel Peace Prize.

Gorbachev was a lifelong communist; he never abandoned the system in which he believed. However, by the time he assumed power he believed the USSR could not remain a world power unless it achieved effective economic reform and parity with the West in the area of technological advances. He and his supporters adopted three routes to reformation: *uskorieniie,* (acceleration); *glasnost,* (openness); and *perestroika,* (restructuring). As a result of embracing those reforms, the Soviet Union collapsed, and ultimately, all the satellite states of Eastern Europe rejected the communist form of government.

Although the events of 1989 originated from conditions in existence long before then, and were probably inevitable, no doubt Gorbachev's reorganization efforts hastened the process.

In June 1989 free elections were held in Poland for the first time since World War II. The Solidarity Party won hands-down, and in August Gorbachev engineered a coalition government led, for the first time in forty years, by a non-communist.

On August 23 the Hungarians opened their borders so that East Germans could escape their country, and on September 10, formally announced that the border was unrestricted. Tens of thousands of East Germans fled to the West. Gorbachev visited East Germany on October 6, and was greeted by massive, favorable demonstrations. From statements made by him at that time, it was clear that Soviet troops would not be deployed to maintain the status quo.

On October 7, 1989, the Hungarian Communist Party rejecting Leninism, became the Hungarian Socialist Party.

Seventy thousand marchers took to the streets in Leipsig, East Germany on October 9, and the communist leadership in Berlin ordered the use of force to disperse the crowd, but local officials refused to obey. A week later there was another demonstration there, numbering as many as 150,000 people, in which some of the local communist officials joined. On October 18, East German communist chief Honaker resigned. A week later Gorbachev acknowledged that the Soviet Union had no right to interfere with events taking place in Eastern Europe, clearly giving a green light to the revolutionaries.

On October 31, the East German border to West Germany was opened, and four days later, 500,000 East Germans demonstrated, displaying their approval. A newly formed East German government announced on November 9 that residents could leave the country without special approval. Thousands did and after twenty-eight years, the Berlin wall came down.

That same day the head of the Communist Party in Bulgaria, who had ruled for thirty-five years, was ousted in a coup.

Police assaulted a student rally in Czechoslovakia on November 17. Two days later, 10,000 protested in Prague. On the 20th, 200,000 marched; on the 22nd, 250,000; and on November 24th, 300,000. That day the communist government of Czechoslovakia resigned.

Finally, in December, after a violent two-week struggle, Romanian dictator Nicolae Ceausescu and his wife, Elena, were ousted from power and on Christmas day, 1989 executed by a firing squad.

The Cold War was over. Remarkably, except among East European refugees, there were few celebrations in America.

Perhaps the War had lasted too long for Americans to grasp the significance of such an onrush of political events in Eastern Europe. Perhaps living for almost forty years under the constant threat of nuclear war numbed us. The Cold War affected every aspect of our lives. Over the years, hostile encounters took place, world wide, in Cuba, Nicaragua, Angola, Afghanistan, Iran and elsewhere, as well as thwarted uprisings in East Germany, Poland, Czechoslovakia and Hungary. Human history had never known a more grave threat of universal destruction than the Cuban missile crisis of October 1962. Sally and I had thought war so imminent then, that we packed our car with necessities and chose a distant location, the antebellum

Episcopal Church in La Grange, Tennessee, at which the family was to reassemble in case of an attack on Memphis.

My sojourn in Germany, from 1953 to 1955, was at a very dangerous time in the world, though not so dangerous a place, as Korea. Unquestionably, it was the most meaningful two-year period in my life. I was introduced to European culture, which I embraced and enjoyed. My work, which I relished, was absorbing and important. From an immature and inexperienced law graduate, I was remade into a mature and competent Army officer and an adroit trial lawyer.

And, perhaps most importantly, I met Sally.

*   *   *

EPILOGUE

Samuel Carver was not executed. After the death penalty was approved by the corps commanding general, it was automatically reviewed on appeal by an army board of review and then by the three judge United States Court of Military Appeals (USCMA). The board of review also affirmed the findings and sentence, but the USCMA reversed and sent the case back to the Judge Advocate General of the Army for reference by the JAG to another board of review for reconsideration.

The USCMA held that the law officer had not properly instructed the court. Specifically, the high court opined that mental impairment, less than legal insanity, might be considered by the court-martial members when they were deliberating upon the element of premeditation and that the law officer should have so instructed the court, but did not. The USCMA further held that, based on the record before the court, the board of review to which the case was to be resubmitted might affirm a conviction for the lesser included offense of unpremeditated murder and approve an appropriate sentence for that crime, or order a new trial. Such a conviction of the lesser offense, as defined by the court, would not sanction the death penalty. If a rehearing were ordered Carver could again be convicted of premeditated murder and under proper instructions, the death penalty reimposed, but I am sure there was no rehearing for there is no supplemental reported opinion of the USCMA. I believe a board of review reconsidered the matter, the conviction reduced to a lesser degree of unpremeditated murder and Carver sentenced to a prison term, probably a long one. So, Lieutenant Addis and Major Ailor achieved what they set out to do; by asserting and supporting the insanity plea, their client avoided the death penalty.

The citation for the opinion of the USCMA in the Carver case is 6 USCMA 258. The case was decided August 19, 1955. A search for reported subsequent decisions to determine the final outcome reveals nothing.

In my view, as a trial participant, that Carver did not premeditate this murder is inconceivable. I do not believe that the technical instruction required by the appellate court was required by the evidence, nor do I think the instruction, if given, would have changed the outcome of the case. That the appellate court did not appreciate or approve of the vigorous prosecution of the case is demonstrated by the following language in the opinion:

As previously mentioned, Captain August, the psychiatrist who had examined the accused sometime after the shooting, was called as a witness by the defense to support counsel's motion to dismiss the charges because of insanity. After discussing the personal history of the accused, the facts of the present offense, and the results of his personal interview with the accused, the Captain expressed the conclusion that at the time of the offense the accused was suffering from schizophrenia and was unable to know right from wrong. Following the direct examination, trial counsel launched into a rigorous cross-examination of the doctor in an attempt to render shaky his opinion. This effort was singularly unsuccessful. (Emphasis supplied).

The members of the court-martial who heard the testimony and saw the witnesses rejected the opinion of Captain August. It would seem to me that such rejection of the defense psychiatric expert opinion signifies the cross-examination was successful, not unsuccessful. Major Fenig had set out to show that the insanity defense was not worthy of belief and, indeed, the trial court repudiated it. Otherwise, the verdict would have been not guilty by reason of insanity and the death penalty would not have been imposed.

In my view these appellate judges, vexed by the vigorous prosecution of this heinous crime, looked for, and found a technicality by which they satisfied their desire to alter the outcome of the trial, which is not to say that I particularly craved that Samuel Carver be executed. By the time the decision was reached on appeal I was six months out of the army and practicing law in Memphis. I did not learn of the reversal until many years later.

*　　　*　　　*

The distinguished VIIth Corps was operational from 1940, through the D-Day Invasion of Europe in 1944 until its headquarters became established at Kelley barracks and from then until the Gulf War in 1990, following the invasion of Kuwait by Iraq. In *Operation Desert Storm* units of the Corps were instrumental in bringing about the defeat of the Iraqi Elite Guard and ending the war. The VIIth Corps was then deactivated and for the first time in fifty years was no longer an operational unit of the U. S. Army.

In 2002, Kelley Barracks, although no longer headquarters for the VIIth Corps, remained an important base for the American Army in Germany. It is now headquarters for the 6th Area Support Group.

*   *   *

With the exception of Eddie Fenig, Dave Addis, George Gallup, Wick Anderson and Bill Bonwell I have not been able to keep track of the officers with whom I served in Germany. Dave went back to the practice of transactional law in Chicago and Bill has a general practice in Wichita. Wick became general counsel to an insurance company in Roanoke, Virginia, and was later mayor of that city. George returned to the advertising business in New York City and Sally and I see him every few years.

Ed Fenig, his wife Maggie and their children visited us once in Memphis and I stopped by to see the Fenigs whenever I was in Washington, DC. Ed ultimately became Colonel Fenig, then retired and began a new career in the Criminal Division of the Department of Justice. He became ill in 1991 and when I received a letter from Maggie early in July of that year I suspected she was sending me bad news.

*   *   *

Dear Maggie,   *July 8, 1991*

I have been thinking about Eddie over the past week or so; when I saw your envelope on my desk this morning I knew what it contained. The funeral is taking place as I write this. I wish I could be there.

Of all the lawyers I have ever known, I learned the most from Eddie Fenig. Not only did he teach me technical skills but he also led me to understand the value and necessity of applying the qualities of honor, ethics, compassion and absolute honesty to the day to day practice of law. He will serve as an inspiration and guide to me as long as I live.

Thank you for writing to us so promptly at this difficult time. I will miss Eddie very much.

Love,

Bud

*   *   *

In 1964 Sally and I toured Europe together for the first time. I sent money to Carl Maul, who had been with me and helped rescue Jerry Hall after Jerry broke his leg. Carl was then living in Bremen. With the money I sent, Carl bought a red and white Volkswagen Squareback, then unknown in the States, and brought it to us at the nearby Hamburg airport. We began our tour of Europe from his home after spending some time with him, his wife and young son. They entertained us and showed us the sights of the Bremen-Hamburg area. On that trip Sally and I returned to Garmisch and the Kreuzeck where we met. We have hiked in the German, Austrian, Swiss and Italian Alps many times since. In 1981 we lived for four months in Blaubeuren, Germany, and Kitzbühel, Austria. Those beautiful snow capped mountains hold a special charm for us. Perhaps we shall return to the Kreuzeck on June 24, 2006, our fiftieth wedding anniversary.

*   *   *

One day in the late 1990s, I was in the high-rise Chicago law office of my friend Dave Addis who had once been my roommate and my most frequent trial opponent when we were stationed in Germany at the judge advocate section of the VII Corps. Dave and I had kept up after being separated from the Army. From time to time I would be in Chicago on business and would usually call on him for a visit. On this occasion we were reminiscing about our experiences as military lawyers in Germany when Dave asked,

"Did you know that under the Freedom of Information Act you can get copies of your old Army efficiency reports?"

I did not know but I was curious. Dave told me how to go about obtaining those sacrosanct and hitherto secret documents so I wrote to the Army personnel records archives at the address he gave me in St. Louis. Several weeks later a big brown envelope arrived.

Reviewing my officer efficiency reports was a journey into the past, a very pleasant journey. Colonel Joseph Guimond, Colonel

Ernst Oeding and Colonel Robert O'Connor were among the judge advocates who evaluated my performance as an Army officer and trial lawyer and signed my periodic efficiency reports. They, and Major Ed Fenig, are among the finest, most skilled and dedicated lawyers I have ever known – in or out of the Army. They taught me how to be a lawyer.

For the sake and edification of my grandchildren to whom this book is dedicated, because in this book I am sometimes portrayed as naïve and uninformed and because I do not think I have ever actually received the unrestricted acclaim and credit I deserve, I have decided to reproduce my efficiency evaluations here. But for this, I am sure, my long overlooked record of superior performance and good character would not again see the light of day.

"A clean-cut young officer; courteous, cooperative and friendly. He appears to be mentally, physically and morally qualified and shows great aptitude and enthusiasm for the numerous techniques and procedures applicable to Judge Advocate activities.

Charles A. Gross, Lt. Col.

Hq 8th Inf Div

Staff Judge Advocate

Ft Jackson, S. C.

10 Feb 53"

*   *   *

"A Young, energetic officer of pleasing appearance and personality. In the brief period assigned to this headquarters

his performance of duty was uniformly superior. This officer appears to be physically, mentally and morally qualified.
William P. Connally, Jr., Col
Section Chief
Judge Advocate Section
Hq Seventh Army
22 May 53"

*   *   *

"This officer is studious, industrious, intelligent and highly systematic. He vigorously, enthusiastically and cheerfully performs any duty assigned in a superior manner. Lieutenant Thomason's performance of duty is outstanding among junior officers. This officer's performance of duty is uniformly superior. For his age and grade I consider him outstanding.
Joseph A. Guimond, Col
Judge Advocate
Headquarters VII Corps
8 Jan 54"

*   *   *

"A well built, energetic officer, who presents a neat appearance. He is a skilled trial lawyer, with a pleasant personality and a good speaking voice, whose ethics are of the highest.
Ernst C. Oeding, Lt Col
Chief Military Justice
JA Section

Hq VII Corps
10 Jan 55"

      *   *   *

"Intelligent, trust-worthy, sensible, effective, hard-working.
An outstanding officer.
Robert J. O'Connor, Col.
Judge Advocate
Headquarters VII Corps
14 Jan 55"

John J. Thomason

ACKNOWLEDGMENTS

In writing this book I have avoided footnotes or endnotes. This is not, after all, a research piece. It is a personal account. Factual inclusions not based on personal experience were primarily obtained from various historical sources on the Internet.

The account of Sergeant Jonah Edward Kelley's activities leading to his death in combat was taken from An After-Action Report for the Second Battalion, 311th Infantry Regiment, 78th ("Lightning") Division for the period 30 January 1945 to 7 February 1945, written by Lt. Col. Richard W. Keyes, Commander of that Battalion, entitled *From Kesternich To Schmidt* and published in Volume MMII, Number 2, of *The Flash*, a publication of the 78th Infantry Division Veterans Association, dated April, 2002. I have slightly edited the account in order to explain military terminology and simplify distances and directions.

The history and information concerning the operations of the Army Special Forces comes mostly from the web site of *Global Security.org. Early Cold War – Army Special Operations*, http://www.globalsecurity.org/military/agency/army/arsoc-history3.htm.

The story about helicopter disaster relief during the Danube flood comes from www.armymedicine.army.mil/history/booksdocs/misc/disaster/ch8.

Information about General W. G. Haan and the history of the troop ship named after him may be found in the Dictionary of American Ships, on the internet at www.hazegray.org.

For an account of the Berlin tunnel and George Blake, see www.usvetdsp.com/story36.htm.

Most of the statistical information concerning popular demonstrations and the collapse of communist states in Eastern Europe was extracted from Robert M. Gates' book, *From the Shadows,* 1996.

Much history and current information about Kelley Barracks is described on the Web at http://www.stuttgart. army. mil/index.htm. and some of the facts reported here were obtained from that site.

The quote of General Gavin concerning the Battle of Huertgen Forest may be found at http://www.wikipedia.com/wiki/World War II/Battle+of+Hurtgen +Forest.

About the Author

John Thomason served as assistant staff judge advocate, VIIth U.S. Army Corps in Germany, 1953 – 1955, where he participated in 168 general court-martial trials, when the Cold War was almost a hot war. This book recounts his experiences as an Army lawyer in a combat ready unit. It is also the sometimes-humorous account of the transformation of a twenty-two year old law school graduate with no military training to a competent military officer and trial lawyer.

Following military service, Thomason was a public defender in the criminal courts of Memphis, Tennessee, then a trial lawyer, frequently defending physicians accused of medical malpractice and representing corporations in commercial litigation. In 1967 he founded a law firm, and in 2002, after fifty years at the bar, retired from the practice of law. By then his firm had grown to thirty-five lawyers.

Selected for the American College of Trial Lawyers, International Association of Defense Counsel, and *Best Lawyers in America,* Thomason tried hundreds of jury trials in state and federal jurisdictions and, for a time was visiting professor of Advocacy at the University of Tennessee College of Law in Knoxville.

Printed in the United States
1002200003B